OKLAHOMA
ARKANSAS
FALLS
FT. WORTH
TEXARKANA
DALLAS
WACO
LOUISIANA
AUSTIN
HOUSTON
N ANTONIO
Gulf of Mexico

TEXAS:
THE LAND
OF BEGINNING
AGAIN

The Romance of the Brazos

By

Julien Hyer

First Printing
1952

Second Printing
1970

Printed By

Waco, Texas

CONTENTS

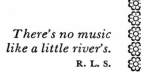

*There's no music
like a little river's.*
R. L. S.

RIVERSONG

THIS SHALL BE A RIVERSONG, set to the musical score of a rivulet where the prelude of a Brazos tributary begins; to the even tempo of the Double Mountain Fork as it winds across the Caprock and on down through the wide plains; to the torrent of a springtime freshet, dashing through the woodlands of the Cross Timbers, with the resonance of brasses reaching a high crescendo; to the downsweep from crashing cymbals to the ripple of a current about a red clay Bosque sandbar; to the cascade of the central River shimmering over the huge limestone slabs; to the notes at the Falls of the Brazos where the stream picks out spasmodic pizzicato among the rocks; to the measures of the wide broadwater flowing majestically through the Brazos bottoms, and then to the full sweep of the finale as it goes to meet in triumph the Gulf at the final curtain.

But the music of this Brazos opera is but the back-ground of the piece. There are many acts to the drama. Scenes of beauty and of fierce conflict were played on the River's wide stage. Arias of arms and obligatos of ordeals have been sung and enacted by a cast of characters.

The fair women and brave men of the Brazos have ever been the players of brilliant roles. The valley of the River breeds stout-souled men; tall and gaunt; lusty and bold; with collars open and sleeves rolled up, a chip-on-shoulder attitude. Varied are their types: red Indian braves with hatred and revenge upon their copper faces as they clash with the white invaders of their homelands; swarthy Spanish *conquistadores* in armor, seeking greedily to gain and keep other men's gold; bronzed Mexican *caballeros* in gay costumes strumming guitars in the Brazos moonlight; fastidious French *cavaliers* following the plume of their Norman explorer as he tries to claim the Brazos empire for his Bourbon liege; hardy Anglo-American settlers, pushing steadily westward as the course of empire wends its way.

They wore many different costumes in their historical procession: men in armor, men in buckskin, men in Osnaburg, men in chaps. They followed various trades: men of the cotton-row, men of the saddle, men of the barge, men of the forest—bold pioneers all—writing the Brazos saga in glittering letters.

And, too, this riversong shall sing of arms as well as of men: flint-tipped arrows and stone tomahawks; lances and long rifles; blunderbusses and Bowie-knives; six-shooters and sabers—arms that men of courage wore by day and kept close to their grasp by night—arms that meant food and security for themselves and their families—arms by which Law was established along the Brazos, by which Order came to her valley and by which the fit of her sons survived.

But, for the continuity of this riversong, one must look to the Brazos herself, winding her way through the heartland of Texas with an exquisite pattern during these last four centuries of traceable history.

Statistics have no place in the story of the artistic side of the Brazos-land. Materialism did not supplant Romance. Instead of extolling her trade and her finance, we hope to summon up memories of her historical greatness that her long valley shall be peopled with the figments and figures of a fancy now almost forgotten.

One is prone in this era of towering sky-lines and myriad smoke-stacks, when the glory of a man or of a city is reckoned in terms of wealth, to look impatiently past the artistic and to ignore the beauty of the scene that is about him. Is one entitled, modern man seems to ask himself, to indulge the luxury of the lovely in so busy a day and in so practical and prosaic a world? Charles Augustin Sainte-Beuvé wrote of his French people once upon a time that they "often wondered if they had the *right* to be moved by something artistic."

This riversong hopes to recapture for the moment the vision of the artistry and romance of the Brazos, each for its own sake, throughout her late brave years.

Since no great and imposing cities of modern magnificence have ever been built upon the Brazos banks, no borrowed splendor of nearby metropoli shall find its way into this tale.

For the River has its own quiet story to be told. The Brazos is among rivers modest and unassuming, even as are the people who have come to settle and live in her valley. The virginal simplicity of the Brazos and her folk is a secret of her charm.

As Virgil in one of his "Georgics" wished:

"Let the fields and the guiding streams in the valleys delight me, Inglorious, let me court the rivers and forests."

JULIEN C. HYER

PART ONE

The Goodly Land

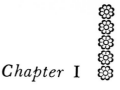

Chapter I

EL RIO DE LOS BRAZOS DE DIOS

"JUANITO, MY HUSBAND!"
Maria called from her place in the rear of the big wagon
as she nursed her babe at her breast. "Tell me, do we reach
yet the river?"

"Ah, *si, cariña mia,*" Juan sang back as he popped his long
whip over the rumps of the small Spanish mules. "I can now
see the trees upon its banks!"

The springtime Tejas sun was setting in a blaze of streaked
carmine and splashing ochre beyond the low western hills.
The wide prairie rolled away on every hand, a carpet with
red Indian-blanket and blue *canejo*-flowers. The recent rains
seemed to have washed each of the petals clean and bright.

Maria was very tired. It had been a long journey up from
San Antonio de Bexar. Last night's camp had been a "dry"
one. Tonight, Juan had promised the cool green trees and
the river.

"Look!" suddenly Maria cried. "Yonder, *hombre,* against
the sun! *Caballos!*"

Juan glanced back over his shoulder and his breathing
stopped for the moment.

"*Los Indios!*" he gasped.

Then he began lashing his mules for dear life. If only he
could reach the river before the savages overtook him. Maria
clutched her *niña* to her and her lips murmured the prayers
to The Blessed Virgin of The Guadalupe.

But on came the Indians brandishing their long lances.

Comanches, Juan noted. He had heard tales of their fierceness and of their treatment of lone settlers.

Soon he was at the river-crossing. The stream was up from the spring rains and still rising. Could he make it? He had no choice but to lash his little beasts until they plunged in. The wagon swayed and rocked as Juan urged them on.

Ah, they were at last to the graveled rise of the farther shore. One more effort and they were clear of the water. And, then, Juan felt a sudden thud.

"What is it, Juanito, *mio?*" Maria called in a worried tone.

"The wagon," he said with despair in his voice. "It is broken. We must fix it before we may go on."

Across the waters of the ford the Indians surveyed the scene and gave little yelps of exultation at the plight of the settler and his family.

The foremost Indian with a shout plunged into the tide of the racing river. But the muddy water was rising more rapidly than he had reckoned and a sudden whirl caught him in mid-stream and tossed him along with it.

His range-pony became frantic, lost its footing and unseated the rider. The others ran up and down the bank shouting in helpless concern, but their companion was already far down in the angry reddish torrent and quite beyond their help. They stood uncertainly on the bank not daring to cross in the mad waters.

Soon the Indian camp-fires were lighted across the river while Juan worked beside his own tiny flame to repair his wagon.

"But *mañana,* Juan," Maria asked, "they will seize us, yes?"

"Ah, my own, we are in the arms of God," he could only reply to comfort her.

During the night, while Maria and the little one slept from sheer fatigue within the wagon and Juan at last finished repairing the axle, a flash-flood came out of the black skies and more torrents of water came down from the upper river. By

[4]

dawn there was a deep and raging flood that flowed between Juan's little family and the hostile Comanches.

In the arms of God, Juan and Maria and their babe were safe.

Felicia D. Hemans wrote:

> *We will give the name of our fearless race*
> *To each bright river whose course we trace,*

but this time a river, in the new Tejas land, was to be named for no man, nor king, nor color. Thereafter, it should bear the name in the Spanish tongue *El Rio de Los Brazos de Dios,* which being translated means "The River of the Arms of God."

For an undetermined time the Brazos has lain like a rusting cavalry saber across the wide breadth of Texas. Beginning very near to the New Mexico line in far western Texas in Forks that converge at the Possum Kingdom Lake in the Palo Pinto country, the River stems singly southward and east, flowing tortuously to the Gulf of Mexico. Near the mouth the water is deep and wide. It is navigable, after a fashion, far upstream.

Many are the lakes that dot the valley of the River and claim her excess flood-water and others are planned for early completion. Truly will this valley be a land-of-the-lakes someday. They are Man's answer to the temperamental whims of the hoyden Brazos as each year she hurls millions of acre-feet of water in flood-season beyond her banks only to dry to a trickle in many places under a torrid summer Texas sun.

But in spring and autumn, the Brazos is a stately lady, flowing with even temper and orderly precision, with silent majesty and appealing charm.

One may find her in many vicissitudes and mutations. Gleaming in the sun of the high, stark bareness in her *Llano Estacado,* as the Spaniard named The Staked Plain of the far west of Texas, tumbling through the canyons of the Caprock country, twisting through the wide, rolling South Plains, gambolling over the vast prairies and the shinnery wastes of sandy soil and scrubby trees, meandering through the forest and woodlands of The Cross Timbers where the cedar brakes cover the high hills, gliding through the deep thickets and tangled bottoms, emerging out into the coastal pastures and the alluvial flats of the river-mouth—it is all Brazos-land, varied though it may be.

Today, at spring, Nature carpets these pleasant banks and valleys with wild flowers from her palette, the great cotton-woods filter the zephyrs through their silvery-green leaves and across the fields a sudden ball of gold is a huisache tree. Wherever one goes, from the tans and sepias of her west to the cool greens and grays of her east, or in her middle counties where Nature flings a brilliant *serape* of many-colored flowers across the Brazos' shoulder, one glories in her beauty.

In 1836 a talented lady came out of New England to visit her kinsman, Stephen F. Austin, who had founded a colony on the Brazos. After dwelling a season in the valley of the River, Mary Austin Holley wrote in her book:

It is impossible to imagine the beauty of a Texas prairie when in the vernal season its rich, luxuriant herbage, adorned with many thousand flowers of every size and hue, seems to realize the vision of a terrestrial paradise. Methinks the veriest infidel would here be constrained to bow and worship.

The valley of the Brazos is the true heartland of Texas. Most of Texas' early history has been made and written along her banks and across her fords. For the span of a golden century (1820-1920) this Brazos-land had the greatest period of advance and progress that it had enjoyed in the four hundred years of its traceable history.

Stalwart men and pioneer women strode up the Brazos valley, unafraid and determined, bent upon building a permanent civilization upon her banks and establishing homes

[6]

for themselves and their children. Cooled and sustained by the River's waters, resting beneath her trees and building their cabins along her course, these early-comers laid the mud-sills of present Texas and began an empire the turrets of which have yet to cease rising.

Lift the Brazos and her story from the Texas narrative and it would be loss indeed. The soul of the State finds its pulse along this River's course. Her tributaries, her lakes and her forks are the heartstrings of Texas.

For the Brazos is essentially Texas' own river. The Red she must share with Oklahoma, the Sabine with Louisiana and the Rio Grande with Mexico, but the Brazos begins and ends in Texas, sweeping entirely across the state to reach from the source at one border to the mouth at the Gulf's edge. Even the tide-lands of the River were reserved to Texas by the treaty of admission into the United States.

A pure-blood people live along the Brazos' course and sharp ethnological bounds have been observed. Although red and brown and white and black men have mingled freely together in her development, they each cleave unto their own kind.

The Indian with his shaven scalp-lock or headdress of wild turkey feathers walked these pleasant paths for a time and then went his way to history and extinction in so far as this valley was concerned. There is scarcely a trace of him now in the Brazos-land.

Of the Spaniard with all of his swagger and bravado, his armor and his velvet, his cowled priest and his adventurous *conquistador,* there is hardly a monument on the banks of the River that he named in his language. Of the Mexican there is here and there a small colony in the laboring-people's section of a Brazos town, but for the most part they are quiet, unassuming people taking little part in the affairs of their community.

The Anglo-American has predominated. Coming in great

numbers across the Sabine, along the Louisiana trail and in boats from New Orleans to settle this Riverland, he builded stoutly and durably, spoke up and claimed the right to govern himself, fought for his independence, fashioned and molded his own destiny and he survives.

With him the Negro thrives and improves his position, educates his children and adds to his stature. Albeit, he keeps contentedly to his fixed line of cleavage and the two races dwell together in peace upon the Brazos banks.

But not without blood and toil and agony have these English-speaking sons of the Brazos accomplished their aim. There were heart-breaking days and nights of deep anguish as they sought to establish their hold upon this valley. Desperately they fought to gain it and many of their brethren died in order to retain it. The midnight skies were red along the River with the fires kindled by the resentment of the Indians over the penetration of the white men into their hunting-land.

The elements, wild animals, hostile marauders, war, disaster and economic depression have each in turn made the lot of the Brazos settler a difficult one. It has been a hard land to settle and a hard one to maintain.

The world outside has not always been tolerant of the Brazos viewpoint. The ethics and opinions of the people along the River have not always jibed with those of their brothers in the United States. Mexican Independence, Indian Rights, Religion, Slavery, States Rights, Secession, Racial Tolerance and Tideland Ownership have been strong points of contention upon which wise and reasonable men have differed with these Brazos folk.

Logic may not have always dwelt in the reasoning of these people but their sincerity and their fortitude, their earnestness and their perseverance have softened their errors in behavior.

Sin and savagery have sounded discordant notes in the

Brazos symphony and they inject themselves into any story if truly told. Along these banks men have hated as well as loved, destroyed as well as builded, killed as well as borned. Human nature has run the course of deep emotions and records grim and pathetic stories of sorrow and loss, fighting and death, tears and sadness.

But, for the greater part, the evil and the sordid have been interred with the past. The natural beauty from Bailey to Brazoria has a stateliness about it that marches proudly, unabashed by too much bitter experience, unshadowed by too much commercialism and with enough dignity, serenity and loveliness about it to preserve its individual charm. The Brazos and her folk are quietly rich in many respects but in no wise blatantly affluent.

There have been singers of songs, painters of pictures, tellers of tales and workers with chisel and pen in the River's land who have set down the artistic history of the Brazos as they have lived and experienced it. One by one they have added their contributions even as the little tributaries— Bosque, Leon, Little, Lampasas, Navasota, Paluxy and Yegua —have hurried through the Valley to give their offerings to Mother Brazos as she winds her way deliberately seaward.

How many gallons of water flow yearly through her banks? How many turbines does she turn? How dense is the moisture in her valley? What is the wealth of her factories?

These answers do not belong in this story. As one seeks for the Brazos' real glory, he thinks of the power she has had to lure adventurous men and their womenkind to brave her wilds, endure her hardships, face her adversities and to wrest from other men and from Nature the right to dwell here in the valley of this stream. What a fascination has been hers throughout the years!

It is the age-old story of Man's primal battle with the elements lived over again in a new scene. Likewise, his strife with his fellows for supremacy has engaged his fighting arm.

It has not always been a lovely sequence nor a smooth and orderly one along the Brazos.

The varied beauties of the Riverland compensate fully for the dross and the dismal failures as well as for the imperfections of Man. The quaint delicacy of the Old South lingers over the lower valley from Richmond to Velasco. Old manor-ruins and marks of departed greatness are all one where early Brazonians courted ease and affluence in the landed estates patterned after Mississippi and Carolina memories.

The eye of reminiscence may look upon the quiet farms of the central River, ringed about with fields of cotton, spotted with copses of trees, with red barns punctuating the landscape and gabled houses rising from prominent knolls. Fences and gates and a covey of quail whirring up from a fence-corner at the approach of the visitor complete the picture.

Then, the sweeping vista of the upper Brazos-land comes to view, where from a flat-topped butte one may see for countless miles to the jagged peaks of the horizon, see the sun glint on the reddish walls of a canyon, admire the rounded form of sleeping hills and marvel at the flat stretch of mesa-land that is almost weird in its absolute bareness.

Variety is the true artistry of the River. Her canvases may include a sunrise out of the Gulf, where one scans the gleaming surface for a pirate ship; sunbeams worked in their intricate exquisiteness through mesquite branches in the Grand Prairie country or a pastel haze in the Plains vastness in the twilight of a Brazos evening.

Tawny in places as she takes her color from the clay of the central Texas banks and sand-bars; crystal-clear there where the Navasota joins up not far from Old Washington, Texas' first capital; a trickle in the hot summer out near the ruins of old Fort Griffin in Shackelford County where the stagecoach once stopped; a flood roaring across the flat-lands in spring like a herd of cattle in stampede. She has her many whims.

To know her intimately one must begin at her source-waters and follow faithfully on through to her delta-land. One must stop and see the flamboyant falls at Marlin, where her rapids dash themselves against the rocks; note the lichens that grow to silvery velvet on the limestone slabs where the Paluxy comes to join her mother River; admire the view from atop Double Mountain just south of Lubbock on the Plains, where a desert sun goes down in a furnace of red; pause in the lingering hush of a Cross Timbers twilight before a million Brazos stars come out to hang low; delight in the sunbeams that dart like arrows through the branches of a pin-oak.

One should learn the simple annals of the Indian; then the intrepid defiance of the First Three Hundred under Stephen F. Austin; in turn, the artifacts of antiquity, the thundering hoof-beats of the Longhorns headed up the trail dripping wet with the waters of the Brazos-crossing; pirates and desperados; outlaws and bandits; buffalo-hunters and Federal troopers; Rangers and Filibusters—they are all of this Brazos history. They were actors in its drama. Their loyalties and perfidies the River saw and noted, their secrets she has kept. They are a part of her mystery and her charm.

Beautiful in one aspect, she is plain in another. Flirtatious and seductive today, she may be stoical and severe tomorrow. Languid and listless in this mood, she may prove vivacious and wanton in the next. But she will always be versatile, presenting a new whim or a new facet at every turn in the River.

It is difficult to reconcile her contrasts: to correlate her huge, square Herefords, grazing on the rolling upper Plains with the long-eared, hump-backed Brahmas of her coastal pastures. One asks how either are related to her famed Longhorns that went up the trail fifty years ago.

One cannot classify her people as Brazos-folk alone. There are the staid dwellers in the lowlands, scions of old families;

her farmers of the midlands, reserved and deliberate; wind-blown people of her Plains, a breezy, gracious type. They are all three native of the Brazos-land.

To each the Brazos has issued her challenge. She has had a fascination for them and for their fathers. They have left the lands of their origins and come to dwell in this new land.

Chapter II

SIX BRAVE BANNERS FLYING

"A FLAG IS THE EMBODIMENT," said Woodrow Wilson, "not of sentiment, but of history. It represents the experiences made by men and women, the experiences of those who do and live under that flag."

On the Brazos breezes of the last four centuries have floated flags and standards of various hues and patterns. First came the blood-red shields of the Brazos Indians. Made of hides, painted with the suns of their gods, they were made to be worshipped. Then came the quartered banner of Castile and Aragon. A new conquest brought to the Riverland the golden *fleur-de-lys* of France on a white field. When they drummed for Freedom down in the lovely vale of Anahuac in Mexico, a new banner of red, white and green flew on the Brazos to show that a government south of the Rio Grande had thrown off the yoke of the Spanish Don.

When a dictatorship appeared under that flag, soon there was flying on the Brazos a Lone Star in a field of blue with red and white panels: Texas had a flag of her own. For a time after annexation to the American Union of States, the starry banner with the thirteen red and white stripes flew over fort and camp in the dry air of the Plains frontier, to be supplanted in the strenuous 1860's by the St. Andrew's Cross of the Southern Confederacy.

Brothers settled their differences, and once again The Stars and Stripes went up to the top of the pole. Since then it has flown for three-quarters of a century.

[13]

These have been the chief Brazos flags. Around them, beneath them and in their name the history of the River and its folk has been made. Indo-American, Latin-American, Anglo-American, Euro-American, Afro-American—they have marched together in grand procession, carrying these banners.

The Banners of Spain. As far back as 1519 a stranger's flag flew at the mouth of the Brazos. A caravel loomed one day off-shore in the direction of the rising sun and wild coastal Indians peered out from under their shaggy brows to fathom this new mystery.

It was the argosy of Alonzo Alvarez de Piñeda and the flag that waved at her fore-peak was the royal standard of Spain. In the name of His Most Catholic Majesty, Charles V, the explorer waved an arm, clothed in slashed velvet, and claimed everything from Florida to Mexico for the Spanish Crown.

His Excellency, The Governor of Jamaica, had sent Piñeda out to map the Gulf coast-line and blaze the trail to this land that he called "Amichel". That others might live there and claim it was of small consequence to the Spanish explorer and his Governor. They discovered first and conquered next.

After Piñeda came Alvar Nuñez Cabeza de Vaca in 1528. He carried no flag in his hand as he and his ship-wrecked comrades came up on the sandy beach near where the Gulf and Brazos meet, but in his heart was loyalty to Spain. She used his explorations for the next three hundred years to strengthen her claim to this land.

Panfilo de Narvaez had been sent from Spain with an expedition to curb Hernando Cortez, who was acting far too officiously in Mexico to suit his Spanish royal master. But the mild Panfilo could do naught with the bold and conceited *Conquistador,* quite mad with his success in the New World, so he set about exploring and claiming land for his liege instead. Cabeza was his High Commissioner and the Treasurer of his expedition.

[14]

Wrecked on the Alabama coast, as today's map would record it, Cabeza de Vaca with Maldonado, Dorantes and Estevan, a black Moorish slave, was able to fare forth in rafts and come on the way to Mexico as far as the Brazos' mouth before he was forced ashore by lack of fresh water and food.

Cabeza writes that when they saw a rusty streak of reddish current enter the green-blue waves and tasted it to find it fresh, they knew they were at the mouth of a river and gave thanks. Some even say that he, thereupon, named it "The Arms of God."

Respected at first as gods by the timid, simple but at the same time ferocious Karankawa Indians, they soon betrayed their feet of clay and were made slaves of the aborigines. Cabeza de Vaca had some knowledge of the medical arts and managed to restore himself in the favor of the Indians and eventually secured their permission to depart westward in the direction of the Spanish settlements on the lower California coast.

Up this river that would bear some day the name "Brazos" in their own tongue, the wanderers made their way in improvised *barcos* of their own fashioning, noting the steep clay bank, admiring the wide savannas, living off the abundant game and the trees bearing fruit and pressing ever onward in their exploring.

Then came a day when the River was too shallow for their boats, when they found themselves out of the woods and onto the prairies and plains. Abandoning their oars and steering their course by the sun and stars, they made their way safely to a port where their people welcomed them as if back from the dead.

Taking a ship for Spain, Cabeza de Vaca, true to the way of a traveller, wrote a book. It was to be the source of both research and impetus for the gold-minded ones of his poverty-stricken compatriots for many a day to come and its extravagant statements were to lure many to their death in the land of Amichel. Estevan's tales were even more lurid than those of his chief. He claimed he himself could lead others to the Seven Golden Cities of Cibolo, for the Indians had given him a secret map to the fabulous land of the Gran Quivera whose streets were paved with beaten gold!

As the result of this advertising, in 1541 the red and gòld flag came again to the Brazos-land. Not out of the sea this time, but out of the west with the sun's-ray glinting on armor and the rich caparisons of the horses—the first that the Plains Indians of the upper Brazos had ever seen.

Grand Captain Francisco Vasquez de Coronado marched out of Mexico, up through the Northern Pass, on to Santa Fé and over to the Brazos plains on his way to the Gran Quivera which he figured to be somewhere in present Kansas. The Comanches and the Kiowas and perhaps the Jumanas tribes stared in wonder at the new-comers on their strange quadrupeds, animals more graceful and faster than the buffalo of the plains. Then, too, there were the fire-sticks of the white men that spoke to a buffalo and killed him instantly.

Questioned as to the Golden Cities, the Indians asked: what was *gold?* It shone in the sun? Well, there were seven settlements that belonged to the Tribe of Seventy that had roof-tops that gleamed in the morning sun. Ah, said the *Conquistadores* of Coronado, that proves that there are Seven Golden Cities of Cibolo. They watered their horses in the Double Mountain Fork of the Brazos, secured a supply of salt from the bed of the Salt Fork of the River and pressed on.

For all of their wanderings and hopes, the seven cities were but little villages with huts that a white man—perhaps one of Cabeza de Vaca's ship-mates—had taught the Indians of the region, the present Texas Panhandle, to build. They used for roofs the mica-bearing rock from the riverbeds. It gleamed in the sun when seen from a distance, but it had no value. Farther on Coronado and his men encountered the mean pueblos of the Zuñis, made of sticks and mud. So disappointed were the Spaniards that they kicked the huts to pieces and returned to Mexico empty-handed.

Back home, Coronado paid the penalty for failure by being stripped of his Governorship of New Galicia by Mendoza and his expedition was written off as mere bungling. The Spaniards still wished to believe that the Gran Quivera existed.

In 1542, Luis de Moscoso brought the quartered flag of Spain again to the Brazos valley after burying his chief, Fernando de Soto, in the waters of the Mississippi, in the dead of night. He was heading for Mexico but he stopped in the vicinity of the Brazos long enough to satisfy himself that there was no gold there.

While they did not feel its oppression particularly, the natives of the Brazos were not to forget the Spanish flag for the next several decades, for traders and explorers, fortune-hunters and gold-seekers came with intermittent frequency up out of Mexico. In 1601 Juan de Oñate, Velasco and Vergara with eighty stout Spanish soldiers came looking for the Gran Quivera in their own right. They would show Coronado!

A failure, but not enough to entirely discourage Oñate, for he was back in 1611 to try his luck again. In 1621, Father Juan de Salas was reported to have been at the Brazos ford in Young County pleading with the Jumanas Indians to adopt the True Faith. In 1629, Estevan Perea and Didaco Lopez, priests of the cloth, working at their missions in the Brazos bottoms to win converts, used the word "Nueces" in their *diarios* to describe the River that is now known as "Brazos."

Alonzo Vaco came with a Spanish banner in 1634 to look for gold-lands and set down in his meticulous records the crossing of the Brazos, citing its beauty and charm, as did Captain Herman Martin and Diego del Castillo in 1650. The latter in their writings place the Jumanas Indians in the Brazos valley south of Waco as do other priests and traders doing business with them. They might have been some of the tribes of the later Caddo confederation.

However, in 1654, Fiego de Guadalajara records that he found them in his trading to be suspicious and inclined to quarrel. They even distrusted the Spaniards. So it is not surprising that in 1662, when the Governor himself, Don Diego de Penalosa, came from Mexico to try his hand at placating the red men, they attacked him before he had time to deliver his speech and thereafter commerce with the Jumanas of the Brazos came to an abrupt end.

That did not apply to the attempted evangelization of the natives by the men of the cowl and the cassock. The Franciscans of Guadalajara were applying themselves assiduously to the conversion of the Indians and one of the priests, Father Morfi, wrote the first History of Texas.

During the century of the 1600's the Spanish flag was kept flying at least over the 39 missions that were established in central Texas, most of them in the Brazos valley. The Spaniard was moving northward. It took him one hundred years to advance from Mexico City, the proverbial stronghold that he had wrested from Montezuma, as far as the Rio de las Palmas (present Rio Grande) and now, as the new century dawned, he was getting to the little river that was called San Antonio and the settlement there of "Bexar".

Once established at San Antonio, the *Gobernador* got out his maps and pointed to a spot farther north, on toward the French settlements of Louisiana and said to his men. "Here we build our next fort—Nacogdoches!"

So, a column sallied forth one day out of San Antonio de Bexar and blazed a trail, the first and oldest fixed road, it is said, on the North American continent—*El Camino Real*—"The King's Highway"—up and across the Brazos and to a place in eastern Tejas where His Excellency had pointed.

Hot it must have been in the humidity of the coastal plain as these soldiers in armor on their tired horses, the priests in their sandals and sackcloth riding small mules, and slaves toiling along afoot under their heavy burdens in the wake of artisans and workmen, made this initial journey for the glory of God and the profit of the Spanish King.

For one hundred and sixty years thereafter the Brazos valley was to know and feel the sovereignty of the Spanish flag and, to listen to the exhortations of the priests who advanced beneath its folds.

The Lilies of France. For eighty contentious years the Dons of Madrid and Bourbons of Paris pointed with avaricious fingers to their inadequate maps of the area north of Mexico and west of Louisiana and each claimed the Tejas-country as his own.

In 1684, out of the old Normandy port of Rouen, René Cavalier, Sieur de la Salle, with his four ships, blessed by his Jesuit teachers, sailed once more for the New World. His most puissant liege, Louis XIV of France, had issued him letters-patent to explore the Louisiana country, but he was either blown off course or else purposely put in at the lovely bay of St. Bernard—now Matagorda—not far from the Brazos' mouth.

He found it a most pleasing place with clear-running streams and flowers of rare beauty. "I am charmed," he wrote back to France, "with this country and the herds of buffalo and deer that we see grazing upon the prairies. It makes us think that we have realized the paradise that we have come so far to find."

On Garcitas Creek, in the benign valley of the Navidad, he built a fort which he called "Fort St. Louis" and began exploring for silver mines in the vicinity of the Brazos. Likewise, he kept a wary eye on the Louisiana settlements where the French *patois* was the speech of the colonists.

Too little is recorded of the stay of the French in the

Brazos-land. La Salle's people were not writing-folk, for George Bancroft in his history describes them as "one hundred men, the scum of French towns, a number of girls seeking husbands, four Franciscans and three priests, one of them La Salle's brother."

La Salle spent only a few years in this delightful environment, then he was eager to be off on more exploring. He had been often in Illinois and the upper reaches of the Mississippi, so he decided to explore it this time by land from the south. Setting forth with a party of his men, leaving the fort at Garcitas Creek to be guarded by the remainder of his party under one of his trusted lieutenants, the Frenchman set off for a two thousand mile trek through the wilderness. He came to the Brazos which he called *"La Malinge"*.

At the juncture of the Navasota with the Brazos, where the little city of Navasota marks the spot today, trouble arose. Nika, Morganget and Saget went out to do a bit of hunting for the party's pot. Hiens, a river-front ruffian out of Le Havre, Duhaut, a pardoned criminal, and Leotat, a renegade doctor in the La Salle party, ambushed and killed all three of the hunters. When La Salle and Father Douay set forth to find out why the missing men did not return, they too were ambushed and La Salle met his death at the hands of his own men there on the quiet Brazos plain.

Leaderless, the little group at Fort St. Louis fell prey to plague, disease, hunger and hostile Indians, until by 1690 the fort was a ruin and all of the garrison dead.

Back in Spain, Philip V had heard of the Garcitas fort and he forthwith ordered his Viceroy in Mexico to dispose of the French threat. Up from Coahuila came Captain Alonzo de Leon with a column of soldiers flying the Spanish flag.

"But, Father Massanet," said the Captain perplexedly as they stood there on the banks of the creek, "here is where it should stand—the French fort?"

The old prelate shook his head and tossed aside a weather-beaten record-book. "Scattered debris, only, my son," he said. "There yonder are the skeletons of the French. Not even buried. They did not build securely enough."

"We shall build a stronger fort. We shall last longer."

"Only if you place a mission beside your presidio," the clergyman warned.

And so they did. Even as they had fortified the western road from Mexico to Santa Fé with mission-forts, likewise did Spain set about throwing a line of such defense from the Rio Grande to the Sabine.

In 1713 the French scare flared again here on the eastern horizon. Louis Juchereau de Saint-Denis slipped over the border from Louisiana, explored for a time at will on the Brazos, wandered down to the Rio Grande and began telling the Spaniards what they were missing by not developing the land up around the copper-colored River in the midst of the Tejas country.

They were shocked. A Frenchman penetrating into Tejas! If Spain found out this some heads would fall. This Frenchman must be arrested and sent at once to Mexico City!

Back came the answer. "El Capitan Domingo Ramon will proceed with a body of soldiers from San Juan Bautista on the south Rio Grande and reopen El Camino Real. Restore the fort and garrison at Nacogdoches and let no one pass without your permission. Grant no permission!"

The Royal Road crossed the Brazos at about where Richmond is today at the great bend, where the banks are steep at places and the foliage of the forest thick. Over this road and across the River came the soldiers and the priests once again. The Franciscans were under Father Hidalgo and they built six new missions in east Texas and flew a Spanish flag over them, some north and some south of the Brazos.

These held the line for Spain against the French except for one little affair in 1719 that was hardly more than a raid or a skirmish, but to which much significance was attached by both of the engaging parties. Captain Blondel and a group of French soldiers dashed over from Louisiana, captured the Spanish mission of San Miguel de los Adaes at Nacogdoches, seized and bore off as trophies of victory the sacred vessels, ornaments and appurtenances to Natchitoches. When it is considered that the entire French force was composed of six men and that the defending garrison consisted entirely of one lay-brother and one ragged Spanish *soldado,* it is difficult to find much to become excited about in the event.

But the Marquis de Aguayo, the Spanish Governor of Coahuila-Texas, was furious. He himself set out to inspect the situation. It resulted in the stationing of one hundred men at Mission San Miguel and the French were defied. Three more missions were added, with their presidios bristling with guns, and the Governor made strong representations to Mexico City that Texas be in a district of its own. The distances were too great for one Governor, he pointed out. But they overruled him at headquarters and lived to see the day when they wished they had not.

However, the far-seeing Governor did establish the Spanish-French border as La Riviere Rouge and La Sabine and placed his own Texas headquarters at Robeline, Louisiana, where it remained until 1772 when it was removed to San Antonio de Bexar. And so the French threat was laid.

All during the 1700's, inactivity, lethargy and nondevelopment marked the Spanish occupation of the Brazos valley and no one seemed to care whether it was Spanish, French, or Indian. While they were ringing the Liberty Bell in Philadelphia in 1776 the missions along the River were closing up. The Spanish soldiers had no one to fight and the priests no one to convert. They deserted and went back to Mexico or to Santa Fé seeking excitement.

Antonio Gil Y'Barbo reestablished in 1779 the old Mission Guadalupe at Nacogdoches, and then went down to La Bahia del Esperitu (Goliad) and set a new garrison there. Spain did not wish to lose entire contact with this vast area, but she was having troubles of her own in keeping the lions-and-castles flag floating over the Zocalo in Mexico City. The fever of Liberty was penetrating to central America.

The Mexican Eagle. A stout old Creole priest, Father Miguel Hidalgo, Prophet of Deliverance, student of French philosophy, acclaimed as the leader of the oppressed Indians of Mexico, had been secretly preaching to his *poblanos* to rise and rebel. The Gachupin-royalists, however, were too strong for him and he was soon a martyr to Freedom's cause.

But he had sown the seed and Bernardo Gutierrez, another patriot of the people, was off to Washington to importune the Yankee leaders in "The Cradle of Liberty" to come and aid the downtrodden of Mexico. Jefferson and the others, however, were busy putting together a government of sorts of their own and they shook their heads.

In 1803 the United States had bought the Louisiana Territory from Napoleon for a pile of dollars and the Spaniards were eyeing the new flag suspiciously as it approached the boundaries of the Sabine and the Red.

Don Nemisco Salcedo, Captain-General of the Spanish Internal Provinces, went on record as saying: "If I had the power I would stop the very birds from flying over the boundary between our Texas land and the United States!"

But before the 1820's were far along there was a new flag flying from the National Palace in Mexico City and likewise over the Brazos forts and missions. It was the banner of The Eagle and The Serpent on a red-white-and-green field.

Two other flags of this era should be included. Gutierrez failing to enlist Washington's aid did interest an ex-U. S. Army officer, Magee, in what was termed "The Fredonia Rebellion"; and they raised a green flag, captured Goliad and San Antonio and came to an inauspicious end on August 18, 1813 when a strong Spanish force of Regulars came against them down at Fredonia.

[23]

Then, too, Dr. James Long had a flag of his own with red and white stripes and a single red star. He came out of old Natchez with 300 recruits and lined up with Gutierrez to take Nacogdoches. When Lafitte the pirate turned a deaf ear to his offers of alliance, he went back to New Orleans for reinforcements. Back he came to Quintana at the Brazos-mouth with a ship-load of volunteers and guns, but he did not last long after capturing the poorly-held fort at La Bahia. The Spaniards came against him with a superior force and aborted his embryonic effort at empire. Ben Milam brought the doughty Doctor's bloody clothes back from Mexico City to the widow as mute evidence that another "Filibusterer" had failed.

The flag of the 1820's and for the first half of the 1830's was the "1824" banner of the Constitutional Government of Mexico in which the Brazos folk had an interest. They had lined up with Santa Anna and his party and were ostensibly loyal to its rule.

Meanwhile, many Anglo-American colonists, perhaps as many as seven thousand, had come to the valley of the Brazos and among them was Moses Austin. He was a Yankee out of New England, by way of Missouri and other stops, and there was the starlight of adventure in his eye. He was man of vision and had a great dream of an Anglo-Saxon colony along the Brazos. He went to San Antonio de Bexar to talk things over with the Spanish Governor at his palace.

"No, *Señor* Austin, *jamás!*" thundered Don Martinez behind his fierce black mustaches. He was thinking of Magee and Nolan and others of the American Filibusterer breed. He had quite enough of *gringos* as colonists.

As Moses Austin walked dejectedly out into the bright sunshine of the *plaza*, he ran into an old friend with whom he had dined and sipped absinthe in New Orleans in an earlier day. It was the Baron de Bastrop, a Spanish nobleman of German lineage.

Ah, yes, the Baron could help—he knew the Governor well
—come on back!

Before they left, the stern old executive had relented and
agreed that Don Austin might receive the grant and bring
a colony, but only if they were loyal to Spain and adhered
to the Catholic religion. Moses agreed readily.

So did Don Martinez, by this one decision, like the base
Indian in Othello, "throw a pearl away, richer than all his
tribe."

Hurrying to New Orleans, Austin began putting his plans
for colonization into effect. But it was not to be given to this
Moses, either, to go up and possess The Land of Promise
on the Brazos banks. He died before he realized his dream,
but he had stood on Nebo and seen in his mind's eye what
someday would be an Anglo-American Texas.

His son, born in Virginia, when 28 years of age, led "The
First Three Hundred" *empresarios* to the wooded banks of
the Brazos.

"This is the place," said Stephen F. Austin to the settlers
who had come on the *Lively* from New Orleans and to those
who had followed with him overland from Natchitoches. "It
is a goodly land and well-watered. The climate is pleasing.
There is timber in abundance. Game is plentiful. We are
far enough from San Antonio and New Orleans so that our
well-meaning friends can not visit us too often. Here we
build!"

When Stephen went to Mexico City to get his grants confirmed by the new Mexican regime under the transformed
government there, he encountered trouble.

"You must wait, *Señor,*" the legislators shrugged. "We do
not know if we will have a monarchy or a republic. Tomorrow, perhaps."

And so he had to wait until January, 1823 before they
finally gave him his clearance, sent him back with his papers
and the new flag to teach loyalty to his settlers and try to

make a reality of the colony that his father had bequeathed him.

He tried his hardest to be faithful to his word and his trust. It was not easy. "My motto," he wrote to Mrs. Holley, his kinswoman, "is Fidelity and Gratitude to the Mexican Government and to be true to the welfare and interests of my colonists."

But these settlers of his had tasted of freedom back in The Old States and they were the sons of the men who had shed blood at Brandywine and Yorktown. Nothing would satisfy them but a voice in their own governing.

The Republic's Lone Emblem.

We, therefore . . . resolve and declare . . . that the people of Texas . . . are fully invested with all the rights and attributes which properly belong to independent states; and conscious of the rectitude of our intentions, we fearlessly and confidently commit the issue to the decision of the Supreme Arbiter of the destinies of nations.

Words of freemen, flung to the Brazos air at Old Washington on March 2, 1836 by a handful of colonists. And flying over the blacksmith shop that day was a flag with red, white, and blue panels bearing a single star in the field of blue.

Unofficially for three years and officially for seven more it waved over the Brazos-land—the Flag of Texas' Republic.

When it finally came down in honor of the banner of the American Union of States it was not relegated to the past. Today, over Texas clubs, public buildings, school-houses and parades, in every stand of colors, it is used. One flew at Bataan and was there when the Japs took over. (The latter looked in vain in their code-books to find out what it meant.)

By 1836 there were perhaps 50,000 Anglo-Americans scattered through Texas and most of them were in the Brazos valley and along the course of her tributaries. Each had brought with him his individual conception of independence. Sensing this, on April 6, 1830 the Mexico government slammed down the bars and forbade any more Anglo-American immigration into Texas. Frantic efforts were made to colonize the Brazos valley with loyal Mexicans from old Mexico. Grants of large land-tracts, subsidies and protection were offered.

Meanwhile, the Mexican officials and those of the United States exchanged suspicious glances across the Sabine. It was an open secret that the United States had designs on Texas. Henry Clay had confirmed this when he offered a million dollars in cash for all the land north and east of the Rio Grande. It was a high price in that day. Today, it would be a fair offer for a moderate-size Texas oil lease.

"The United States is not dangerous as a conqueror," said the irate Governor of the State of Durango, "but as a greedy, aggressive knave."

Noah Smithwick, contemporary blacksmith-historian, wrote of the attitude of the Brazos-folk at that time:

I can't remember the distinct understanding as to the position we were to assume toward Mexico. Some were for independence, some for Mexican Constitution of 1824 and some for anything just so it was a row. But we were all ready to fight!

Almost as soon as Don Antonio Lopez de Santa Anna, self-styled "Napoleon of The West", was ensconced in the highest office south of the Rio Grande, he forgot his Texas friends and his promises and began belaboring them by passing oppressive laws. This they resented bitterly and evidences of revolt began to appear along the Brazos.

The idea of Texas independent of Mexico was no new thing. In 1811 Captain Juan Bautista Casas with a few San Antonio sympathizers began a revolt and set up a government that proclaimed free trade between the United States and Texas. But the Spanish authorities in Bexar soon captured and shot the brave Captain and hoisted his head on a pike in the public square as a warning to other revolutionists.

Now, twenty years later, it was different. The colonists called a meeting of the leaders of the settlements at San Felipe on April 1, 1833. There they drafted certain resolutions and petitions to be presented to Santa Anna's government. Stephen F. Austin was off to Mexico to deliver them in person and then was when the Mexican President made his greatest mistake. Austin was always his loyal advocate and follower, bent upon holding the colonists to the Mexican line. Santa Anna clapped him in jail as soon as he arrived in the Mexican capital.

When the word got back to the banks of the Brazos, heads became hot and speeches sizzled with resentment. The idea of Austin imprisoned for seeking the constitutional right of petition!

William Barrett Travis, a South Carolina lawyer, began making himself heard. Jim Bowie, who fought his duels with hunting-knives, was speaking up in meeting; and a quiet, serious man from across the Red, who had dwelt in the tents of the Cherokees, named Sam Houston, was airing his views.

It was not until September 1835 that the Mexican jail-doors swung open and Stephen F. Austin was allowed to limp back home to the Brazos, sick in spirit and in body, but with a new decision on his lips: "Only by union and resistance can Texans survive!"

When that word came from his Peach Point plantation-home, the Brazos folk threw their hats in air. That was what they had waited to hear.

Forthwith, the Texas leaders formed a temporary government, recruited an "Army" and marched to take Goliad fort on October 9, 1835 along with $10,000 worth of Mexican Army supplies. Austin was at the head of them and seven hundred followed him on to capture San Antonio.

Flushed with military success the Brazos people gathered at San Felipe on November 3, 1835 and "declared war on Mexico".

"Volunteers from the United States will receive liberal bounties of land," they sent the word back to the old States. "Come with a good rifle and come soon! Liberty or Death! Down with the usurper!"

Up in Cincinnati, over in Louisville, down in New Orleans, men of action buckled on their knives, grabbed their rifles and started for Texas "to fight for their rights." These martial movements called for a flag. On that topic there was division. They had used the "1824" banner of the Constitutional Government of Mexico over the meeting-place at Old Washington when they wrote the Declaration and the Constitution. At Velasco, when they captured the fort, they had flown the "bloody arm and sword", or the Troutman flag, as it was known. The Georgians had a lone star flag they wanted to fight under and the Kentucky volunteers had their own private banner that Jack Sylvester of the Newport Rifles, fighting in Colonel Burleson's First Regiment, would carry at San Jacinto. The Ohio and Pennsylvania contingents had their own flags, but it was left up to Sarah Dodson to be the Betsy Ross of Texas.

In 1823, Edward Bradley with his wife and eleven year old daughter settled on the Brazos between Richmond and Columbia. The Dodsons from North Carolina settled nearby. Archelaus Dodson and Sarah Bradley met; courted, and wed on May 17, 1835. When volunteers were called, Arch and Andrew Robinson organized a military company with Andrew as Captain, Arch as First Lieutenant and James Ferguson as Second Lieutenant.

They wanted a flag, so Sarah made them one out of calico, a tricolor with a single star in a blue field, with panels of white and red alternating. It was used by the new company when it followed Austin into San Antonio on December 10,

1835 and it flew in the battles of Cibolo Creek and Mission Concepción. It shared honors with the "1824" flag over the blacksmith shop at Washington when the convention was declaring Texas free. Arch Dodson's boys carried it in triumph on April 21, 1836, when, on the flat coastal plain of San Jacinto, a new Republic was born in battle and blood and the Texas conflict of a half-hour's duration became one of the sixteen decisive combats in the world's history.

They had not adopted it officially, however, when Sam Houston was leading his men through the Brazos bottoms in "The Runaway Scrape". His arch-enemy, Santa Anna, twitted him about it as they talked beneath the tree after the battle was over.

"Why, you have no government," said the Mexican President haughtily. "You are fighting under no recognized flag."

The grizzled old Virginian grunted. "Tell him," he said to the interpreter, "so far as the first point is concerned, the Texans have a government and they'll damned soon get 'em a flag!"

But it was not until 1839 that they adopted Sarah Dodson's flag officially, changing only the arrangement of the red and white panels to the horizontal instead of the vertical. Now, the Texas Republic had a flag of its own.

Santa Anna had flown a scarlet flag over the San Fernando Cathedral in San Antonio that fateful day in March, 1836. Barrett Travis wrote from the Alamo:

A blood-red banner waves from the church of Bexar and in the camp above us in token that the war is one of vengeance against rebels. They have declared us such.

In 1842, Santa Anna flared up again in a discussion about flags with Sam Houston, President of the Texas Republic, who was dickering with his Washington friends about annexation of Texas to the Union.

Santa Anna still had hopes of avenging San Jacinto, did

not want the United States as his neighbor across the Rio Grande, and gloated over the financial difficulties of the new Texas Republic. So he addressed an icy note to President Houston as to what *might* happen if Texas were to contemplate annexation to the United States.

Houston replied heatedly after telling his old adversary off and making it plain that annexation was none of Mexico's business. He wrote:

With these principles, we will march across the Rio Grande and, believe me, sir, ere the banner of Mexico shall float upon the banks of the Sabine and the Brazos, the Texas banner of the single star, borne by the Anglo-Saxon race, shall display its bright folds in Liberty's triumph on the Isthmus of Darien. With the most appropriate considerations, I have the honor to present you my salutations.

(Signed) SAM HOUSTON.

On February 19, 1846 the Lone Star flag came down at Washington-on-the-Brazos into the waiting arms of President Anson Jones and up went the starry banner of the American Union. There it was to remain at the high mast on the Brazos until sixteen years later when it was replaced for a season by "the Bonnie Blue flag that wears the single star"—the flag of The Confederate States of America.

The Confederate Bars. Over the Brazos forts and strongholds, where U. S. Cavalrymen in blue-and-yellow had been in garrison since Annexation, the flag of the United States flew. In the early 1860's men went to war—brother fought against brother in a bitter struggle to decide who was master in his own home. A new flag went up.

During those dark days of Civil War the men of the Brazos land went east to fight under the guidons of Terry's Texas Rangers or the gold-fringed banner of Hood's Texas Brigade. The fires of this war did not burn in the Brazos valley, but did scorch and singe its edges for many years.

[31]

Galveston fell early to the Federal gunboats, but Jeff Davis sent General J. Bankhead Magruder from Richmond, Virginia to organize a local force and recapture the town and the island. The guns boomed in ear-shot of the Brazos and on January 1, 1863 the Confederate flag went back up over the Island's fort. Federal blockaders stood off the mouth of the Brazos, but the guns of Quintana and Velasco threatened them if they dared to venture within range.

There were fights at Sabine Pass and Palmito Hill in Texas, but the Galveston affair was the closest that the Brazos knew of war. The conflict, however, took a heavy toll of the River country. It depleted the man-power, the crops went untended, the houses fell into ruin, the cattle went wild on the unfenced ranges and women wept over news-bulletins up and down the River's course.

Then, one day, up in Virginia at old Appomattox Courthouse, General Robert E. Lee, who had soldiered on the Brazos line of forts in the old days as a Lieutenant Colonel of Cavalry, handed his sword to General Grant and they brought word to the Brazos that the war was over.

Many Southerners along the River, as well as in the other Confederate states, would not accept it and went to live in Mexico, Europe, South America and elsewhere rather than serve under any flag by force. In July 1865, General Joseph O. Shelby with his brigade marched across the Brazos and on down to the Rio Grande, buried their battle flag with the Cross of St. Andrews and thirteen stars in the middle of the river across from Eagle Pass, and continued on to Mexico City. There they tendered their services to Emperor Maximilian, but that Austrian gentleman was a bit timid as to what Washington might say and courteously refused their offer. So, they came back home, one by one, to defeat and to suffer the Reconstruction hardships.

The Stripes and the Stars. Once again, in 1865, the flag of the Union came back to the Brazos and its forts.

The years that followed were hard ones for the Brazos folk. Carpetbagger Government was onerous and distasteful to these freedom-loving people. Disenfranchised of their vote, dispossessed of their land and their rights they paid the penalty of defeat and the edicts of the conqueror were merciless.

Abbé Seyes was asked what he did during the French Revolution and he replied, "I endured!"

It was so with the people of the Brazos valley. They endured, suffering bitter reprisals. These men and their sons who had fought at San Jacinto were now enslaved in their own homeland, living under a flag and a Constitution that they had sworn to defend and accept, yet afforded none of the rights that it was supposed to guarantee. They endured . . .

It was not until 1870 that Independence and normalcy returned to the Brazos valley for its own people. A new generation came along, soon forgot the burdens and insults of Reconstruction Days and by the time the nation needed soldiers in 1898 to fight Cuba's war for independence, the boys and men of the Brazos-land were ready to go.

With Teddy Roosevelt's Rough Riders they trained at San Antonio, coming from the farms and ranches of the River country. When it was over and won, they mustered out at Texas City not far from the Brazos tide and came back home to the pursuits of peace. All Americans were together again.

In 1917, the next call came and to World War I the men of the Brazos marched as volunteers. The War Department selected a campsite on the banks of the Brazos at Waco, named it for General Arthur MacArthur, the father of Douglas MacArthur, and here many troops were trained for war. Nearby, an Army airbase—Rich Field—was set up and at these two installations thousands of American infantrymen, artillerymen and airmen came to do their preparing for overseas combat.

Meanwhile, the Brazos young men were going to Camp Bowie at Fort Worth to form the 36th National Guard Division from Texas and Oklahoma, while others went to the 90th National Army Division at San Antonio. Soon, on the plains of Picardy and in the depths of the Argonne, they were spilling their blood for the flag.

A quarter-century passed and up and down the River, from Lubbock to Brazoria, the bugles sounded again. Armed camps and airfields sprang into being overnight. Before long the men from the Brazos were marching once more to the battle-fields of France and Flanders, of Leyte and Manila. The streets of the cities and towns along the River were filled with men in uniforms.

The sixth flag of the Brazos moved forward again "to the sound of the guns." The descendants of the men who had served under the various banners of the Brazos valley were following where it led.

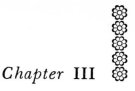

Chapter III

HER ORIGINS, ORNAMENTS, AND OCCUPANTS

A HUNDRED YEARS AGO AND more, in 1836, when Mrs. Holley wrote to her Kentucky friends after sojourning with her kinsman, Stephen F. Austin, at San Felipe, she said:

Here, as in Eden, man feels alone with the God of Nature and seems in a peculiar manner to enjoy the rich bounties of Heaven in common with all created things. The animals which do not fly from him; the profound stillness; the genial sun and the soft air . . . fill the heart with religious emotion.

The Brazos holds many deep, intriguing secrets for the naturalist, the botanist and the archaeologist to study. There are many hieroglyphs and pictographs along the banks and in the caves, smoke-dimmed by fires that went out thousands of years ago. Limestone slabs remain that enticed prehistoric artists and writers. In the security of the River's rocks is found Nature's own artistry as she preserves the outlines of a fern or snake; or perhaps, the foot-print of an animal that lived in untold cycles past.

At Glen Rose in Somervell County, the Brazos is fortunate in having an archaeologist, Dr. Ernest T. Adams, who brought from Oxford, as a Rhodes scholar, a keen interest and a hardy perseverance to the caves and gravelpits here where the Paluxy joins the Brazos in the region local to his home.

He has unearthed the jaw-bone of a giant woman whom he contends lived here on the Brazos 30,000 years ago. He claims that she was seven feet tall, that she died in child-birth and that her remains were in a sleeping-compartment made of stone that could be warmed from beneath. In addition, he has brought forth the tracks of dinosaurs from the limestone beds of the Brazos, one of which is exhibited in the Glen Rose public square.

Upon the High Plains are found artifacts that W. C. Holden of the Texas Tech History Department tells of in his "Alkali Trails":

According to recent archaeological discoveries (West Texas) has been inhabited longer than any other part of Texas. Pleistocene Man lived here, fashioned his exquisitely-shaped arrow-points and hunted the gigantic bison whose species has now been extinct for 10,000 years. Another race of men lived in the Canadian valley of the Panhandle, built substantial homes of stone and cultivated fields several centuries before the coming of Columbus.

Other authorities state that in the Folsom epoch these upper Brazos plains and prairies were inhabited by mastodons, prehistoric horses, elephants, bison, camels, turtles, sharks and other long-extinct animals.

Students of archaeology debate the influences of certain civilizations upon the early life of the Brazos valley. Some say that it is Mayan and that the people from Mexico and Central America came bringing the culture and arts of Yucatan and Chichen Itza, kinsmen of the workers in gold filigree whose handiwork Cortez was to find near the pyramids of Teotehuacan. There is a similarity between the Brazos artifacts and those of the Mayans. At some time or other these people may have tarried beside this River.

Others are positive that the invader of Brazos culture came from the Northwest and that the Pueblo style predominates, while others argue for the inroads of the Mound-Builders of the Mississippi valley. Kitchen-middens have been found on the lower Brazos that correspond with those in the country to the North and East. Likewise, definite mounds, circular, with depressions in their centers have been discovered on the upper Brazos plains with ancient ashes beneath them.

Perhaps these rocks were used for cooking and heating. At least we know that the people were hunters. The fact that they had stone huts or permanent pueblos indicates that they were not entirely nomadic nor lived solely in wigwams and tents.

There are traces of the Nassonis, a pioneer tribe of Indians, who once roamed the Brazos banks. Why did these early peoples only draw pictures of birds and beasts and illustrate their stories with pictographs instead of leaving us some of their language in their own handwriting? Was it because they did not use writing as such? Apparently they were well advanced in the civilized arts otherwise.

Where did these ancient folk come from? Did they come out of Asia, down through Alaska and Canada, pausing here before they went on south to Mexico? Many of these Mexican Indians have definitely-marked Mongoloid attributes and features. Did they cross on dry land that is now sunk into the sea, leaving the Aleutians as the tops of its mountains? Did their ships come to the California coast and the explorers trek east in search of better climate, hunting, gold or adventure until they stood on the Brazos?

Professor Edgar B. Howard of the University of Pennsylvania claims that he found in 1935 evidence within a hundred miles of the Brazos of a hunter and a musk-ox that he had killed dating back 15,000 years.

It is accepted that, prehistorically, the Shumla Cave-Dwellers of the Rio Grande region emigrated north to the Brazos; and evidences of their rope-ladders, which reach to the high caves that they once inhabited, have been found. Their skeletons are remarkably well-preserved by more than ordinary mummy methods and their weapons were of the Australian boomerang variety. Over fifty different articles of daily use have been identified. The Witte Memorial Museum's party of San Antonio explored their caves in 1933.

That these people were long of head, short of stature, dark-haired and smoked something through a reed is established with fair certainty. That they could carve and illustrate their thoughts is apparent from their pictographs and petroglyphs. Their arrows show that they were adept at flint-work and in the textile arts they were most proficient.

So much for the peoples, now, what of the land? From its geological and physiographic attributes we have named the Brazos Valley successively: Llano Estacado, South Plains, Caprock, Rolling Prairies, North Central Plains, West Cross Timbers, Grand Prairie, East Cross Timbers, Blacklands, Post Oak Belt, Coastal Prairies and Plains.

These diverse belts and sections are filled with varied soils and minerals that men have mined during the years and some which are yet to be developed. Strange to relate, the one mineral that the Spanish explorers sought most assiduously has not been found along the Brazos course—Gold.

Coal is found in Young, Palo Pinto, Parker and Stephens Counties. It was being mined in 1880 with as many as 30 carloads a day moving to the outside world with the gins, furnaces and railroads, locally, depending upon it for fuel.

Salt has been another product of the Brazos since the days that the Indians camped in the vicinity of the Salt Fork and the California travellers stopped to stock up with it. Down near Velasco at the mouth of the Brazos, the lagunes produce salt in merchantable quantities and have for a long time.

The entire lower Brazos valley, geologists claim, is one vast alluvion with a surface of black mold formed by the decomposition of vegetable matter in long past ages. The banks of the River show universally a rich soil where cotton thrives and the truck-farmer is assured of a ready harvest.

The Brazos rock is a volcanic one. How many thousands of years ago it was thrown up from the earth's center or tossed about as molten lava, one may only guess.

There are many peaks along the upper half of the course. Comanche in Hood, Double Mountain and others on the Plains. They have yielded many ores.

The Brazos is an old river. How many millions of years minerals have awaited the diamond drill or the steam-shovel is anyone's guess. On the Brazos banks is found one of North America's seven granite shields. Huge blocks of this indigenous stone, sparkling in the sun with its mica, were piled here one on top of the other, to form these limestone hills.

While we have a most exact knowledge of almost every part of this valley today as the result of the oil development that has occurred in this present century, it is interesting to note what an early geologist wrote of the Brazos:

It is on many accounts a most interesting river . . . Its head-waters spring in the Comanche country and consequently are but little known. It has the peculiar feature . . . which has no parallel in any part of the world—a salt water river running from the interior toward the sea . . . When the rains are copious an extensive Salt Branch is formed, its waters being at times salt enough to pickle pork.

The physiographic province of the Grand Prairie—McLennan, Hill, Johnson, Parker, Hood, Erath and Eastland Counties—is perhaps the most mild and temperate of the entire valley. The hills are soft and rolling, grass-covered and landscaped, with groves of oak and cedar and with plenty of native stone. It is possessed of none of the dry aridity of the upper Brazos nor of the heavy humidity of the lower River's region. It is adapted to all sorts of farming, productive of trees and vegetation, covered with native wild flowers, yields excellent timber, furnishes abundant grazing and the multitude of its settlements attests to its perfection.

Enough of the physical origins of the Brazos-land. What of the name? How did "Texas" come to fasten itself on this area? Piñeda called all of this country "Amichel", but it was not popular. "Florida" they tried vainly. "Nueva Felipinos" was too long. "Quivera" drew a smile after a time. "Llano Estacado" was inapplicable. But the Caddos had a word for it.

As the Spanish explorers approached the friendly Caddo Indians they would duly raise their hands to show that they did not have weapons and utter the greeting "Tejas", which being interpreted was "Friendly". Captain de Leon of the Spanish force that was building missions in east Texas began using in his dispatches the words "Tejas-land" and "Tejas-Indians". He called the Brazos "Espiritu Santo". Coronado had called them "Tejas-natives" in his earlier *diarios*. That was what it finally became: Texas—The Friendly.

Even as there is diversity of rock and earth, of elevation and terrain, so the Brazos brings forth trees and flowers, each after its own kind, in the various parts of the valley that it waters. The botanist, the horticulturist and the lover of flowers for their natural beauty will find many kinds and species in the Brazos country.

Down at the River's mouth the traveler meets with tangled wildwood, morass and forests with trees of giant size. In the midlands, there are clumps and copses of woods, interspersed by wild-flowered prairies and open landscapes. High on the plains, where infrequent patches of grass must do for vegetation and a solitary cedar against a bare hill must suffice to feast the eye for miles, there is a contrast that gives the visitor the impression that he knows three different lands.

There is the tall yucca of the upper River, a bleached Christmas tree of blossom-bells with sharp spikes shooting in all directions . . . or a serious old cypress, coloring a bayou-pool in the swampy area around Oyster Creek, with purple water-hyacinths blooming nearby in a patch of secluded sunlight . . . or a giant pecan by a Bosque stream waving its leafy green and sporting a family of squirrels playing hide-and-seek among the grapevines that dangle from above. The three seem to be quite strangers to each other.

The pecan is Texas' state tree, duly adopted by the Legislature. Governor James Stephen Hogg, a famed Texan, left in his will the desire to have a pecan tree planted at the head of his grave and a black walnut at its foot.

Vying with the pecan are the oak, the mesquite, the walnut, the willow, the hackberry, the cypress, the pine, the elm, the cottonwood, the cedar and the bois d'arc. There are others, but these are the elder statesmen of the Brazos forest.

After the woodlands are left behind, the mesquite is the typically Brazos tree on up through the prairies and the plains. Cabeza de Vaca mentioned it in his writings and appreciated its protecting him from the hot sun of the high country. It is indigenous to the southwest, hardy, inured to sun and drought and roots its way down to water, husbanding what little it finds over against the long dry spells.

Mesquite-gum was found to be an excellent substitute by the early chemist for arabic and acacia. Thorny and tough, durable and lasting, it makes a good post, fits to an ox-yoke, and resists decay. It came in handy for the early settler who had to be resourceful with but little at hand. Early colonists along the River used its sap for tanning leather and preserving hides.

Pin, post, live and a dozen other kinds of oaks thrive along the Brazos' course. Some are huge and majestic, others scrubby and low, depending on the soil and moisture. Some are a thousand years old and others the seedlings from last year's acorns blown along by the wind.

There are many historical oaks along the River. Not far from the Brazos' flow was the oak under which Sam Houston received Santa Anna the day after the battle. Just out from Old Brazoria, there in the silent parliament of many huge trees, all of them gray-bearded with moss, stands an ancient landmark. Here the first Masonic Lodge of Texas was tiled beneath its bough.

Along the creek banks stand huge pecans and cottonwoods. The latter shed their lint in season and the birds use it to line their nests. The bois d'arc is a fence-maker of note. They were planted originally in long rows to mark a road, or a land-line, to border a property or to act as a wind-break. Surveyors, lacking monuments of a more substantial nature, wrote down "thence N to bois d'arc tree in the NE corner" and had confidence that it would be standing years later. It usually is.

Old Texas deeds in the Brazos valley are filled with such descriptions. It is vicariously known as Mock Orange, Buzzards' Apple, Osage Orange and other such names, but no useful purpose has ever been discovered for its abundant fruit and no animal or bird savors it.

Said Roemar, a German writer, in 1847 after a visit to Texas and a sojourn on the Brazos, when he got back to his native Rhineland and published his book:

The richest and most fertile soil which Texas has, suitable for cotton, sugar-cane and corn, not to mention the wild flowers and trees, comes to be found on the Brazos below San Felipe.

He saw, undoubtedly, the undulating fields of bluebonnets. Each tiny blossom is a replica of the pioneer woman's sunbonnet with a small red fleck in the heart of the flower. They grow everywhere in the Texas spring. There are many stories . . . one is of the little Aztec maiden who, to deliver her people from a dreaded plague, offered her life as a sacrifice to the gods. Ascending the altar she tossed aside her bonnet of blue and gave her life for her people. Ever since; says the legendist, about the Brazos-land in the springtime these little bonnets bloom in her honor with a tiny drop of her blood in their center to commemorate her sacrifice.

In the spring to the Brazos come the little Canterbury

bells. Yucca blooms and wild purple sage garnish the plains and in the swamps of the lower River magnolia and water-hyacinths bloom.

One wonders what the earlist *fauna* of this region looked like. We do know that the buffalo is a carry-over from the huge mammalia of an earlier unknown era.

The *cibolo,* as the Spaniards called him, survived all of his natural enemies including the Indian. He outran them, outbred their raids on his herds, and doggedly withstood the pitfalls that were set for him. But with the gunpowder and the ruthlessness of the White Man he could not cope and to-day he is a specimen in a museum or a zoo when found outside the picture-books.

He was the Indians' portable commissary. The red man used his flesh for food, his hide for robes and clothing, joined pelts together for tents and burned his chips for fuel. The Indian lived by and off the buffalo herds that ranged up and down the River. Even as far south as Richmond in the 1840's, herds of buffalo crossed the Brazos at a shallow ford.

At first, the Indian hunted on the edge of the herd, lay in wait and shot down a young calf or an old bull with his bow and arrow. When he got the horse from the Spaniard he could ride alongside, select his animal and speed an arrow into its heart. But when the Anglo-Saxon settler came and he got a trade-rifle and gun-powder he could kill wholesale. It was that which spelled the death of the shaggy beasts. The word went out that the eastern and foreign markets would pay good hard dollars for the buffalo hides and Indian and White Man joined in the slaughter. They stripped the hide where they shot the animal and the air above the Brazos was filled with buzzards coming to feast upon the abandoned carcass.

When the whitened bones dotted the prairies, the white man found a use for them. Gathering them and shipping them to market for fertilizer, a profit was made even on them. Once the herds were so big that they covered seven square miles at a time of tightly-pressed bodies, and they ranged from Montana to Mexico. At times the summer found some of them as far north as Hudson Bay.

But a day came when, instead of having to pack the hides to market in single mule-teams, an enterprising merchant, Lobenstein, by name, set up an assembly-point at Fort Griffin on the frontier and the market came to the Brazos. Hunting outfits poured in and began peddling their hides locally. In one month, March 1876, the freighters hauled a half-million pounds of hides from Fort Griffin to Dallas and Denison to the rail-heads. A hundred wagons a day passed through Weatherford on their way east. The far-shooting Sharp's rifle had supplanted the small-bore standard gun of the early 1800's to increase the slaughter of the buffalo.

There was a time when the market demand was strong for meat and over the slow mesquite fires they cooked, cured and then stacked the buffalo flesh like cordwood, selling it to the Government to feed the soldiers at the forts, or to be shipped off to foreign parts for the commissaries of the world. Refrigeration was an unknown factor then but when it did come, it but served to speed the end of the buffalo on the Brazos.

And with the buffalo's passing went the Indian.

That may be considered an extravagant statement, but it is one that General Phil Sheridan stood sponsor for when he commanded the Army Department at Fort Sam Houston. There was a bill before the Legislature at Austin to protect the buffalo from wholesale killing. Cook in his book, *The Border and the Buffalo,* quotes the General:

It will settle this Indian question that so vexes Texas. When you destroy the buffalo you destroy the Indian's commissary. It is a well-known fact that an Army losing its base of supplies is at a great disadvantage. Send them powder and lead if you will and let them kill, skin and sell until they have exterminated the buffalo. Then your prairies will be covered with speckled cattle and the festive cowboy will follow the hunter as the forerunner of civilization.

Whether he was unkind or merely logical, time has borne him out and on the old home-range "where the buffalo roamed and the deer and antelope played", high on the Brazos Forks, the buffalo has gone, the antelope are very few and the Indian has disappeared. Instead, thriving towns, silos, huge compresses of cotton, cattle pens by the railroad tracks bawling with fat Hereford steers, gin-yards with a hundred cotton wagons waiting . . . these have been exchanged for the buffalo of General Sheridan's prophecy.

The deer, too, have gone from the glen and the shinnery wastes of the Brazos. Now and then a plane pilot will see a herd of antelope on the bare high Plains. Prairie-chickens and wild pigeons of the olden days have gone. What are left have drifted south to the Edwards Plateau country and seek shelter in the hills of the Llano and on the banks of the Guadalupe. Great herds of wild game dwell no more on the Brazos.

John Duval, early Brazos biographer of Big Foot Wallace and chronicler of the lore of the River, when escaping from the Mexicans at Goliad during the Texas Revolution and making his way through the Brazos bottoms near Columbia, saw great droves of deer, painted grouse, prairie-hen and wild turkey. He states that he could get within fifty steps of an hundred feeding deer at one time and that they were far tamer than the wild mustang that fled at human approach.

It was a magnificent sight, the old-timers say, to see a drove of wild mustangs on the top of a plateau at sundown, forming a line against the setting sun, seeming like a cavalry troop in maneuver and precision, their thick manes waving and long tails sweeping the ground.

The hunters, both Indian and white, walked or rode them down in relay teams or by indefatigable stalking. It might take a week to exhaust a selected mustang and pen him up in a dead-end arroyo or canyon and capture him. If he stopped to graze for an instant the pursuer would come steadily on and the wild beast would run on again with only a stop now and then to look back. The man was always coming. The tracking would be on the full of the moon so that it could continue all night. When captured and broken they were used for mounts, eaten or sold to horse-dealers to be shipped to markets in the east.

There was no dearth of "critters" in the Brazos valley in early days. Wolves were said to be so plentiful that they accounted for as many as one hundred head of cattle each every year. Some were crafty enough to avoid poisoned meat set out for them. They were hunted, along with the cougar and the wildcat, for damage they did to young deer and yearling colts.

But the mustang was a match for them. If a wolf or a panther sought to attack their young, these wild horses would form a circle and if the varmint got within range of their flashing hooves, he was quickly bested. But today they are both gone from the Brazos—the mustang and the wolf—and only now and then is an isolated lobo heard howling up in the lonely hills.

Many of the little fellows survive. The pole-cat, the fox, the squirrel, the 'possum, the coon, the prairie-dog, the ground-squirrel . . . they stay on and multiply and replenish the land with their kind. Many are the amusing tales told of the time when cowboys lived in dugouts or slept beside a chuck-wagon and the numerous little skunks came foraging. Woe to the cow-poke who woke up too suddenly and flung one off his blanket. It got so that the favorite pastime at sundown was to hunt these little creatures as they left their warrens and shoot them before they came within smelling distance of camp.

The prairie-dog persists in spite of the war that man and rattlesnake have made on him and his kind. They are said to consume in a year enough Brazos grass from the plains and prairies to feed out 3,000,000 cattle. Their holes caused many a broken horse-leg. Rattlesnakes are found in their villages, seeking to devour the tiny prairie-dogs' young, about the most practical use that a rattler has ever been to a Brazos resident.

There are accounts of alligators being on the Brazos in the old days. Even as far north as The Falls of the River in the vicinity of Chilton, near Marlin, it is recorded that Newton B. Maxey was out hunting one day when an alligator "charmed" his young puppy and before Maxey could interfere had swallowed it. Becoming very angry, the old Brazonian killed the 'gator and cut him wide open to recover the puppy who grew up to be a fine hunting-dog and lived out his days.

There is little game along the Brazos today, perhaps because the River's people used it up for food in the early days, or did not protect it from needless slaughter. There was a time when outside his cabin, or at least in his smokehouse, come wintertime, the Brazos settler would hang a dressed deer, bear or buffalo carcass in the cold air and slice off steaks when he needed them. They had an old saying: "The hogs ate the farmer's corn and the bears ate the farmer's hogs."

There is one lively survivor—the jackrabbit. He stays on despite the drives, diseases and continuous open season against him. Target-practice and auto headlights have taken their toll of him but he persists and his numbers seem never to grow less.

The books and accounts, newspapers and old-timers' stories are replete with tales of the abundance of the early Brazos game trails. Deer, antelope, mustang, buffalo, bear, panther, wolves, Mexican hogs, wild turkeys were all here then but now they are gone. Doves and quail are hunted in the limited season, with a short shot at wild ducks and geese that pause on their way to winter-haven in the Gulf. The Brazos hunter has to go afield now to other parts of the country for his game . . . his predecessors did too thorough a job.

Coyotes, armadillo, an occasional wolf, a small wild-cat and the crow—the old reliable "Gentleman-in-black"—are all that are left. Birds of many kinds and colors fly in the air above the Brazos and nest in trees beside the stream. Eagles were bad in the old days up in the Caprock country. Roosting on the jagged peaks, they darted down into the plain and carried off newly-born calves and young deer or pecked out the eyes of the aged or ailing animals who could not run. A few only are seen now in the high air of the Double Mountain region on the upper River.

Another bird fading out of the Brazos picture as the years pass is the wild turkey. At one time they were thick in the Cross Timbers and on down to the mouth of the River. The cowboys, careful of their gun-powder, found out where they fed and watered and hunted them on horse-back, running them until they were exhausted and came to ground to make easy catches.

There are serpents in Eden, too. The outstanding one is the Texas rattlesnake. Nature put him and his kind along the River from Bailey to Brazoria, sunning on the Caprock, slithering through the limestone slabs, hiding in prairie-dog holes or whirring in the dank undergrowth of the lower River. They hunt him along the stream's course with forked sticks and crocus-sacks, catch him and extract his oil, preserve his skin for market and can his flesh for *hors d'oeuvres,* but not to be eaten by Brazos folk who know him far too well.

He is the common enemy of man, bird and animal along the River's run. The deer or goat will attack him with their sharp hooves, the *paisano* or road-runner will stand up and fight him with its long beak, and the hog, tame or wild, will wade in and try to gobble him up.

In April 1685, the first surgical operation in Texas was performed by Leotat, the rascally French surgeon with La Salle's expedition. The patient was M. le Gros who had been bitten by a rattlesnake. An amputation of his leg was attempted but the poison had spread to the blood-stream and the patient died two days later.

The fish in the streams of this present day are no great lure for the angler. Abundant in earlier days, catfish, bass, alligator gar, perch, gasperoo and buffalo fish take chances with the uncertain depth of the Brazos current and usually lose. Only in well-stocked lakes may the fisherman find plenty.

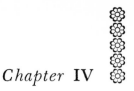

Chapter **IV**

CITADELS, CHURCHES, COLLEGES

IN THIS COUPLET OF RYAN'S is the story of many a Brazos church and citadel:

> *A land without ruins is a land without memories,*
> *A land without memories is a land without history.*

When peace does reign up and down the River of The Arms of God, when her sons are not at war, when the midnight air is not disturbed by the screams of massacred settlers, when the six-gun is silent on the Plains and the bugles are but memories through the thickets of the Cross Timbers, it is hard to believe that this was a land won through battle and blood-shed and held by the might of arms.

The old forts of the Brazos-land are in ruins or the site marked by historical shafts. The old missions have fallen with the weight of years and have been supplanted by other temples and spires. Colleges have burgeoned and bloomed from the buds of the small schools of the earlier days.

When the River's folk were compelled to fight with gun and sword for the survival of themselves and their families they "forted-up", fired back and gave the enemy as good as he sent. That they were good fighters is attested by their survival.

They have been a devout people "whose God is the Lord". For more than a hundred years they have followed the paths of righteousness as a people.

They have fought steadily against ignorance. Schools have

thriven from the earliest day and education is a foremost industry in the valley. Few rivers can boast of as many institutions of higher learning upon their banks.

Citadels and forts . . . They were necessary in the early
days. When Austin and his First Three Hundred came to the
banks of the Brazos in the 1820's and built their rude cabins
they had to have loop-holes between the logs out of which
a rifle-barrel could be thrust to draw a bead on a besieging
Indian.

There had to be stockades, centrally located, where the
settlers could seek haven and refuge when the redskins went
on the war-path in numbers. Later, the Indian depredations
became so savage and the settlers' cabins were so strung out
along the River, that the Government had to send Rangers
and cavalrymen in to patrol the wooded area, chase the war-
parties of the Indians and teach them that they could not
raid the settlements with impunity.

A line of forts went up from the Rio Grande to the Red
and moved steadily westward with the wagon-trains and the
cabins. Troopers had to accompany surveying parties and
respect for Law and Order had to be taught the Indians and
outlaws who preyed upon honest folk.

There were two kinds of forts in the early days. One
gained the name but had no soldiers to garrison it. They
were stockades or earthern ramparts where the settlers could
hie in time of danger for "forting-up". The others, such as
Quintana and Velasco at the Brazos mouth, Fort Graham in
Hill, Fort Belknap in Young and Fort Griffin in Shackelford
bristled with sabers and housed men who rode out on the
Brazos Forks behind the guidons of the famous cavalry troops
of the Army.

The Spaniard built *presidios* from the first time of his oc-
cupancy of the Brazos valley. Beside this fort he built a mission and hand-in-hand, the Church and the Military evange-
lized the Brazos country, each after its own fashion. Their

first was at Nacogdoches, for the *padres* and the *soldados* had made it to the Brazos and beyond into eastern Tejas to establish an outpost for Spain. South and west of the River, they established another at La Bahia del Esperitu that was later to be known as Goliad, about which history would swirl.

But, strange to say, it was not until 1762, two hundred years and more after Cabeza de Vaca, Coronado and Moscoso, that the Viceroy of Spain in Mexico City gave earnest attention to fortifying the Brazos-land for his King.

Iturrigaray decreed that no strangers to the Spanish flag should cross the Arroyo Hondo. To enforce that edict he ordered the Brazos mouth fortified. Out of his San Antonio de Bexar central headquarters he directed the garrisons there and at the mouth of the Colorado River and on the sandy keys of Galveston Island. These forts and their successors were to have a come-and-go existence keeping pace with the threats to Spanish sovereignty in the Brazos-land. When Aaron Burr would make a gesture toward Texas, or the Filibusterers would come adventuring across the Sabine or out of New Orleans to match swords with the Don, there would be a strengthening of the garrisons, the hasty erection of more fortifications and a column would start North from Monterrey.

Once, when Governor Antonio Cordero was to be installed at San Antonio, the Governor of Nuevo Leon, Simon Herrara, marched 1,500 of his crack troops up from Monterrey to put on a show of power and pomp for the Tejas Indians.

But, when the threats died down so did the garrisons.

The Brazos always demanded its fair share of garrisons and redoubts. The fort at Velasco was one of the earliest. Anahuac was not far away and about these two one of the earliest inimical advances of the colonists for freedom took place. It was in 1832, when Colonel Blackburn commanding at Anahuac told William Barret Travis, Patrick C. Jack and Monroe Edwards that there was no justification for the colonists to transport cannon and forbade it. A hostile argument arose and the Velasco commander, Colonel Ugartichea, was warned to keep hands-off. He agreed but the settlers on the Brazos suspected him of breaking his pledge.

After the arrest at Anahuac of Travis and his associates, the colonists moved in force and on a May morning in 1832 William J. Russell and a man named Harrison fired on Mexican troops and the first blood was spilled. "The first germ of Texas Liberty was planted" and the issue was joined.

When the perfidy of Ugartichea was discovered the colonists moved against him. Blackburn at Anahuac, Colonel Piedras at Nacogdoches and the commander at Fort Tenoxtitlan up the Brazos had all struck their flags and were falling back on San Antonio for reinforcements, leaving the Velasco commander at the mercy of the settlers.

John Austin and William Russell led their followers to the storming of Velasco. By land and by River they attacked, using Captain John C. Rowland's cotton-boat with a cannon mounted behind the bales. At Calvert's Labor, two miles from the fort, there was a sharp engagement between the land forces and the fort surrendered before the main attack ever came off. The colonists were jubilant that there was not a single soldier in Mexican uniform left east of the San Antonio River . . . that was a full four years before San Jacinto.

After the coming of the *Lively* with Austin's first colonists, the building of a fort of sorts became the issue. The place selected was at the great bend of the Brazos near the site of present Richmond. It was selected because it was midway between Nacogdoches and Goliad, near to El Camino Real, which was the main road from Mexico to Louisiana. The road crossed the Brazos above Big Creek and below the Bend where the Richmond bridge is today.

The Indians had a regular passage here and the buffalo used a ford nearby. William Morton would later install a ferry here and Austin's *empresarios* would build a fort of sorts—naming it "Fort Bend". It was neither old nor a fort, but came popularly to be known as "Old Fort".

The Mexicans established a fort later on at Tenoxtitlan, ten miles north of San Felipe, fifteen miles below the mouth of the San Andres River on the right bank of the Brazos, twelve miles above the upper road leading from Nacogdoches to Bexar. The Brazos was navigable then up that far and furnished an advance post against marauding Indians who cast avaricious eyes at the settlements that were beginning to sprout on the lower River.

As the regular Brazos forts came to be established they followed a pattern. One writer in 1856 gives a general description of them:

. . . our nominal Indian forts had no structures for defense . . . a stockade of mesquite trunks, surrounding the stables, which were open thatched sheds. There were . . . officers' quarters, barracks, bakery, hospital and guard-room. All were rough and temporary, some being merely *jackals* of sticks and mud, but all were white-washed and neatly kept by taste and discipline.

Texonlet was, in 1832, the farthest up the Brazos of the recognized forts where a Mexican garrison was established and would be in present Burleson County. Many forts, such as Fort Parker near Mexia, ungarrisoned, were stockades built of logs capable of caring for many families and their live stock. Fort Graham in Hill County on the Brazos was near Whitney and eighteen miles from Hillsboro. It was established in 1849 on the site of an Indian village where old José Maria, a "bad" Indian Chief held forth, and it lasted for four years. The 8th Infantry garrisoned it in 1849 and it was named for Colonel W. M. Graham who was killed in the Mexican War. Only a few ruins of native stone remain. Since the troopers from Fort Richardson at Jacksboro patrolled the Brazos valley in Palo Pinto, Hood and Parker

Counties for hostile Indians and frequent trips were made to that fort, it has come to be accounted as one of the Brazos chain although the River does not run through the county of Jack. Here there were forty imposing buildings of rock and stone in the garrison-days and General William Tecumseh Sherman dignified it with an inspection on his trip to Texas as Chief of Staff of the Armies.

Fort Belknap near present Newcastle in Young County flourished as an important fortification of the Army in 1855. To this post in September of that year, Colonel Albert Sydney Johnston with 750 men and 800 horses moved from Jefferson Barracks, Missouri with the 2nd Cavalry to form the garrison. A long string of mule-drawn supply wagons followed. Arriving at the Cross Timbers in mid-December, Companies B and C were sent down on the San Saba River where the Comanches and the Lipans were giving trouble, while the remainder of the regiment went into garrison at Fort Belknap. Lt. Col. Robert E. Lee was serving at nearby Camp Cooper at the time.

Fort Murray was a forting-up redoubt about eight miles from Belknap and used by the settlers when the Indians came down on their monthly raids. During the Civil War when the border forts were inadequately garrisoned, these earthern fortifications were about all that the settlers had. At one time the Indians got so bad, with the men fighting with Lee in Virginia, that every resident of Clay County moved out.

Fort Phantom Hill was situated between present Albany and Anson and was an important one for a time after its establishment in 1851. But by 1854, Fort Belknap was garrisoned and the Army abandoned Phantom Hill in 1854. The Butterfield Stage Line took over one of the fort's barracks and some of the buildings still stand. The powder-house of native rock and River-mud is well preserved as a monument to those who dared to keep the vigil in the early days when the Indians made it highly necessary.

[55]

After the Civil War was over and the Federal troops came back to the Brazos forts, Fort Griffin became of primary importance. Set up on a high hill over the Brazos Fork in Shackelford County, it had a commanding view of the country roundabout and became a settlement of considerable size. The buildings were of native rock and stone put together by the Army's best artisans and masons from Fort Sam Houston down at San Antonio. There was an officers' row of one-room-and-kitchen size houses with the Commanding Officer having a great log structure of importance. The old bakery with its high chimneys and fire-brick ovens still is the object of much interest to the visitor. The arsenal and hospital buildings are distinguishable in the ruins. There were no wash-houses nor bathing facilities and the kitchens were frame shacks, long since gone. The stables, it being a cavalry post, were the most de luxe accommodations on the post, of course.

Near the foot of the hill on which the Fort stood and along the Brazos was a town that sprang up overnight. Traders and gamblers, buffalo-hunters and dance hall girls, surveyors and soldiers, adventurers of all types came and went. It was a lively boom-town while the Fort lasted. Thirty-seven miles west of Fort Belknap and eighty miles east of the Double Mountain, it was strategically located and gradually the other fortifications were abandoned in favor of Griffin. It was called Camp Wilson when first officially recognized on July 31, 1867 for a Lieutenant of the 6th Cavalry, but when Congress made it a fort, they named it for General Griffin who commanded the District down at Fort Sam Houston.

The country around the fort was wooded and rolling. It belonged to the string of forts to which Bliss at El Paso, Quitman, Davis, Stockton, Concho and Richardson belonged. The prospectors, overland travelers, buffalo-hunters and stage-coach drivers looked on Fort Griffin as their last jumping-off place before hitting the Indian country and never failed to make it to Fort Griffin to stock up. It was also the center of amusement and hell-raising for the rough men of the frontier in those early times.

The frontier moved gradually as the Indian and the buffalo drifted farther and farther west. Surveying-parties were treading on the heels of both, guarded by soldiers from the forts and little cabins of settlers began to appear on the Brazos Forks in the shinnery country. There was a great buffalo-hide industry at Fort Griffin and in the valley north of the Fort—"The Flats"—were many stores, a dozen saloons, eating-houses, dance halls and dives. Picket-houses made of poles and hides with dirt-banking served as living-quarters and at a safe-smelling distance from town there was a tipi settlement of Tonkawas. Night and day the trading went on. Barter and sale, loading of wagon-trains, coming or going of a hunting or a surveying party, drunks and gamblers whooping it up to constant music . . . robberies and murders occurring in broad daylight and everyone went armed with his eyes wide open . . . or else . . . such was the Fort Griffin of the '70's.

Company I of the 6th Cavalry was the first Army unit there and the troopers had to haul water from Collins Creek by wagon. But it was alkali-bitter in summer and brackish in winter, so they went to the Clear Fork of the Brazos instead. They used Collins Creek for a bath-house. Vegetables and fruit came by wagon from Weatherford and Jacksboro. Calvert, way down on the Brazos was the nearest railroad. It was eight good days to San Antonio for the mail and twelve to Washington, D. C.

A writer in 1877 gives a pen-picture of the Fort there at Griffin:

The post, on a hill a quarter-mile south, is almost depopulated, one company of Negro soldiers keeping the garrison . . . This is a frontier town with all of the usual characteristics but it is orderly. The picket-houses are giving way to rock. The buffalo industry has reached huge proportions, 200,000 hides having been received here last season. It is a gay and festive place, night is turned into day, the dance and the flowing-bowl is indulged freely while hilarity and glee range supreme from eve until the morning hours. Lager beer is 25c a glass.

If one wished to see a celebrity of that day or if a sheriff wanted to catch a criminal, he went to Fort Griffin and waited. The rendezvous would usually be made. Pat Garrett and Bat Masterson were frequent visitors. Old Indian fighters strolled down the streets of Fort Griffin town—Shafter, Miles and Mackenzie—from up at the Fort. Great cattle names were called in the trading and stock-pens as greetings— Goodnight, Slaughter, Chisolm, Potter and Loving. There were two hotels for the transients and a boot-hill for the permanent folk.

But, one day in 1881 the end came . . . the Indian menace was laid, the buffalo had moved on west or been exterminated in that region . . . the gamblers and the fancy-women found the pickings too slim . . . so the troopers lined up for the last Assembly on the top of the hill. The Adjutant read the order, the flag came down and the bugle blared. The column swung into fours and off behind the guidons of the troops. Fort Griffin was washed up and done.

The Brazos forts underwent a change of management in 1861. The State had gone for Secession and on a cold February day, Colonel Ben McCulloch in his new gray uniform called on General David E. Twiggs, USA. He demanded that the Texas forts surrender to him in the name of the Confederate States of America.

"We shall have the honor of accepting your surrender, sir," said McCulloch, "or we shall be compelled to take action against your garrisons and seize the materials of war that you have."

"You are aware, sir, that we are prepared to defend our nineteen Texas forts?" the Yankee commander asked.

The Texan nodded and drawled, "We figured on that, General, before we seceded. I'll make you a proposition, sir. Move out peaceful and we won't make prisoners of your 2,328 men."

"You seem well informed."

"That's how we do business in Texas, sir."

So, on February 18, 1861 almost $3,000,000 worth of Federal property and nineteen forts passed to the control of the Bonnie Blue Flag, Texas' choice of the Confederate banners, because it "wore the single star."

They cashiered Twiggs out of the United States Army for "treachery to the flag of his country" by surrendering his forts without firing a shot and he joined up with the Confederates, but he did not last long. He retired shortly because of "illness."

But the flag of the United States came back to the Brazos forts in 1865 and stayed there until the forts were dismantled one by one. In 1917 a new fort or camp was known to the Brazos. At Waco, the War Department set up Camp MacArthur, where the 32nd Wisconsin and Michigan National Guard Division trained for World War I over-seas duty and where Generals W. G. Haan and J. D. L. Hartman came to command this huge cantonment on the River.

In World War II, at Mineral Wells in Palo Pinto County, through which the Brazos flows in snakelike meanderings, the War Department set up its great Infantry Training Center and thousands of young Americans tramped through the thickets of the Brazos to learn how to fight on New Guinea and in the Ardennes. General William Simpson, later commander of the 9th U. S. Army in Germany, and himself a native Brazonian, commanded this camp as the first officer in charge after its inception.

There were many airfields strung out along the Brazos' course during the days of 1941-45 where glider, bomber and pursuit pilots were trained in the River's sky.

[59]

Churches and missions . . . After the settler and his axe, came the soldier and his rifle. Along with each . . . shoulder-to-shoulder . . . strode The Man of The Cloth. Priest, preacher, rabbi or minister, they have been there in the River's valley to bless the efforts, minister to the distressed, marry the lovers and bury the dead.

The Brazos folk have ever been a religious people, but not notably pious. The red Indian was deeply devout as he worshipped his Sun-god and invoked the blessing of the "Great Spirit" or of the "Grand Captain", to whose Happy Hunting-Ground he believed his blest would surely reach. In his burial-mounds that we desecrate today in search of artifacts and curios for our museums, we find many attestations to the Indian's belief in immortality.

The dead brave was dressed in all of his finery, accoutred for a long journey and into his ear the Medicine-Man of the tribe whispered: "Work there in the great house until we have all assembled." They had the idea of waiting for each other until all the tribe had come when they would unitedly go on to the final Nirvana of the gods. He venerated fire as did his Mexican counterpart and feared that if it ever went out completely it would never be restored.

They had trouble with the faith of these Spanish priests in their cowls and sack-cloth, bare of foot and shaven of pate. When the *padres* held up the image of their god, wracked and tortured on a cross, slain by the perfidy of his own people, and told them to adore it, the Indians hesitated.

Then, when the Jesuits came no more and the Franciscans were sent into Texas by the order of The Holy See—"Francis, repair ye my church that falleth into ruin"—the Indian found that he was supposed to go out of his way and build for these religionists great houses for The Persecuted Figure on the Cross. It was not long until the mission bells were ringing in the valley of The River of The Arms of God, but the Indians did not reconcile the differences. Enslaved, they had a kindred feeling for the tortured Christ, but never seemed to find relief at the hands of the relentless *padres*.

It had been Austin's solemn pledge that those who came in his colony would be of or would embrace the Catholic faith. That was a condition precedent. But it was a hard rule to enforce and men do not form their religious convictions by reason of political or economic obligations. Many masses were mumbled in those early colonizing days along the Brazos that were only upon the lips of the devotees. Clandestine Protestant services began to be held along the River at an early date. In a century and a half that has elapsed . . . over sixty sects are now in the valley . . . 1,600 churches and more than three million followers of the various faiths.

The priest and the preacher always have figured prominently in the history of the Brazos. Father Douay was there at the death of La Salle in the forests of the Navasota . . . Four Franciscan fathers marched with Captain Alonzo de Leon to bless his bullets as he came to destroy the French at Garcitas Fort on the Navidad . . . every expedition that came out of Mexico, Brazos-bound, had one or more *padres* in its train from Coronado on through the years.

The Spaniards built a fort against the hostile Indians and then caused the friendly aborigines to build a chapel or mission next door. The first of these was dedicated to St. Francis and named "San Francisco de los Tejos" and was between the Brazos and Nacogdoches. It had many varied fortunes but was never fully abandoned. When Captain Domingo Ramon—he who called the Brazos "San Xavier" in his reports for some unknown reason—brought the re-establishing movement to the land of the Brazos in 1713 after St. Denis, the Frenchman's surprise visit to the Rio Grande, he had twelve friars, three laymen and a number of religious artisans, all committed to the building or repair of missions, with him. Then was set up San Francisco de los Tejos at Nacogdoches, Nuestra Señora de la Guadalupe at the Neches,

La Purisima Concepción for the Assinais Indians and Nuestra Señora de los Dolores for the Aes Indians on the Brazos.

They built well. Dormitories, barracks, cells, court-yards, colonnades, dungeons . . . political prisoners, war-captives and Indian slaves working hard all day under the directions of the priests and sleeping at night in pits and dens hardly fit for human habitation . . . it was a hard penance to pay in so noble a cause . . . but the Spaniards believed that it was good for the souls of the Indians.

Efforts were made unceasingly to bring these benighted folk who were found living upon the Brazos to the True Faith. There were two groups according to the *padres*—*"Reducidos"* were the ones who were converted and *"Bravos"*, the ungrateful sinners who ran away into the woods and hid from their "benefactors".

Many of the missions built on the Brazos and along its tributaries were elaborate affairs. Artists from the Grand Mission Colleges at Querétaro and Zacatecas came to do the fresco work, carve the doors, turn out the panels, line the niches with shells, adorn the holy objects, fashion the grill-work, lay the tiled floors, erect the Moorish columns and set the pebbled mosaics. The heavy work was done by the slave-labor of which there seemed to be no shortage in the Spaniards' chains and shackles.

There was wood along the Brazos banks and in the lime-stone quarries there was stone in abundance. Thirty-five elaborate missions were builded in the 1700's and one priest records that he baptized 5,000 Indians in a single day!

There usually was a wooden chapel at first with a crudely-fashioned cross atop it, patio and transept open to the sky. But later there were stables, granaries, mills and a *Gran Iglesia* of cathedral porportions with imported bells—The Voice of the Angels—ringing their message to the Brazos folk at Evensong.

Father Solis' diary, written about the Brazos folk, says:

In the afternoon before even-prayers with the stroke of the mission-bell the padre assembled the Indians, small and large, in the cemetery. He had them do their devotions, explained the mystery of the Holy Faith, adjured them about the Commandments, gave them food and clothes for their bodies and lessons for their minds.

Images were sculptured from Brazos wood and painted with the vegetable dyes that the Indians revealed to the Spaniards. In turn the *padres* taught the aborigines to make candles of animal-tallow for their devotions to The Queen of Heaven. In 1762 a visiting Franciscan includes this in his report when he returned to Mexico City:

The employment of the Indian women and children is to spin, work with the *malacates* and to comb the cotton. All of this labor constitutes no impediment to their spiritual welfare.

Whether the Indian enjoyed this scourging of his soul may be judged from one example. One winter the Indians of the San José Mission deserted *en masse* and returned to their native woods and gods. The *padres* reported in great concern to Mexico that "there was no way at the disposal of the priests to compel them to return."

But there was not all drudgery and penance along the Brazos in those days, for there are many accounts of devotion manifested by the Indians and these old missions had a sacerdotal air about them that must have given peace to many of the troubled hearts of the red men. The impressive churches, the rich garments of the priests and the candles with their shadows falling upon the surplices of the small Indian acolytes serving the Mass undoubtedly resulted in the conversion of many of these people. Father McGill states that he won 80,000 Indians to the Church, travelling alone through Indian countries "all with no defense except a Crucifix raised on high."

There is a story that one hears often of "The Lady in Blue". . .

[63]

Maria Coronel de Agrada lived in Spain and when Father Massanet came North with Captain Alonzo de Leon to build missions and dispel the French threat he wrote to this lady back in Spain of his experiences. The account that she read was constantly with her and she organized a society in her home town to sponsor the heathen Indians of Tejas.

She corresponded with Father Massanet intermittently until she had a good understanding of the Indians and they of her. Finally, she was convinced that the saints had transported her across the waters and allowed her in a dream to visit in the tepees and wigwams of these people. Some of them reported that they had actually seen her. Thereupon, the priests declared a miracle, built a chapel in her honor, fired off a salute with the cannon on her Saint's Day and added her story to the folk-lore of the Brazos.

The Church did more than the government to strengthen the Spanish hold on the land of the River in the first two hundred years of the Spanish settlement on the Brazos. On October 4, 1730, the Viceroy at the instance of the Querétaro Missions, gave the oldest land-grant in Texas to certain Indian tribes for "having been reduced to Christian and civilized communities."

The Catholic attempt at evangelization of the Brazos began with Cabeza de Vaca, who boasted many converts and his claimed success caused Fra Juan de Padillo in 1541 when he came with Coronado to seek a ministry among the Plains Indians whom they encountered. He won the permission of the *Gran Capitan* to be allowed to remain behind and work on the tribes.

But, alas, when the expedition came back that way it was found that the good *padre* had been killed by some Indians up on the present Canadian River, who claimed that the men of Coronado had used them ill. There were few attempts at converting or "reducing" the Comanches on the part of the *padres*. They were most unreceptive.

[64]

The Catholic faith has lasted and persisted along the River throughout the years and at Waco it has known eighty persistent years where it operates schools and missions. It owns about one million dollars worth of property there today all stemming from its first mission on the banks of the Brazos in 1873.

But other faiths and sects and creeds have been as stoutly proclaimed on the banks of this River. As early as 1815, William Stevenson, a Methodist missionary in Arkansas, ventured down across the Red River and preached his doctrine in Texas, perhaps holding the first Protestant service in the neighborhood of the Brazos that there is any record of today.

In 1828, a little Protestant band under Elias R. Wightman came from western New York to Texas. They landed in the Matagorda Bay region and went to work on the Karankawas but with little encouragement. They ate Christmas dinner with some of Austin's colonists and then scattered, by pre-arranged design, all through the settlements up and down the Brazos preaching their doctrines when they could get an audience.

However, Joseph Bays, a Baptist from out of Ohio came in 1820 preaching in the wilderness of the Brazos-land and was promptly jailed for his heresy by the Spanish authorities. They were taking him to San Antonio de Bexar for trial when he escaped and made his way to Louisiana. Later, after the Revolution, he returned and Houston made him Indian Commissioner of the Republic of Texas.

In 1832, Needham J. Pilgrim, a Methodist, and Sumner Bacon, a Presbyterian, held services in Milam County not far from the Brazos and with the aid of the Protestant missionaries from New York who were already in the colony, made plans to establish the Protestant faith despite the opposition of the authorities. Josiah H. Bell and Stephen F. Richardson of San Felipe gave them support and encouragement. They gave out that they would organize a Sunday-school and the people came from ten miles around until thirty-two had gathered.

"But, *Señores*," said the Alcalde. "Thees ees *contre la ley. El Señor* Austin promeez. . ."

The members of the new body nodded gravely but went on with the meeting. D. W. C. Baker gives us this account of it:

This first Sunday school was held in a blackjack and post oak grove near the center of the town in a rude log cabin . . . the logs unhewn, the cracks neither chinked nor battened, a dirt floor and across it are several logs hewn on one side for seats. At one end stands the superintendent, a mere stripling, and before him about one half-dozen gentlemen and ladies as teachers with about thirty-two children.

Daniel Parker, a long-bearded old Baptist patriarch came in 1834 to San Felipe and dared the authorities with his predestinarian doctrine . . . the Hardshell Baptists set up on the Colorado about the same time . . . the Presbyterians in 1833 . . . the German Lutherans in 1839 . . . the Episcopalians in 1843 with Caleb S. Ives as their missionary, who reported his first service at Richmond "postponed because of rain" . . . the Baptists met that day! The first Jewish synagogue was established in 1854.

William B. Travis wrote in 1835 to *The New York Christian Advocate and Journal* to send Methodist missionaries to Texas "as it is destitute of religion." He wrote:

Texas is composed of the shrewdist and most interesting population of any new country on earth. The people you send to exhort them must be respectable and talented.

Two years before San Jacinto was fought, there was a big trial at the county-seat of Fort Bend County and old Parson Woodruff, a Baptist, stood up in the tail-gate of his wagon and preached hell-fire and brimstone. A Mrs. Stafford and Mrs. Rose are said to have stood nearby and when the brother paused for wind, sang lustily "On Jordan's Stormy Banks

I Stand." The Brazos, miffed and offended, that year went on a rampage and her flood-waters reached clear to Buffalo Bayou, the newspapers report.

Then, there was "The Canebrake Preacher," Rev. Z. N. Morrell, of whom Dr. J. M. Carroll says in his *History of Texas Baptists*—"There was a man sent from God and his name was Morrell." He left Tennessee condemned to die of consumption. Sam Houston had told him that "Texas was a good, healthy country and that few people there die in their beds." So, he made a date to meet Davy Crockett, a neighbor, at The Falls of the Brazos on Christmas Day, 1835 and hunt bear.

When they told him he had better turn back as a Revolution was brewing in Texas he allowed: "Naw, I've druv two hundred and fifty miles and I seldom ever turn back. I'll trust in God and travel on."

He got to the Brazos on December 30 and rose up and preached a sermon before he descended from his wagon to settle. When he got the word of how his old friend, Sam Houston, had licked the Mexicans at San Jacinto he preached a great sermon on "There is still a God in Israel" and sat down to write a book.

He established the first Baptist congregation at The Falls in 1837 and in 1844 he built and dedicated old Antioch Church in Anderson County that still functions.

"Do you still believe what you preached when you first hit Texas?" they heckled him one day. He thought a moment, spat reflectively and said in reply:

"Yes, I believe that the wilderness of the Brazos will blossom as the rose and the solitary places be made glad with the presence of the Lord!"

Rev. Joseph P. Sneed and his fifteen faithful Methodists began their church in Waco in 1850, while Noah T. Byars was the Baptists' missionary from South Carolina who settled in the Brazos midlands in 1851. It was he who owned the blacksmith shop at old Washington where the Declaration was signed and the Constitution written. He had a Baptist church going there at the Capital in 1837. In all he organized sixty-four Baptist churches along the Brazos, many of them up in the bad Indian country now in Palo Pinto and Young Counties. He was a fearless old roundsman of the Lord.

The Presbyterians came up the River to Waco in 1855 under Rev. Samuel Taylor and in 1876, Major William Penn, a lawyer from Jefferson, held a revival in Waco and is said to have preached one hundred and eighty-four sermons. Captain Sul P. Ross, Waco's first citizen, joined the church as the result of one of them, it is reported.

But on the upper Brazos the religious going was decidedly slow. Distance—Indians—lack of towns—few settlements—general hardship, these were the factors that prevented any concentrated effort in the early days. They could not locate enough timber to build a brush-arbor, in which many of the other congregations in this mild climate held their church-gatherings in the Cross Timbers. The circuit-rider and the missionary-on-horseback had to do the job on the Grand Prairie and the Plains.

Rev. J. T. Bludworth in June 1886, a Methodist circuit-rider, blazed the trail up on the Forks of the Brazos. The Methodist bishops in the North had taken heart after San Jacinto and sent a delegation of young preachers to Texas under Rev. Martin Ruter. With his main headquarters at Mobeetie, Rev. Bludworth toured the Plains and the Panhandle on horseback, preaching the doctrine of the Wesley brothers in the valleys of the Canadian and the Brazos. He recorded that if he got ten or twelve people together he held a service no matter what day of the week it was.

After the Republic was set up, there was no religious conflict along the Brazos thereafter and churches lived in harmony. The newer and more radical doctrines have never taken hold. The tendency has been toward the older and more established faiths. Methodists and Baptists predominate now but the other churches are well supported.

Colleges and schools. . . . There are three major educational institutions upon the Brazos banks where the enrollment runs into the thousands every year. In addition to these in the counties of Brazos, McLennan and Lubbock, there are numerous junior colleges, academies, institutes, high and preparatory schools.

The tradition of the Little Red School House is one deeply fixed in the Brazos-land. From 1503 when the Spaniards ordered their priests to school the Indian children to the end that they might be "reduced" from their ignorance it got its start. Soon the little black-haired redskins were speaking in the Castilian tongue and parsing the irregular sentences. They did not like it, it is recorded, any more than their parents cared for the ecclesiastical teachings, so that it became necessary for the Viceroy to issue his decree to *padre* and Indian alike that the children *"must* be educated in the arts."

When the Anglo-Saxon settlers came they had to teach their own children at home, send them back to the old States or depend upon classes taught by itinerant teachers who came along now and then, going from settlement to settlement. In 1866 at Quintana the first "free" school was established. Held in a log building, chinked with mud, clapboarded from the outside, it burned the driftwood that the small pupils picked up on the beaches. Little wooden pegs were there to support the caps and lunch-pails on the wall of the single room where the dominie taught those of all ages.

But it ended in a note of tragedy . . . the children crossed in a boat from Quintana every day. One day the teacher, bell in hand, watched the boat approach when something happened. It capsized and all of the children were drowned before help could get to them. The school closed and a few months later a hurricane swept the little school-house away

[69]

and ended the first chapter of the colony's education under the free school system.

Education has had its stumbling-blocks throughout the long years. Paucity of funds, bi-racial difficulties, distances between schoolhouse and home, Indian menace, need to work in the fields, low pay for teachers, the parochial schools sharing in public funds and the religious question, have all arisen to plague the people who tried to advance the cause of knowledge. The Mexican authorities during the days of the pre-Revolution used land-grants and other means to encourage education after their own ideas and conceptions but with scant success. Then, there was the aversion to the Spanish language, the objection to ecclesiastical background, the preference for private instruction and other reasons why the settlers from back in the United States did not choose to send their children to the Mexican state schools.

In Mirabeau B. Lamar education found a warm ally. Poet, writer, scholar himself, as well as soldier and statesman, he set about, as President of the Republic in 1838, building a State public school system. Said he:

If we are to establish a Republican government upon a broad and permanent basis, it will become our duty to adopt a comprehensive and well-regulated system of mental and moral culture.

Under his supervision and urging in 1839 the Texas Congress set aside grants for county school systems and prescribed two colleges or universities under the sponsorship of the new government. Those grants with their vast oil holdings make the system of the Texas State University the wealthiest in the world today.

Public or Free schools were set up, private and denominational seminaries and fraternal order colleges came into being. Churches and national groups began to think of institutions on the order of those in the old countries over the waters . . . the land became education-minded for its children.

But the devastation of Civil War put an end to the advancement and it was not until 1876 when the new Texas Constitution was written that a State Board was provided whose duty it would be to foster the education of the youth, make land grants and put into being Texas Agricultural and Mechanical College.

After the U. S. Congress made available 180,000 acres of Government land to each state establishing an agricultural school, the Texas Legislature, on April 17, 1871 appointed three commissioners to select a site of 1,280 acres of good land and $75,000 was set apart in the Special School Fund for buildings.

The Brazos boasts of three great colleges upon its banks. Texas A. & M., at Bryan in Brazos County is the first that the traveller meets as he journeys up the River. "Aggieland" has numerous buildings, a huge campus, superior experimental-stations, a large student-body, football teams studded with All-Americans, a large contingent of Regular Army personnel on duty with the Cadet Corps, diversified military instruction in every arm of the defense system, high standards of agricultural and engineering curricula.

In World War I there were more officers of Texas A & M in the American Army than West Point boasted . . . in 1942 when World War II was at its height, over 50% of all living graduates of Texas A & M were in uniform . . . seven General officers were old-time Aggies.

From this four hundred acre campus with over sixty buildings along with three branch colleges over Texas and many experimental-stations, A & M's influence is far-flung. The plant is located on a part of Stephen F. Austin's old original grant.

There is another State school hard by . . . Prairie View State Normal and Industrial College for Negroes near Hempstead, which is the largest Negro Land Grant college in America, owned and operated by the State, with a property value of two millions of dollars covering 1,437 acres of ground and boasting eighty-seven buildings.

Far up on the Brazos at Lubbock on the North Fork of the River is Texas Technological College—Texas Tech, as it is known—the Pride of the South Plains. Here flock the young men and women of the open spaces and the high *mesa* to learn textile and agriculture, engineering and fine arts, science and animal husbandry. Begun in 1923, during the administration of Governor Pat M. Neff, a Brazonian, as the needs for a great western institution of learning on the upper Brazos grew, it has progressed until it ranks high among the colleges of its kind.

On the middle River the towers of Baylor University rise . . . a Baptist school at Waco where the red tide of the Brazos flows beneath the high bluffs and where, for more than an hundred years, higher education has thrived. Baylor is the largest Baptist educational institution in the world.

It came into being down at old Independence near Washington-on-the-Brazos in 1845 under the sponsorship of Rev. William Tryon and Dr. Robert Emmett Bledsoe Baylor, a Baptist divine and lawyer, and got its original charter from the Texas Congress. Unbeknown to the Judge, Rev. Tryon put into the bill that the college should bear the name of "Baylor" and it was so passed. It opened on May 8, 1846 with twenty-four students and one teacher, at Independence. That town had won out over Travis, Grimes Prairie and Huntsville. The winning bid offered the following inducements:

1 section of land,	1 cow and calf,
1 bale of cotton,	1 bay mare,
1 yoke of oxen,	20 days' hauling,
5 head of cattle,	$200 in cash.

Baylor became the lengthened shadow of a great man— Rufus C. Burleson—who became President in 1851. He took it to the fore of denominational schools and kept it there. In 1857 the Waco Classical School was set up that was merged with Baylor in 1861 and the entire institution moved together and located at Waco.

Committed to the Spartan way, Dr. Burleson led Baylor students down a strict path for half-a-century. His monument on the Baylor campus carries the thoughts of the traveller back to the ruins down at Independence upon which this institution was based.

Citadels . . . churches . . . colleges . . . there are many of them in the River's land.

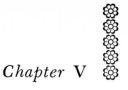

Chapter V

WE, THREE KINGS OF BRAZOS ARE

BUT . . . WHENCE COMES the industry and the wealth of these people? From what do they derive their livelihood? Upon what is the native wealth of the Brazos valley based?

Three great products of the Brazos-land stand out above all others. For one hundred and thirty years people have served these monarchs in the valley of this River. They have contested and battled with each other at various times, but today they live together in accord. Those three kings are Cotton, Cattle and Oil.

Grazing herds and lowing cattle in the pens may be found in all parts of the Brazos' course . . . silvery sheen of a cast-iron gin or the broad vista of a cotton-patch "white unto the harvest" are as familiar in Bailey as in Brazoria . . . gray steel of oil derrick above the plains or the tree-tops is as accustomed in Scurry as in Stephens and the pumpers are pulling their lines from Hempstead to Garza.

Except in the wild parts of the Forks country, where only cactus and broom-weed thrive, one is never out of sight of gins and cotton-fields.

Basically, Brazonians are people of the soil . . . they may raise other crops, they may stray off after other economic gods . . . but out of cotton, cattle or oil, they derive chief sustenance.

Up the River from Quintana one might start and see the modest little cotton stalks, knee-high and some of them bale-

to-the-acre in quantity . . . then he will encounter around
A & M the tall stalks that are queerly different . . . depending on the season, he will see little two-leaf plants growing
just out of the soil . . . and then he is on the Grand Prairie
and the Blacklands where he senses that the yield is more
abundant . . . there is a wealth of cotton here, he admits
. . . and then he reaches the high Plains country.

Certainly, he argues to himself, there can be no cotton up
here. It is bare and not even the trees and other vegetation
grow well . . . but he suddenly begins to find himself in cotton . . . acres of it, multiplied sections under cultivation and
he frowns in wonder.

Bales of it strung out as far as the eye can follow from the
level, row upon row. No warehouses can accommodate the
excess so it must be left here by the compress, the gin or the
railroad out in the open. And then the wagons at the gin.
No cues forming up, just wagons left there until the ginners
can reach them, running night and day during picking time.

And about the farm or ranch-house there is a huge dune
of fresh-picked cotton awaiting the wagons coming back,
tractor-drawn, from the gin. There is nothing else to do with
it but pile it here.

King Cotton is not new to the Brazos. When the men of
Hernando Cortez marched into Mexico City to see the Aztec
followers of Montezuma wearing cotton garments of finer
weave than any they had seen back in Spain they were amazed.
Cotton had gotten there ahead of them and it is contained in
their reports to the Spanish Crown. Of course, when the
Spanish *padres* and soldiers came to the Brazos they brought
cotton-seed and had the Indians plant and cultivate it. Later,
they came in handy in carding, seeding and weaving it.

There have been evidences of textile-work even among
the prehistoric aborigines that show cotton to have antedated
the Spaniards on the banks of the River of The Arms of God.
When the Anglo-Americans came across the Sabine they

[75]

brought their cotton-seed and their slaves to found the plantations of the lower Brazos and repeat their successes back in the land of Dixie.

Limited as was the Spanish-Mexican *algodones* production, the Anglo-Saxons coming in 1820 made it the first commercial crop by 1850, when over fifty thousand bales was the annual yield of the River's valley. Noah Smithwick says that Jared E. Groce of South Carolina brought an hundred slaves and set them to clearing new-ground for cotton and corn. He hired two hunters to keep his field-hands supplied with food and Noah adds significantly:

. . . the wild mustangs being the largest and easiest to kill, the Negroes lived on horse-meat until the corn crop was made.

Likewise, Jared Groce built the first cotton gin in 1825 and shipped the first Texas bale out on a Brazos barge to the Gulf to meet the ocean-going ships. As soon as they had a roof over their heads, Austin's First Three Hundred planted a stand of cotton. Despite what they had done in trade or profession back in the old States, here they had to have something they could barter and trade. Cotton was legal tender the wide world over.

Gradually, from this early beginning in the 1820's, Cotton crept up the valley of the Brazos. By the year 1823, 5,000 bales were pressed and sent to market. By 1833 there were thirty gins and an annual production of over 8,000 bales. England was interested now in Brazos cotton and New England wanted Texas in the Union so that the cotton raised along her longest river would come there to Massachusetts and not go to Manchester across the waters.

Sam Houston used cotton as a trading-value in Annexation and by 1855 with a slave population of 105,974, there was an annual yield of 105,111. But by the time Fort Sumter was fired on, the Brazos fields and those of her tributaries ran the yearly crop to half a million bales.

The Civil War wrecked this economy. After the four years fighting was concluded the slave was the share-cropper, the non-plantation owner was the tenant-farmer.

Cotton was produced by the few before the War, but now it came from many. A small farmer had a few bales that he *had* to sell. Book-keeping, credit, boll-weevil, pickers-shortage, drought, weather, price, marketing, were the problems of those who served this King.

By 1917 the counties of the Brazos west of the 100th meridian were raising close to an hundred thousand bales and by 1927 the upper Brazos was sending a million and a quarter bales to the markets of the world. The boll-weevil can not live in that high Plains country. They found out that it was only a few inches down to water up on the Plains and they stopped looking up for rain-clouds and looked down to the under-surface water for irrigation. The roads came and the railroads ran their steel rails over the flat Plains country to take the crop to market. Cotton-fields increased and the land bloomed whiter.

Blackland, Plains, Prairie . . . there was no difference. It was all cotton-land—eleven million Blackland acres and seven million Grand Prairie acres.

Within one hundred miles of the Brazos banks is the largest inland spot-cotton market in America and in that area the world's largest production of cotton machinery is turned out every year. Cotton mills, gins, factories for cotton goods with processing plants for cotton-seed and its oil abound all up and down the valley, while nearby Galveston and Houston furnish adequate ports to ship that portion of the yield of the Brazos crop to foreign markets by water that the rails have not claimed.

Waco at the midway of the River was early The Cotton Capital of all Texas and in 1911 was the world's largest inland cotton market with upward of a million bales handled through its cotton yards. Today the figure is doubled and it ranks with the largest of the inland cotton centers. Back in the early times of the town Captain Thomas H. Barron owned the first mill in that section and in 1860 added machinery for the carding of cotton. Bayliss Earle ran the Yankee blockade in the Civil War to bring over a cotton mill from England, spirit it in through Mexico, ox-cart it to the Brazos and establish it in East Waco. It made so many Confederate uniforms that the Carpetbaggers confiscated it when they took over.

These later days have seen the Negro passing from the cotton-patch . . . the Mexican *bracero* gladly takes his place. Admitted to Texas under special immigration treaties which provide that they may pick cotton and then go back to their homes across the Rio Grande, the migration North comes in the fall of the year. An ancient jaloppy loaded with an entire Mexican family of all ages, headed by the bewhiskered *padre* of the group, comes up the highway. Attacking a cotton-field, every member of the family drags a sack down the row and many an American dollar goes into the family pouch that will last them all winter back in their sleepy little village in Coahuila. This modern Mexican invasion is netting the folk from south of the Border far more than their efforts did the *conquistadores* when they searched for gold in the Brazosland. These later-day invaders have "struck gold" on the Brazos!

Cotton battled for kingship with Cattle for a time when the post-Civil War days made quick money imperative and the trail-drives beckoned to the Brazos men. For a few decades the attention was directed to beef-on-the-hoof, but with money gained from cattle the farms were rehabilitated, the land put back in shape and soon cotton was growing again. Then came transportation in the form of the railroads and Cotton was secure. It is interesting to see what they thought back in 1880. *The Fort Griffin Echo* for February 21, had this to say:

The subject of raising cotton is being agitated by a number of our farmers who believe that the staple has never been tried in this country and that it would be well for those who do engage in it to place their reliance on other crops until they can thoroughly test the adaptability of our soil to this new crop.

"The cattle upon a thousand hills" . . . the psalmist was rhetorical. Perhaps his Judea did not have a thousand hills, but the Brazos valley has and there will likely be cattle grazing on them all. Usually if a man owns a hill in the River's land, somehow or other he will manage to have a few cattle.

You see them high on the *mesa* cropping the brown tufts of grass with patches of flinty or sandy soil showing in between . . . a group of Herefords gathered about a windmill holding convention around salt or sulphur blocks or, perhaps, a feed-trough . . . not a tree in sight to seek shelter beneath . . . or down in the shinnery chewing a cud under a mesquite bush as they nibble at a bean of that plant . . . splashing in the shallows of the forests of the Bosque . . . mooing at the gate of a dairy in Falls . . . enjoying the shade of the big trees in the coastal pasture, their hides impervious to the mosquitos and pests of the low country.

The Brazos plays the Herefords for beef, the Holsteins for milk, the Brahmas for hardiness, with a straying off to other breeds on the part of an occasional "foreigner" or newcomer to the valley.

They claim that the first Spanish cattle came to Mexico in 1521 when Captain Gregorio Villalobos experimented with them there. But it took the adventurous Dons two hundred years to get them on to the banks of the Brazos in sizeable numbers. Coronado's chronicler records that in 1541 they included five hundred head of cattle in their first expedition. Many of them escaped into the upper reaches of the Brazosland to run wild and breed the herds that were to be found there in a later day.

The Indians never got interested in raising cattle. It was

too confining, they did not know milk or its use and would far rather have deer, buffalo or mustang meat for eating purposes. They took to the white man's horse but, as far as his cattle were concerned, the Indian slew them for the sheer deviltry of it, or for a meal when he was extremely hungry. The Brazos-land had many wild cattle when the settlers started their march up the River's course and "cow-hunts" were very usual ways to start a herd.

The Spanish expeditions into Tejas brought cattle for use at the missions and presidios. Long, lean and rangy Spanish-Mexican breeds were quite a contrast to the European and American varieties that the settlers from the old States drove in when they came. A union of the two produced the Longhorn possessed of much endurance and hardihood. He was fit for the trek up the trail and few sedentary breeds of the present day could take what the Longhorns did when a distance was covered such as the Texas-to-Kansas trip in the latter days of the 1800's.

Colonel Shannon in 1866 brought the first Brahma stock into the lower Brazos country where the breed now abounds. J. A. McFadding of Victoria started the first real herd from a pure-bred *Bos Indicus* cow and bull, born in India, and purchased by the experimenter from Hagenback circus. But it was Captain Mifflin Kennedy in 1874 who began crossing the Brahmas with native stock and interesting breeds developed. That has not been popular, however, and one may see on the lower Brazos today some fine registered herds of Brahmas with their silky gray coats and high humps against a background of great oaks and Spanish moss that will delight a lover of good stock.

The Brazos is a cattle-land and its people are cattle-minded. On the high plains, where there is grass and shelter in winter in the canyons and draws, down in the forested country of the middle River, or on the coastal plain, where there is much water and lush grass, Brazos cattlemen ask no more than a break with the weather now and then. If he has a little money ahead, he will get a small ranch on the outside of town . . . run a few head of cattle . . . wear a tan hat with an extra-size brim . . . have a fancy shirt and a pair of narrow-toed, spool-heeled boots in his closet and . . . a yen to talk cattle whether he makes a dime out of them or not. It was bred into his bones and will not out . . . a native Brazonian is a cattleman at heart and if he is not in the cattle business, he *wishes* that he was and aims to be—and how he loves a rodeo!

The Spaniard taught the Mexican Indian the art of the *vaquero* and he, in turn passed it on to the buckaroos of the Brazos. Cowboys were a necessity in a land of wild cattle that had to be rounded up and driven out of the woods and thickets. Branding, cutting out of the herds, bull-dogging, roping and the other range requisites called for skill and, when the trail-drivers came, it was a new art that had to be mastered.

After the Texas Revolution, a number of the Mexican sympathizers left the Brazos-land and went to live in Mexico. Many of them went so quickly that they left their herds behind them and the cattle strayed into the woods and prairies and reverted to a wild state. The Texas Congress sagely deliberated and decided that they belonged to whomever captured them since they were forfeited to the State. Thereupon, began cow-hunts through the bottoms and thickets for the spoils of victory.

Cattle throve in the valley until the Civil War and then all was suspended until the men came home to begin the cattle-drives. After that era, the cattlemen were to come upon hard days. The farmers and "nesters" were moving into the open range, fencing it and making little farms out of the unlimited pastures. It resulted in a cattleman-nester war that raged for a long time. But the compelling influence of civilization was too strong for the men of the herds to withstand.

They yielded after a time. Today, some of them even plant cotton. Their fathers would have scorned to do that!

At one time there were round-ups engaged in by several cattle outfits that would extend over several counties. Then there was no barbed-wire, no settler's cabin with its fences. The cowboys would begin slowly sweeping across a great area, driving the accumulated herds before them, picking up a stray calf or cow here and there to add to the string. Now and then they would yank a milking heifer out of a farmer or nester's barn-lot that had one of their brands on her flank . . . but he would pick up another in a few days and begin milking her.

There were some famed cattle ranches in the old days of the Brazos-land's rule of King Cattle . . . in 1867 the Slaughter brand came first to Palo Pinto County. Oliver Loving used the Brazos and its water, its crossings and its pasturage until one day on the way to New Mexico he stopped an Indian arrow. Colonel Charlie Goodnight of the JA took over what he left. Major George Littlefield came from down around Austin to be converted to the Plains and Forks country as the place to run cattle. He is said to have branded five thousand calves a year at his Yellow House Ranch in Lamb County.

W. V. Johnson of Lubbock was the man to first introduce windmills in the upper Forks country and that brought the near-surface water up to slake the thirst of the herds. It made the Plains a real cattle country for the first time. The cattle raised themselves when the water-situation was settled.

The XIT—Ten-in-Texas—Ranch was an empire of three million acres at first and many of those acres were swapped for the Texas State capitol building. The Slaughter coverage was half-a-million acres by 1916 and had come from an 1850-start with less than one hundred head of cattle. The McCord-Llano Cattle Company; the 10-A, just south of Lubbock; the Cross-C; and a string of other great Brazos cattle-kings, such as Merchant, Parramore, Matthews, Simpson, Hastings, Hobart and Borden, gave to the hide-and-horn its real impetus in the early days of the River land. In nine of the upper River counties and those adjacent, the SWS brand of the Swenson Brothers has been active since 1883.

Dependent on the cowboy and his horse, the cattle industry went through its colorful period, saw it wane and settled down to specialization and modern methods. They died hard, the men who raised all they could and depended on the Lord and the banker to help them get the choice stuff to market . . . everything was mortgaged.

"They've got the market on the radio," bemoans Ab Crabtree. "They've jumped the price of boots and shirts clear out of sight with all these square-dance costumes. A cow-poke can't afford a new Stetson any more. They try to substitute a jeep for the cow pony. But what have they done for the cowboy's hours of work, his pay, his chow, his old age pensions and his loneliness. Oh, they print a lot of Western magazines and make these bookity-bookity movies to show him how glamorous he is, but as far as he is concerned, he's not any better off than his grand-pap was who went up the trail in the '70's."

They have night-lighted arenas for open-air rodeos in most of the Brazos towns—upper, middle and lower—for it is a sport that Brazonians choose. The square-dance, now all the vogue, perpetuates the old songs and dances of the ranch-house. The movies will not let the world forget the days when men rode hard and fought bitterly over a few buttes and sage-grass hills out in the upper Brazos Forks country.

"The land of the heart," said George Pope Morris, "is the land of the west." They must think so for in all parts of the country they seem to love the things that perpeuate it and it is the most characteristic brand of true America-lore that the country boasts in the two centuries of its history. This Brazos cow-country has lived through the greatest attempt at mass-herding since the days of Abraham and Lot and it has come, through science and experiment, to make of the industry a workable source of economic supply. A few fat and well-bred cattle today supplant great droves of skinny Longhorns. Not how many, but how good. A single bull to-day will bring more on the auction block than a whole herd did in Abilene, driven up from the banks of the Brazos.

King Cattle has ceased to be a jealous master. Registered hogs are now in vogue, with a little cotton, some expert chicken-laying, a few head of mohair goats, a flock of fancy sheep, milking-machines, walking-horses, big-breasted tur-keys and rotated crops . . . the cattleman is not carrying all of his eggs in one basket any longer.

Gone are the days of "moonlighting," when unscrupulous rustlers hid beside a water-tank as the cattle came to drink and rushed them off to change their brands and add them to their herds, or sell them in a distant market. The practice of "mavericking" a calf that had strayed away from its mam-my and could not be identified was abused by the actual stealing of the young-un as it ran with a branded cow. "Judge Colt" and "Sheriff Winchester" long ago put an end to that.

But, nowadays, it takes money to raise calves, where in the old days "they raised themselves". Back in 1858 they said:

It costs $25 to raise a cow in Connecticut, $15 in Indiana, $2.50 in Illinois, while down on the Brazos you can raise one as cheap as you can raise a chicken.

The difference is that while it takes more to raise one today, it brings more at the market. In that day a whole steer could be bought for the price of a modern moderate-priced steak. On the Brazos the prime beef of the nation is being scientifically raised, fed and marketed. It is not guess-work any longer. It has taken one hundred and thirty years for it to come to pass, but as Berta Hart Nance once said:

Other states were carved or born,
Texas grew from hide and horn.

"Boys, she's blowed herself in!"
That was, is and will always be good news along the Brazos
to the ear of the oil man. When a guy jumped out of his
beat-up Ford and ran down Main Street, covered over as he
was with mud and slush-pit oil, shouting that bit of glad
tidings, every one came a-running.

In practically every Brazos county, at one time or another,
they have spudded in a well and tested her out to see "if
there was oil there." It began in the old century and it is a
lively issue today from up in Garza and Scurry on the Caprock and the Plains, on down through the Ranger oil belt in
Stephens and Young and the other middle counties, down to
Raccoon and Hempstead—Oil is a King and a powerful one!

"Oil is where you find it." That is the prime maxim of the
industry, the shibboleth of the independent operator and of
the big company. But the starry-eyed "Wildcatter" is the man
who speculates, who takes chances, who shoots his hard money
on the chance that there is oil where it has not been produced
before. He will work up a block of leases in the most out-of-
the-way places, sell himself on the idea that he will get oil
at that spot, start drilling on a shoe-string, sell and trade
acreage for tools, fuel and wages. Then, one day, he strikes
and is a millionaire over-night. Immediately a thousand other
wildcatters are born. "If he could do it, so can I!"

Then, the big company will take proven acreage with all
of the geology pointing to a sure thing . . . plan to log the
well by many other tests . . . have access to sub-surface surveys and government reports on the structure . . . spend
large amounts . . . use the most scientific methods . . . and
get a dry hole. Oil is where you find it!

The records say that oil was discovered in Texas in 1889,
but 1543 would come closer to it. When De Soto's men

[85]

came through Texas on their way to Mexico after losing their chief and their battle over on the Mississippi, they were bothered with mosquitos as they tarried on the Brazos and explored for gold. The Carancahuas showed them how to grease themselves with a substance that they skimmed off the springs and creeks with broom straw, wrung-out and saved.

Gil Y'Barbo, who kept an accurate diary back in 1790 while he tarried in the country between Nacogdoches and the Brazos valley, mentions an oily substance and says that they used it both for medicine and greased their axles with it. They skimmed it off the water and barrelled up some of it. One barrel went to England and was thrown into the harbor at Liverpool because they had no duty-schedule for its admission. The other went to Germany and they analyzed it in their laboratories. Thereafter, whenever a German emigrant came to the Brazos-land he made searching inquiries about oil and mineral rights to the land he took.

After they got oil in Pennsylvania in 1859, Lynis T. Barrett in 1866 in Texas took a big auger and bored a shallow well to 106 feet and got a showing of oil. He reports that "oil and water gushed from the top of my well," but nothing came of it in the little Brazos town where he experimented. They claimed a showing near Graham in Young County in 1871, not far from the Brazos when wet gas showed at 136 feet and in 1888, near Gordon in Palo Pinto, they brought in a shallow gasser at 384 feet while drilling for water. It caught fire.

"Hell's-bells!" exclaimed the farmer. "I was drillin' for water and got fire!"

But in 1895 over in Corsicana, about fifty miles from the Brazos, using water from the Navasota, a tributary of the River, they got a real producer at 1,027 feet and a refinery went up there. Oil was definitely in Texas. Texas was in the oil business!

By 1901 near the Gulf and not far from the Brazos down

at Spindletop and over by Beaumont and Houston they had oil . . . a decade later, Colonel W. K. Gordon, up in the Brazos Cross Timbers brought in the big field at Ranger with an initial producer of 1,200 barrels at 3,484 feet . . . that made Stephens, Young, Palo Pinto and the other Brazos counties hot for oil. Down at Liberty in 1918 and over at Mexia in 1920 oil came very close to the Brazos-land and caused tests to be made in all of her counties. Colonel A. E. Humphreys proved up his hunch and sold his Mexia holdings for $80,000,000 not far from where the Indians took little Cynthia Ann Parker a captive. Then Dad Joiner brought in the East Texas field that was only a county away from the Brazos valley—the biggest in the world up until then!

While there have not been any great discoveries on the Brazos until oil broke loose in Scurry in recent months, here and there they have been bringing in shallow fields, with small production, and occasionally a deep producer. Oil is now a steady industry that keeps on testing and proving up the land. In Scurry there are many derricks at work today and oil is making rich men and women. King Oil is holding court there just now.

In 1891 they got a showing of oil near Fort Griffin. Near Mineral Wells earlier they had a small gas field. Down in old Washington in 1888, William Seidell produced gas, commercially, and Colonel William I. Prather had a good little well he claimed at Waco in 1890. There is oil production in Archer, Shackelford and Throckmorton and they are still trying in Hill and Falls.

Down in Austin County at Raccoon Bend they have many derricks against the sky and much production to show for it. Likewise, in Brazoria, they have a lively field. Up and down the Brazos the sound of the pumper and the gleam of a steel derrick shows. King Oil holds up his head and shares equally his throne with the other two kings.

He had a great day back in 1919 when a well came in within forty miles of Ranger town in Eastland County—and the Brazos was within that scope. Ninety million dollars worth of oil was produced that year and the rush was on. Gamblers, speculators, wildcatters, and all the boom-town gentry moved in and the whole area watered by the Brazos was fired with the desire "to get rich in oil."

Since that day there has been a persistent, never-ending search after oil along the River. Big companies and little independents, conservatives and wildcatters, genuine oil men and fly-by-night promoters, doodle-buggers and willowstakers, experts with divining rods and wiggle-sticks, miracleworkers and "lucky guys"—they have all committed themselves to winning the big money before they quit. And they have in Scurry, up on the Brazos Fork and the end is not yet told in that region.

There's a good story of Juan Ximines and his grant. In 1835 he was one of the Mexicans in old Mexico who was sent to the Brazos-land to overcome the predominance of the Anglo-American settlers. They gave him a section and told him there would be soldiers and protection and subsidies and everything furnished if only he would go there and settle.

But when Juan, in his big wagon with his wife and little *muchachos,* got as far as the River of The Arms of God he found that his kind were being talked about and shunned. "The Runaway Scrape" was but a few months away and it was not an hospitable welcome that Ximines got. So he sold his section for $50 and figured that he made a profit of $4.44 on the deal. He signed his name with an "x" and went back to Bexar.

About one hundred years later there came another man that way and he had faith that in Juan Ximines' old grant there was oil. He was about as poor as Juan had been, but he knew the oil business and a lot of people. So he started in promoting, borrowing, trading, "liberating" and managing for tools and equipment to drill a hole for oil on the Ximines Grant. He sold "interests" in his lease, scribbled on pieces of paper that were used to pay for groceries, cord-wood, second-hand mud-pumps and used drilling-bits for "making-hole."

Finally he got started. In a little unpainted shack he housed his rickety old engine, stacked what wood he had outside and hired a boy on "jawbone" to stoke his boiler-fire. With "borrowed" pulleys and steel-cable that he had "managed for" he lined up his tools. Some he got while the boss of the supply-yard was at dinner and had left a friend in charge while he was gone. Some of his stuff came out of junk-yards . . . fish-tail, diamond and rock drills . . . but never once did Dad Joiner give up.

One day after heart-breaking delays he spudded in and was on his way down to the fresh-water sand on Juan's old original section. Getting his casing "on time" to use for his surface stabilizing, he watched the cuttings as they came up to the ground-level, flowing out over the top into the troughs and slush-pits. Day by day, night by night, tower by tower, the monotonous drone of the traveling-block, the clank of the pipe-elevators told him that he was slowly going down.

He had to promise and placate his tool-dressers, drillers and supply-men a thousand times, feed them on breakfast food and raisins with "borrowed" milk from a neighbor's cow, but he kept them at it.

Then, one day, when it looked hopeless, there came a gurgling sound from down under and the driller cocked an ear.

"Put that damn fire out!" he yelled to his crew. "Go get the Old Man. I think he's got a well!"

And he had, and there on the section of land that Juan Ximines sold for fifty dollars in a Brazos bar, Old Dad Joiner brought in the biggest field that the oil people ever saw in all their history. Somebody else made the fortune—not Dad. He had sold his birthright to the last bit to get the hole made.

They made $20,000,000 out of Juan's section and all that the hapless Mexican got out of it was $50 and the glory of having his name on the title-papers. Oil is where you find it in the valley of the Brazos!

These are the Kings of the Brazos . . . Cotton, Cattle, Oil.

PART TWO

The Lusty Years

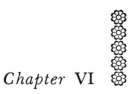

Chapter VI

WARWHOOPS ALONG THE BRAZOS

LONG ERE THE FIRM, DETER-
mined tread of the white man's boot came to the Brazos-
land it had known the silent moccasin of the red man.
In the shade of the great cotton-woods, down by the glistening sea, or up on the wide *mesa* dwelt the people whom the
white men called "Indian". Here he hunted, fished, loved,
mated, moved with the seasons, fought and died. Here his
soul took reluctant leave of a land that he loved.

There came tragic days for the Indian. One, when he saw
the strange white sails of a ship off the shores of what is now
Quintana. Another, when a ship-wrecked Cabeza de Vaca
came stumbling through the midland woods. A still later
one, when he saw the glint of the sunshine of the Plains on
the breast-plates of Coronado's men. He did not know it but
they were coming to serve the death-warrant of his race in
the valley of the River of The Arms of God.

They uttered strange words in an unknown tongue. Were
they gods to be adored? Friends to be received and with
whom to exchange gifts? They puzzled him at first, but he
soon learned that they were as greedy as the worst of his own
people; that they had little to trade and naught to give; that
they were seeking a substance that they called "Gold" and
what they coveted they took . . .

*"We here unfurl the banner of The Holy Cross and claim
this land for His Most Gracious Majesty, The King of Spain
. . . or France . . . or England!"*

[93]

He did not understand what they were saying, but to the Indian the gestures and the manners were decidedly unfriendly toward the native people who claimed this land of the River as their homestead.

As he saw the assumptive white man become more and more possessive, the red Indian asked his Medicine-Man, "Why must I give him my land, my hunting-ground, my services to build his forts? Why can he abuse me at his will and if I attack him, I am punished? Why?"

The Medicine-Man shook his head. He did not know the answer. So, the Indian ran away into the forest to hide, moved on and left the land to his enemy or else, with bow and hatchet of stone, he fought back to protect his fathers' graves and his forest-home. For this he was denounced.

Sons of the men who had drummed for Liberty at Bunker Hill said that the Indian was "a wild, ignorant savage" to wish to resist the foreign invasion. If he retaliated by burning the home of his enemy, he was "a cruel, bloodthirsty brute." When he and his fellows went out and fought *en masse,* trying to rid their land of this oppressor, they were called "inhuman red devils" and their few victories were dubbed "massacres".

But the new-comer of whatever flag or tongue looked enviously at this red Naboth's vineyard and made up his mind that he would possess it for his own. Under the sacred symbol of The Cross and with the aid of the righteous bullet, he went about "civilizing" the aboriginal Indian and succeeded in pushing him farther and farther west until to-day he is gone from the banks of the Brazos and the place knows him no more.

Of course, the Indian was cruel. He scalped his enemies. He broke his word and violated his flag-of-truce. Depredations and inhumanities without number were charged against him. But are these not many times a matter of view-point? Is there any consideration ever invoked for him and his war for survival and self-defense? No proper brief has been filed in his behalf.

The white man found the Indians living in a sort of territorial pattern along the banks of the Brazos. The boundaries were loosely fixed but strictly observed.

The Low Country Tribes dwelt from the mouth of the River up to the Blacklands. The Karankawas, or "Cronks", were littoral people and the date of their origin is not recorded. They were fish-eaters for the most part, crude and primitive and very ignorant. Cabeza de Vaca fell in with them, amazed them with his learning and healing and managed to escape them after a time.

Noah Smithwick says of them:

Theirs is a fierce tribe whose hand is against every man. They live mostly on fish and alligators with a man for fête days when they can catch one. They are the most savage human beings I ever saw. Many of the bucks are six feet in height and their ugly faces are rendered hideous by the alligator grease and dirt which they are besmeared with from head to foot as a defense against mosquitos.

They would have no part with the Caddos of east Tejas, but roamed the coast from Galveston Bay south, lighting their fires up the Brazos as far as Fort Bend. Their sub-tribes were many—Cujanes, Copanes, Coapites, Cocos, Caranquases and several others.

When David Ingram, Richard Browne and Richard Twide, seamen of Plymouth, barely escaping with their lives near Vera Cruz while engaged in the slave-trade with the Spaniards, passed through Texas, traveling overland to the English settlements in Canada in 1568, they said this of the coastal Cronks:

The people . . . about five foot high, somewhat thicke, with their faces and skins of colour like an olive . . . they are naturally very courteous if you do not abuse them, either in their persons or their goods, but use them courteous. The killing or taking of their beasts, birds, fishes or fruits can not offend them . . .

The Cronks continued on until the 1820s in the valley of the lower Brazos when the white men began arriving in numbers. Trouble arose and in 1824 they killed several of Stephen F. Austin's colonists. Captain Randall Jones with twenty-three soldiers was dispatched down the Brazos from San Felipe to determine if the Cronks were guilty and if so to punish them. There was a fight and the Indians lost fifteen, the whites three, with many wounded in the fray.

They fought continuously with Lafitte and his pirates at Campeachy and when James Long saw them coming against him at Bolivar Point, he fired his single cannon at them. They were badly frightened. In their hollowed-out log *bateaux* they hunted deer far up the Brazos and traded for corn as far west as Navasota, but always came back to the Coastal Plain as their basic homeland.

Good bowmen, fine wrestlers, Sun-god worshippers, cannibals. In 1839, the historian Atkinson says of them that they wandered south and west and were not heard from again:

Perhaps the oldest inhabitant of the Texas soil, he was the first to be driven from it by the merciless settler . . . the remaining tribal remnant, a mere handful of old men, women and children were last seen begging their way into Mexico and oblivion.

Next came *The Midland Tribes*. These covered the territory from The Grand Prairie to The Rolling Plains and left off where the trees did. They were primarily a forest-abiding people, farmed in a small way and were more cultured and civilized than the other Brazos tribes. They were mostly of the Tonkawa derivation.

They approached the Caddo settlements on the east and the Comanches on the west. To their south were the Lipans and the Apaches. Their lesser groups were the Ervipianies, Mayeyes and Yojaunes, but the white man called them all

"Tonks". They ranged from the Trinity to the Rio Grande, but looked upon the Brazos and around the site of present Waco as their home council-fire. They were the friendliest Indians to the Brazos whites and General R. S. Mackenzie used them as scouts against the Comanches in 1872 when he was warring up in the Brazos Forks section.

Gatchet says that "Tonkawa" means "staying-together", just as "Caddo" meant "confederation". It was a way of the white man to use the Indian word that he heard for the thing that he wished to name. The Indian who raised an empty hand to show that he carried no weapon and said in his native tongue "Tejas", meaning "friendly", was thereafter "The Tejas Indian" to the Spanish explorer.

The Tonks lived in conical huts of light branches, covered with tanned buffalo hides and built them in the center of groves. They were adept with tools and made excellent arrows. They were such good hunters that they had many deer-hides to trade to the white men.

Father Douay of the La Salle Expedition wrote of them:

Their houses are fine, 40 or 50 feet high, of the shape of beehives . . . they live in round dwellings that look like cupolas and are very warm . . . they sleep between tanned bison skins.

They were quite susceptible to the *padres'* religious experimentation. One of their sub-tribes, the Wacos or Huacos, were at Waco Village on the Brazos as late as 1824 and Austin alludes to them in his writings. He states that they had thirty-three grass houses, with a second village a half-mile away and corn was growing in abundance.

The Caddos, Anadarkos and Ionis had a sort of Confederation that grew from time to time by the joining-up of lesser and weaker groups. They lived on the Brazos in Hood, Palo Pinto and Young Counties as they are known today.

Major George Erath comments in his surveys about the thriving peach trees that the Huacos grew near their villages, but he was of the conviction that the Huacos (or Wacos) were a tribal group of the Wichitas and used that language.

The Tonks had their grand council-fire at *La Tortuga* (The Hill of the Turtle) in Limestone County, as we now know it, but the Tewakanas came along and battled them for it, took it and used it for their own thereafter. Today it is a wild butte with no trace of human habitation about it and goes unnoted by the passer-by. To one who knows its history, however, in the haze of a Brazos twilight he can fancy that he sees the spirals of Indian camp-fires on the high mound.

Smithwick records that the settlers and Rangers used the Tonks as their allies in the famous Plum Creek Fight, when a decisive victory was won over a band of marauding Comanches. He vouches for the fact that the Tonks ate Comanche meat after the fight in token of their triumph. It was the last great Indian battle on the lower Brazos. They did not venture that far south again.

The Spaniards sent Athanase de Mezieres y Clugny, a clever French diplomatic agent to the Tonkawa councils in 1762 to make friends with the Indians for them. Mezieres was from Natchitoches, in Louisiana, and was well received by the red men up as far as Waco and the mineral springs in Palo Pinto. From there he worked down toward San Antonio de Bexar to report to his principals.

But he was to find that when chiefs changed so did the policies of the tribes and although he was constantly among them in the latter part of the 1700's and the early years of the 1800's, he did not accomplish his purpose. The encroachments of the Anglo-Americans alarmed the Spanish Governor of Texas, Baron Riperda, and he welcomed the visits of the chiefs whom Mezieres brought to his capital to see him.

Waco, as we know it now, was intensely Indian in these

days of the early nineteenth century. The nomadic tribes came there to trade, visit, stock-up with essential supplies, learn the news and amuse themselves. Dr. Robert Hill, a noted Texas writer, speaks of a Spanish explorer called "Mosco" who came to Waco (or "Guasco" as he called it) in 1542. Since the Waco (Huaco) tribe did not come to the Brazos until the late 1700's, the Indians whom Mosco and Cabeza de Vaca saw there might well have been Apaches, or even a sojourning band out of Oklahoma, possibly the fierce Osages.

When he came along, Mezieres in his report described the Tawakoni as "good horsemen, cruel to a fault, polygamous, cannibalistic and given to the sadistic torture of their enemies." The Indians pronounced the word Tay-way-ko-ni. The two middle syllables, perhaps, made the word "WACO". But Mezieres called the town "Quiscat" in his journal and the upper village "Flechazo".

Then, when the westward-moving Yscani tribe came from east Texas to join up with the Tawakonis, they were possibly called "Wacos", for when Erath and his surveyors came in ahead of the Anglo-Saxon settlers to the village on the Brazos mid-river, they always considered the Wacos and the Tawakonis as the one tribe. *172184*

Small-pox killed many of the central Texas Indians in the latter days of the 1700's and so reduced were the Tonks that a one-eared Apache named "Tosche" became their chief. He figured in the fight at the San Saba Mission. Mezieres did not like him, called him *El Mocho,* The Maimed, but he was so smart that the Frenchman had to deal with him to accomplish his mission.

At that, Tosche outlived the French-Spanish diplomat, but was murdered at La Bahia del Esperitu in 1784 by a cold-blooded Spanish act of treachery where the flag-of-truce was flagrantly violated. The presidio-captain claimed that he killed Tosche on the express orders of the Governor at Bexar.

It was quite an old Spanish custom to play the Indians against the Anglo-American settlers along the Brazos. Once the Mexican Governor ordered Stephen F. Austin to go to Waco and wipe out the entire Tawakoni village. Then, he sent word to the Indians that Austin was planning such a raid. Then, he cancelled Austin's order. . . .

There was bad blood between Austin and the Indians there on the mid-River thereafter.

The Wacos were a strong people and while reputedly wild and hostile, sly as horse-thieves, powerful as warriors, bold and overbearing, they loved this land of the Brazos and left it only after much opposition. Then they withdrew up into Young County and set up there for a time.

The Tonks as a rule got along with the white men but the Wacos did not. The Spaniards found the Tonk to be a mission-Indian, easily enslaved and willing to build forts and churches in the valley. They also taught the explorer to hunt on the Balcones Scarp and how to catch fish in the Brazos.

Their docility was not rewarded well. Governor Throckmorton of Texas wanted the Legislature in 1884 to spend $4,000 for a section of land for the Tonks in Shackelford County, but it was voted down. Congress finally located them in the Indian Territory. When they came to Waco to the *Maifest* in 1877 and to Albany to a fiesta in 1883 from their tepees near Fort Griffin, it was to be their last appearances on the River they had known so long. They were removed to the Territory in 1884.

Lastly, come *The Plains Indians*. These tribes roved and ranged in the high, bare country of the Caprock. They were Comanches, Apaches and Lipans for the most part, but the Comanches dominated. The latter had come from the old Shoshoni stock high up in the Rockies of Wyoming and were wild and never tamed. They tolerated the Apaches but made no alliance with them. The Apache was an Arizona Indian.

Thrall wrote in 1879 about the Comanche:

This is the Indian that fills our ideal of true savage life—The Arab of the Prairie—the model of the fabled Thessalian Centaur, half-horse, half-man, so closely joined and so dexterously managed that it appears but one animal, fleet and furious. The Comanches are considered the best horsemen in the world.

General Phil Sheridan, who should have known, said: "Never was there a Cavalryman the equal of the Comanche."

He never knew what a horse was until the Spaniards came, but when the wild mustang began to rove in droves across the prairies and the plains of the Brazos Forks, the Comanche stalked and captured him. Mounted up he rode the wings of the prairie-wind and he could be found down in old Mexico raiding the villages of Chihuahua, or on the Pecos following a buffalo-herd, swooping down on the peaceful tepees of the Tonkawas, warwhooping along the Brazos, making the midnight sky red where he had fired a settler's cabin on the Trinity or robbing a wagon-train or a stage-coach near Fort Belknap.

Wild and proud of it, he never made friends with the white man. He stole for the sheer love of it. He was Hitlerian in his treaty-breaking, acted without principle, called himself "The Child of the Sun" with the scalp as his symbol of conquest. To keep his own and take that of his enemy was his highest aim. He had two gods — a good one and a bad one — and he served the most convenient one according to his whim.

He buried his dead, fully-accoutred, sitting-up, ready to ride on his slain pony in The Happy Hunting-Grounds for a hundred years, then be reincarnated and come back once more to his own people. The Comanche was never lost to his own . . . as many as the stars or the leaves on the tree were his seed . . . of this he was convinced.

Not only did he cherish this ancient East Indian belief of

the rebirth of the soul but he used the symbol of the Serpent, common to Egyptian, Hebrew and Mayan.

The Comanche shot an arrow straight, learned to rope and ride as a child, studied strategy in battle just like a general officer of modern times, learned well the care of the wounded, was versed in signals and smoke-signs, scouting and trailing and was imbued with the doctrine of Eternal Vengeance to his enemies. As soon as the young brave was schooled in the Art of War, he went out in his war-paint to demonstrate it. Fighting was his joy, peace troubled his soul.

He was an orator. Colonel Dodge in his book in 1883 mentions:

Knowing that he will be obliged to speak in public, every Comanche man speaks well, spending no little time, not only in the preparation and elaboration of his speech, but by frequent rehearsing, satisfies himself in this manner.

His marital relations were loose and lax, women were slaves and chattels, gentleness toward them was a sign of weakness. In winter he loafed and relaxed with his tribesmen in a sheltered canyon. His youth horse-raced, broke wild mustangs, engaged in buffalo bull-fights, turkey-lassoing, and — it is hard to credit — tracked honey-bees to their hives. He had a sweet tooth.

The elders bet on the prowess of the young contestants, planned next year's campaigns and boasted of last year's contests and victories. Meanwhile, his munition-workers fashioned bows and arrows, shields and lances. The Rangers said that a Comanche shield could turn a bullet and bear only a smudge of lead to show where it had hit.

Coastal — Midland — Plains . . . these were the great tribal boundaries across which other Indians dared not trespass. To come into the high Brazos-Forks country the lower tribes had to get permission from both the Comanches and the Apaches or else the one overlooked would attack them on sight. If the Plains Indians came to the Cross Timbers without permission they were warred on.

So, when they came into each other's domain they came bringing gifts, just as the Greeks did in ancient times. But the Comanches even with their gifts were to be feared for they are reported to have stolen more than they donated.

The Caddos and the Asinai of east Texas were never allowed on the Plains because of a feud with the Comanches. The Lipans and the Apaches had no amity with other tribes, but roved from The Plains to the Pecos, from the Guadalupe to the Canadian, homesteading on the lower part of the Brazos Forks in the short-grass country.

These tribal boundaries held for a time, but when the white men began slowly advancing the frontier and those back in the South and East started the Indians of that country moving westward, a new problem arose. Where would the Delawares, Seminoles, Alabamas, Cherokees, Kickapoos and Coushattas find haven since they had been forced west of the Mississippi?

Among their own redskin people? "No", said the Comanches, "not on The Plains!" The others were as adamant. The Caddos tolerated them for a time, but they were soon on their way to Oklahoma and to their final camping-ground in the "Territory." Today all of these tribes are out of Texas except for a few hundred Alabamas and Coushattas, wards of the State, living on a small reservation in Polk County.

There were sub-tribes of the Comanches, but the white man rarely differentiated. They were all "Comanches" with their hard looks, straight top-knots, hairless faces, bronzed bodies, dark sun-baked skins and without a kindly bone in their tall, tough, wiry bodies. The Comanche had no friends save among his own people and gloried in it.

After the winter "hole-up" in the canyon country, they came out in the spring up on the Salt Fork and the Double Mountain Fork, ready to skirt around the forts along the

Brazos and swoop down into the wooded areas of Palo Pinto and Parker. Scalping, stealing, burning, raping, killing little children or taking them captive and practicing the most unheard of cruelties on their prisoners. They tried to work ahead of a buffalo herd so that the animals would trample out their hoof-prints and lose the trail for the pursuing soldiers.

There was a long-standing distrust between the Comanches and the whites due to broken promises on both sides and after a time they gave up all attempts at reconciliation.

In 1827 a party of Comanches wandered down as far as present Burleson County on the Brazos. When Captain Sims of the Rangers stopped them they explained that they were going down the River to steal horses from the Lipans and asked for a paper from him to give them safe-conduct.

He wrote: "I am inclined to think that they are headed for the Colorado to steal from the white settlers there." Next Colonel Shap Ross and his Rangers stopped them farther down the River. He examined the paper and told them to head back whence they had come. When they refused, he and his men attacked them and only two of the Indians got away. They took the word back to the Plains and the other Comanches took the war-path.

Of course, they never forgot the Council-House Fight. It did not happen on the Brazos, but the little settler there in his cabin was to pay with his life and the safety of his family for the perfidy of his politicians down in San Antonio de Bexar.

In March 1840 a big pow-wow was called by Secretary of War Albert Sydney Johnston of the Texas Republic to try and settle all Comanche-white man disputes. Each side was to bring in its captured children and an exchange would be effected.

When they arrived at San Antonio, the Comanche chiefs laid aside their arms and came into the Council House. They had a single white child with them. The white leaders were

irate and began berating the thirty or forty Comanche chieftains for their bad faith.

A fight ensued in which the Comanche chiefs were slain
almost to a man, despite the flag of truce under which they
had come. The few Indians who escaped got back to the main
party camped some distance away. They beat a fast retreat
to their own country carrying the word to the lodges of the
Comanches. The breach made at the Council House never
healed and ever after the Comanches practised reprisal for it.

The raiding redskins rarely came except on the light of
the moon. The settlers learned to look for them on bright
nights. Hiding the *remuda* — string of horses — down in the
woods, they would lie in wait to catch a lurking redskin
sneaking up on the cabin to steal or burn.

In 1869 it was figured that the Comanches, Kiowas and
Lipans along the Brazos could muster 5,000 braves for war.
During 1865-7 it was claimed that they scalped 162 Whites,
wounded 24 more badly and took 43 prisoners besides stealing and destroying much property.

Juan Antonio Padilla in his *The Barbarous Indians of
Texas*, published December 1818 said:

The Comanches are the most numerous of the Indians who
cover the greater part of the vast region toward the North, treach-
erous, revengeful, sly, untrustworthy, ferocious and cruel when
victorious, cowardly and low when conquered. They are inclined
toward rapine and murder of their fellow-beings. It is certain
that they are not reducible to the Catholic religion.

Enmity was so marked and prevalent that between the
white man and the Comanche it was a shoot-on-sight proposition and the woods of the Brazos in Parker, Hood, Palo
Pinto and Young came to be known as "The Dark and
Bloody Ground".

Among the tales that are told along the River of Indian
depredations none is so full of romance and pathos as that

of Cynthia Ann Parker. It happened on a Brazos tributary — the Navasota — and is a definite part of our River's tradition.

An Illinois colony in 1833 settled and built a stockade for "forting-up" on the Navasota near the present town of Mexia and called it "Fort Parker" after the family of the leader of the expedition.

One afternoon in May 1836, while the men were away in the fields a party of Indians, mostly Kiowas and Comanches numbering about five hundred, appeared at the Fort. They demanded food and water. After bickering with the old men and the women they attacked the settlers and a massacre followed.

When the men returned that night to sift the ashes and try and revive some of the more badly wounded to learn the story, they figured that the war-party of Indians had gone on west, following the course of the Brazos. Among the children carried away captive were Cynthia Ann Parker, 9, and her little brother John, 6.

The two white children were reared in the wigwams of the Indians and became full-fledged members of the tribe. John, when on a raid into Mexico, fell in love with a captive native girl and when he contracted small-pox and was about to be abandoned by his Comanche friends on the way home, the girl begged to be left with him. She nursed him back to health and they settled down to stock-farming. He served in the Confederate Army, but refused to go outside of Texas and never associated with his relatives back on the Navasota.

Cynthia's annals were not so simple. Four years after her capture, Colonel Len Williams and some Rangers tried to buy her from Chief Pan-ha-u-ko up on the Canadian, but he would not sell her nor would she agree to leave. She later married Peta Nocona, a war-chief of the Comanches and bore him several children, "loving him with a fierce passion and wifely devotion."

Several parties of white traders tried to persuade her to go back to her own people but she refused to desert her husband and children.

At the battle of Antelope Hills in the high Panhandle in 1858, when her husband led the Indians against Captain Shapley Ross with his one hundred Rangers and one hundred and eleven Tonkawas, she rode with Peta and his five hundred Comanches into the thick of it. One of the Indians participating in that fray was Phebits Quasho, who wore a suit of mail, a relic of Coronado's day, which earned for its wearer the name of "Old Iron Jacket." When the day went against the Indians, Cynthia fled the field to safety with her husband.

About a year later when Sul Ross, son of Shap, both of them residents of Waco on the Brazos, commanding a detachment of one hundred thirty-five Tonkawas, reinforced by a troop of Cavalry from Fort Belknap under Major Karl Van Dorn, located a Comanche village in the Wichita Mountains and attacked it, Cynthia Ann and her family barely escaped capture.

In that fight, however, a little white girl was taken from the Indians. She was raised by the Ross family and given their name. Lizzie Ross, as she was known, married and went to California to live in later years. Both Ross and Van Dorn were wounded in that battle and were carried by litter back to Fort Belknap for treatment. It was from this battle that the Second Cavalry got its famous "Wichita March."

Peta quieted down for a time but the autumn of 1860 saw him back, pillaging and burning in Parker County with Cynthia Ann riding boot-to-boot with him on his raids. Her old uncle Isaac Parker lived there at the time.

Young Sul Ross was back from college in Alabama by now with his diploma so Governor Houston gave him a Captain's commission in the Rangers and sixty men. He was told to go by Fort Belknap and get some soldiers to help him and take the field against the marauding Comanches. With a Sergeant and twenty troopers and a band of volunteer citizens he set out for the Pease River. Captain Jack Cureton and seventy militiamen from Bosque County went along to have a part in the fun.

On December 18, 1860, taking advantage of a wild Texas sandstorm they surprised Peta Nocona and his village. Not having time to stage a fight, Peta sought refuge in flight, a fifteen year old girl mounted behind him on his pony and Cynthia, carrying little Prairie Flower, on a horse at his side.

Captain Ross and Lieutenant Tom Kelliher of the Regulars took after the pair and Kelliher rode Cynthia down and captured her. Ross dropped Nocona's horse with a shot, but when the Indian hit the ground, he hit fighting. He shot an arrow at Ross and another at his horse. The Ranger demanded that he surrender.

"Only when I am dead," the Comanche defied back. "Never to you!"

"I can't shoot a brave man like that," said Ross to his Mexican cook who had run up to the scene.

"I can, Captain," said the Mexican. "He killed my whole family and kept me captive for months." Thereupon he fired the shot that ended Peta's life.

Cynthia Ann, her daughter and two sons were captured but her husband and another daughter were killed. Ross sent her and her children to Cooper, notifying her Weatherford relatives. She was then thirty-four and when Colonel Isaac Parker tried to explain their kinship she could not comprehend it. She went to live with white people over in Anderson County, but pined for her former life. When Prairie Flower died of a disease within a few months, Cynthia Ann did not survive her long.

Her son Quanah became a famous Indian character, attending the World's Fair in 1885 and visiting many Texas towns. At the old Pickwick Hotel in Fort Worth he had a narrow escape when his room-mate, Yellow Bear, blew out the gas before retiring. Parker was revived but the other Indian died. Up at Anadarko, Oklahoma, Quanah lived to a ripe old age with his three squaws. A Texas town in the Plains country bears his name.

Even as Cynthia became Indian so did they tell a story of a little Indian girl who became "White." Colonel J. C. Eldridge, Texas Commissioner of Indian Affairs was sent by President Houston in 1843 to deliver two little Indian children who had been captured in 1840 down around the Falls of the Brazos to the Comanches.

The boy, Bill Hockley, was still very much Indian and welcomed the exchange of homes, but the little girl, Maria, aged 11, begged Colonel Eldridge to let her remain at his home.

"I bring these children at General Houston's command, Chief," the Commissioner said to old Pay-ha-u-ko, "but the little girl wishes me to take her to my home and I will gladly do so."

"She is the child of our long-dead chief," the Indian answered. "She is of our blood and her ancient grandmother is here to receive her. But she has evidently forgotten her people. She does not want to come to us and if the White Chief has only sent her to show us that she is fat and well-cared for, tell him I thank him. She can go."

Hope revived in the little girl's heart, but it was short-lived. The over-conscientious Colonel said, "I was ordered, Chief, by General Houston to give you the child. I have done so and my duty is fulfilled. You see she is no longer a Comanche. I implore you to let me take her home and care for her."

"No," said the Chief, "if she is ours, we will keep her."

Thereupon, he thrust her into her grandmother's arms who bore her screaming from the council-tent. But in time she was reconciled and became an interpreter for her people.

It is customary to gloss over the times when the Indians were victorious, but the fact is that they often won encounters with the whites.

In the winter of 1863, six companies of Confederate troopers rode out of Fort Belknap on the Brazos to investigate the activities of a band of Kickapoos who were reported to be raiding. They followed the trail up the Clear Fork to a point near Fort Phantom Hill and caught up with the Indians near Dove Creek. About nine hundred were penned up in a thicket surrounded by high bluffs.

Captain Totten with his three hundred Bosque County militia and one hundred ten Confederate Regulars attacked the picket-lines and captured about one thousand horses. Captain Fossett with his command attacked the camp of the women and children to divert attention from the main attack. But the rifles of the troopers when fired had to be laboriously re-loaded and before they could accomplish it, the Indians counter-attacked and recovered over half of the horses.

Meanwhile, a snow-storm had blown in on the heels of a "Norther" which confused men and animals to the extent that both sides beat a retreat from the battle. The whites lost fifty men killed in action, but did not pursue further. The Kickapoos always claimed that they were a peaceful party proceeding south to their winter hunting-ground when attacked without provocation. It was highly probable.

Down in Burleson County on the Brazos if you will take an old abandoned road from The Yellow Prairie neighborhood to the site of former Nashville in Milam County, you can walk through an oak thicket on the south side of Cedar Creek and be at "Battle Ground Prairie."

In 1844 some Indians were camped on Cedar Creek, about twelve miles from Caldwell, roasting terrapin, when they were attacked by a band of white men and a lively fight ensued. The Indians retreated to the creek-bottoms, where the settlers tracked them with dogs. The Indians took to water sniping at the whites with a rear-guard action that killed two of the settlers.

This loss dampened the ardor of the pursuers and they quit the attack. Thereafter, the place was known as "Battle Ground Prairie."

Then, there was the famous victory of the Indian tribes over the whites on the Mississippi that became a great Indian legend. Summoned by smoke-signals and runners to send warriors to cope with De Soto and his soldiers, many of the Brazos tribes sent war-parties to participate in this fight. They never let the later Brazos white men forget the outcome of that encounter which was a defeat for the Spaniards.

The Indians fought among themselves as well. One of the most noted Indian feuds along the Brazos was the Waco-Cherokee. The Wacos had a very prosperous village at the site of present Waco, where the bluffs gave good protection, the land was high and safe against flood and the corn and maize grew easily in the blackland. The white men had settled no closer than the ill-fated Nashville Colony in 1829. It was a large Indian village and the Keechis and the Wichitas came to live there for the protection afforded them as members of a larger group of Indians.

One season they made a foray up on the Red River and stole all of the Cherokees' ponies. The latter were migrating at the time and were sorely crippled by the loss of their transportation. On the advice of their chief they waited to gather a short-crop and then sent a war-party of about fifty-five warriors on foot to Waco. They came near making a surprise-attack at dawn, but an early-riser of the Wacos gave the alarm and the fight was on. The Cherokees had rifles, however, and laid many a Waco low on the first volley.

The latter retreated to their limestone fort where they shot arrows at the enemy who ventured out into the open.

During the day up rode two hundred mounted Tehuacanas on the Waco side of the Brazos to the rescue. They yelled and whooped but were careful to keep out of range of the Cherokee rifles.

During the day a Cherokee chief's son was captured and the Tehuacanas scalped him and hoisted his scalp on a spear to taunt the enemy. The old father, armed only with a knife and a tomahawk, prepared to attack the entire enemy camp.

"What will you do, Chief?" his followers asked.

"Go with my brave boy," the Indian replied. "I shall die slaying those cowardly thieves who have killed the last of my family!"

He charged out alone and killed many of his foes before he was slain.

That night, seeing that they were outnumbered, the Cherokees withdrew back to the Red River, carrying the scalps of fifty-five Wacos, losing only three of their men in action.

But the next year in 1830 they were back again, one hundred twenty-five strong, attacking the Tehuacana main village, which was located in present Limestone County and they all but erased it. They returned home with plenty of horses, spoils and prisoners. There are other accounts to the effect that the Cherokees drove the Wacos out of their village beside the springs on the Brazos and forced them to go up into the Painted Pole country around present Mineral Wells. At any rate, for some reason, the Wacos did that and the conclusion is not improbable.

Under Sam Houston's government the Indians throve for he understood and valued them and their friendship. He never forgot how the Cherokees and the other Indians stood firm during "The Runaway Scrape" and refused to join the Mexican attack on him and his Texas Army. Sam tried again and again to get the Texas Congress to reward the Indians' faithfulness, but he could never muster the votes. Republics have a way of forgetting.

Mirabeau B. Lamar, on the other hand, Houston's arch-rival, hated the Indians and made life miserable for them whenever he could. In 1839 he sent a punitive expedition to drive the Cherokees over the Red River. Great Bowl, Houston's friend, was killed in battle and Houston never forgave Lamar for that.

It was a matter of constant reprisal. Plum Creek, Linville, Guadalupe, Council House . . . one side or the other always said that they "were getting even" with the other and the warring continued.

Attempts at converting the Indians to the white man's religion were never very successful. In 1715 the first Catholic missionary, having read Cabeza de Vaca's *Relación* story about how the Indians had embraced the True Faith at his preaching, came from Mexico to work with the Indians on the Brazos and around Nacogdoches. The mound-building Caddos were more inclined to the white man's saints and ceremonies than were the other Indian tribes. The Comanches would not even listen.

After all, the teachings and the actions of the Spaniards were highly inconsistent to the Indian's viewpoint. After listening to the soft words of the *padres* about Love and Humility, they could not understand when Francisco Garay, who had sailed with Christopher Columbus, came in 1527 to the banks of the Brazos with Niño de Guzman to take their young people as slaves. All of the good work of the *padres* in "reducing" them to the Catholic religion went for naught and the red men ran away into the forest and hid. The slavers finally went to the Rio Grande and preyed on the Panuco tribes.

From Piñeda's visit in 1519 up until 1731 there were ninety-two expeditions of Spaniards who came to the Brazos to see what they could trade the Indians out of or could exploit from the land and its people. Some of the visitors preached and prayed, others bargained and bartered, others stole and cheated, while some murdered and enslaved. None of the expeditions during this period stayed very long or contributed much to the permanent rule of Spain on the River of The Arms of God.

But along in 1718 the Spaniards decided that they had better set up some form of government in Tejas if they hoped to keep it from the French. *Alcaldes, ayuntamientos* and other officials were named by the Viceroy in Mexico City and rules of law were imposed on the settlements up in the Spanish triangle — Bexar, Nacogdoches, La Bahia del Esperitu — in Tejas. The Indian never understood or submitted to the white man's law except when he was made to. He preferred to withdraw westward and avoid it. But it pursued him.

There was little intermarriage between the Indians and the whites. Extermination and domination rather than amalgamation was the preference of the new-comer. We find no traces of Indian-Americans along the Brazos. The Spaniard and the Frenchman were not the marrying sort and the Anglo-Saxon wanted marital-alliance only with his own kind.

Other races were to come later; other nationalities that would find homeland along the River left their imprint in name, in custom and in blood-strain — German, Irish, English, Czech, Polish, Norse, and many others — but not the Indian. You never encounter a family along the Brazos that boasts that there is Caddo, Waco, Comanche or Keechi blood in their veins. Perhaps, in Oklahoma, but not here in our valley. Nor is there any trace of the architecture, art, song or poetry of this romantic people left to us today.

There is pathos in many of the stories about the Indian. And a whimsical note of tragedy, despite the terrible sins that are laid to his name. He was called smuggler, rapist, killer of little children, arsonist and cannibal. But not all of his people were culpable. A few crimes committed by a few Indians should not indict a whole race.

[114]

Once the Brazos Indians found a meteorite that had come whizzing through the air as a fiery ball to bury itself deep into the ground. His Medicine-Men told him it was a message from the Sun-god. The red man believed it even as the *padres* pointed to the rainbow in the Heavens and told him that it was a message from the white man's God to the white man.

Digging it out with great effort, the Indians carried this Ark-of-the-Covenant about with them in their wanderings until one day the dominant white masters said that the tribe should go to dwell in Oklahoma on the reservation. Then the masters decided that the message from the Sun-god had better be placed in the museum of the University of Texas, so they took the holy-stone of the red man and made of it a curio.

There was an Indian fight in old Hood County one day in 1871. Eight Indians had stolen a string of horses and William Weir organized a posse and took out after them. The twenty-five whites hemmed the Indians up in a ravine and picked them off one by one. Getting a shot at the Chief, Weir dropped him and shouted triumphantly,

"Say, boys, I got the Chief! He's the last one!"

As the victors ran over to view their conquest, a lone shot rang out and Weir dropped with a bullet in his chest. The Chief's faithful squaw standing over the body of her man had avenged his death before she herself was killed. A Wagnerian climax, but no composer to commemorate this theme in an Indian opera.

A grand attempt was made in 1846 by the United States to consummate a treaty with the Indians of the Brazos country. Annexation had been accomplished and the Government decided that it was time to settle the Indian question once and for all. Congress appropriated $15,000 for a mission to go and meet with the Indian chiefs at Comanche Peak in Hood County.

It was a glorious junket in the true Congressional fashion. Ex-Governors, Army officers, Judges, Department heads, secretaries, assistants, servants, clerks, scouts, soldiers and flunkeys made up the large party. They were to proceed from Shreveport in Louisiana to a point about forty miles southwest of Fort Worth, as it is now located, in Texas.

To do this, they traveled all up through Arkansas, Oklahoma and the Texas Panhandle. Finally, on January 17, 1846, they reached the Trinity and in another month's time managed to arrive at the Peak, just outside of the present town of Granbury.

Here is an item from the Committee Clerk's diary:

We find many bear, deer, turkey, buffalo and fish. The Comanche Peak has been found at last, but it is destitute of enchantment. It is a brushy hill.

There not being enough Indians to justify a conference, the Committee and its entourage pitched camp, sent down to Bucksnort (Marlin) for supplies and went game-hunting. They ordered their own Indian scouts to send up smoke-signals and invite the tribes to come in. The clerk's entry for March 13, 1846 states: "Eating breakfast of turkey-breast, biscuit and coffee."

A Lipan belle in the Indian encampment celebrated her nuptials, the report goes on to state, to a Keechi brave which furnished some diversion and amusement. Indian singing, drinking, dancing, feasting and music enlivened the monotony for the gentlemen from Washington, while drums and trade sleigh-bells added to the noise and color of the occasion.

After many delays delegations of Kickapoos, Caddos, Cherokees, Creeks, Delawares, Seminoles, Choctaws, Chickasaws, Lipans and Tonkawas came in. But the one for whom they waited came last. Old Buffalo Hump with two hundred of his Comanches arrived and immediately, in true diplomatic fashion, moved for a postponement of the conference until May.

After several delays and more exhaustion of the Congressional rations to feed the visitors, on May 15, 1846 an elaborate treaty was drawn up and signed whereby the United States Government would grant its protection to the Indians (whatever that meant) and they in turn agreed to release all of their white and Negro captives by coming November.

The Committee returned in triumph to Washington, but by November the treaty was quite forgotten.

The Indians' homeland was the subject of envy by the white settlers. They were neither of them content to share it. They wished to possess it. Once when Noah Smithwick, a very versatile person, took five important Indian chiefs to see Governor Houston about establishing a reservation-line — one side for the Indians and the other for the whites — the old fighter shook his head.

"No use, Noah," he said. "If I could build a wall from the Red to the Rio Grande so high that no Indian could scale it, the damned white people would devise some means of crawling under it or getting around it."

Then, one day in 1852, the Texas Legislature in its wisdom decided that the Indians must be disposed of, so they set aside 37,000 acres of very poor land in Young County near Graham, washed by the Brazos Fork and moved the Tonkawas, Delawares, Caddos and others to it. They must stay there and obey the Indian Agent and yield all of their rights and properties to the whites. Up on the Clear Fork of the Brazos there was a similar reservation for the lordly Comanches.

The Indians went. But they did not stay. Using the reservations as a base for their depredations, they would steal down into "The Dark and Bloody Ground" of Palo Pinto and Hood, steal and burn and plunder and then run back to the reservation and claim protection. The settlers took it up with the Indian Agent, but he always found the Indians blameless. So, the settlers buckled on their pistols and organized a "Reservation War," going onto the preserves and battling the marauding redskins, recovering their property.

It was not until after the Civil War that General Phil Sheridan, the Military Governor, had to remove the recalcitrant Comanches, Kiowas and Apaches to Fort Sill and put them on the reservation there under military watch and supervision.

But the Comanches were rovers and rangers and they always found their way back to their depredating-grounds. It was not until 1874 that they were finally broken of the habit of raiding down on the Brazos. In that year Richard Coke of Waco became Governor and drove out the last remnant of Carpetbagger rule. He sent General R. S. Mackenzie, a noted Indian fighter out to match battle with the Comanches and their allies up in the Tule and Palo Duro Canyon country. After a decisive defeat the Indians settled down on their reservations and never gave any more trouble on the banks of the River.

The frontier forts could now be dismantled . . . the buffalo was gone . . . the Indian was pacified and on the reservation . . . the troopers had mown down the flower of his young warriors . . . he had fought his last battle . . . his warwhoops would be heard no more in "The Dark and Bloody Ground". . .

But he made one last convulsive effort. The General of the Armies, William Tecumseh Sherman, was down in Texas inspecting the Army's forts. He had heard of the Indian atrocities and he was treated by the Comanches to one in his honor.

He had landed at Galveston and proceeded by buck-board with military escort on to San Antonio and then up the line of western forts to the Brazos. Fort Phantom Hill — Belknap

— Griffin — on into Richardson at Jacksboro where they were giving a dinner for the high brass at the Officers' Mess.

In the midst of the levee in one of the long native stone buildings that still stands, a worried soldier came in and whispered to the Post Commander.

"What is it, Colonel?" the General inquired.

"Sir, it's the Comanches," the Colonel replied. "They're off the reservation up at Sill. Attacked a wagon-train of ours over the same road you came today and killed twelve teamsters — burned one poor devil at his wagon-wheel."

A shadow crossed the dour face of the General.

"Order a detachment to take the field at once — tonight," he ordered. "One hundred and fifty men with thirty days' rations. Don't come back until they have brought these red devils or their hides in."

He could barely be decent to the delegation from the Brazos counties who waited on him to discuss this very Indian subject. Hurrying on to Fort Sill the next day he ordered the Comanche chiefs brought before him. It was not difficult for they were drawing rations at the time at the commissary there at the Fort.

When accused of the massacre of the teamsters, they proudly admitted it.

"If anyone claims that we did not do it," said Chiefs Satanta, Satank, Kicking-Bird and Lone Wolf when the military man questioned them, "he lies!"

Sherman ordered them in arrest to the great fear and apprehension of the Indian Agent — to whom the Indians could do no wrong. They were to be taken back to Jacksboro in irons and tried for murder. On the way down, Satank gnawed his hand loose and when about to escape was shot and killed by the guards. The others were duly tried. (An account of their arraignment is elsewhere in this narrative.)

Thereafter, there were no more raids down into Texas and the Brazos-land by these reservation Indians. He was through. He had fought to his last warrior and had yielded only to the superiority of numbers.

He had been guilty of occupying a land that the white man coveted and found good, along a pleasant stream that the Indian called "Tockanhono", but which the *conquistador* called "Brazos."

This is a brief resume of his last stand along the River, the story of which is written by his enemy's descendants. No stroke of his own pen, stylus, chisel or brush leaves his side of the story to posterity. The places where he fought for the green mounds that were his people's graves is marked by no monument of bronze or marble. The groves which were the temples of his gods are silent today.

No Indian composer has come forward to write the *gotterdammerung* of bronze braves along the Brazos . . . no Verdi has composed a ballad for an Indian maiden to sing in her buckskin and beads high above the Brazos' russet tide . . . no redskinned Beethoven has caught the rhythm of a sonata that the River sang to the ears of the Indian before the white man and his "civilization" came to disturb the idyll.

The taps of this once-proud people has sounded. A few beads in the sifted ashes, a mound here and there containing old bones of men who were great in their day, broken bits of pottery on which an artist poured out his inspiration, an arrow-head that missed a buck deer in the alders and willows . . . these are the faint traces of him and his day — the Brazos Indian.

Let him who knew the Indian best and loved him most pronounce his requiem. Sam Houston, a Senator from the State of Texas, arose one day in the Senate of the United States and said this:

As a race they have withered from the land. Their arrows are broken and their springs have dried up. Their cabins are dust . . . Slowly and sadly they climb the mountains and read their doom in the setting sun . . . They will live only in the songs and chronicles of their exterminators. Let these be faithful to their rude virtues as men and pay tribute to their unhappy fate as a people!

Chapter VII

"COME TO THE BOWER"

THIS WAS THE BATTLE-SONG
of the Brazos:

> *Will you come to the bower I have shaded for you?*
> *Our bed shall be roses all spangled with dew.*
> *Will you come to the bower I have shaded for you?*
> *Our bed shall be roses all spangled with dew.*
> *Will you, will you, will you*
> *Come to the bower?*
> *Will you, will you, will you*
> *Come to the bower?*

If a crow were to flap his ebon wings eastward for a distance of about twenty miles on a straight line from the Brazos banks he would perch atop a high, dead tree and look down upon a level sward beside a little stream that is called "The River of St. Hyacinth" — San Jacinto, in the Spanish tongue — where, one day in 1836 a battle was fought. In one half-hour it was won and they said of it that it was one of the sixteen most decisive battles in the world's history. There, that day, Texas was born . . .

The fires of Revolution had been smoldering in the valley of the Brazos for some years. The settlers from the old States found it intolerabie to submit to Mexican imperiousness where they were granted no voice in government. And, so, no sooner had they unpacked their wagons, their boats or their saddle-bags on the banks of the River of the Arms of God than they began talking of a "Free Texas." It was treason, of course, but they had seen it work before at Cow-pens and at Saratoga and they were willing to try it again.

They would whet-stone their Bowie knives to help Santa Anna set up his democratic government, free of the Spanish rule, and they would fly his flag with "1824" in its center — a tri-color with red and white and green panels — and they were willing to cheer Mexican Republican troops on parade. They would sit at a feast where Stephen F. Austin and the Mexican Commander, General Mexia, would bandy their toasts of Mexican-Texan amity, but the Brazos sun shone upon men who wished to govern themselves and who would have none of Santa Anna's dictatorship.

Austin had sensed this and came hurrying home from Saltillo where the Legislature of Coahuila-Tejas was con-vening. He welcomed the five ships of the Mexican President as they came into the mouth of the Brazos that day . . . he took the salute of the march-past . . . and he told himself that it was his duty to caution his colonists to be loyal to the Mexico City authority.

But he could not handle the passions of his men. One man in particular saw things differently and spoke plainly. He had had a queer history . . .

A soldier under Old Hickory, Virginia-born, Tennessee-reared, a Congressman, a Governor, then an exile in the lodges of the Cherokees, where he had consorted with an Indian princess and "worn the blanket," Sam Houston, queer creature of Destiny, had ridden across the Red River, un-bidden and unheralded.

He had not stopped at the Brazos but had ridden on to San Antonio de Bexar, hitched his horse in front of the Governor's palace and went in to talk with Don Veramendi in person. Then, when he had listened well, he rode to San Felipe and introduced himself to the men he found there and at Nacogdoches. Finally, he was ready to write Andrew Jackson in Washington:

The people of Texas are determined to form a state government. Mexico is involved in civil war. Now is a very important
crisis for Texas. I may make Texas my abiding-place.

Shephen F. Austin was away when Sam arrived but he met
Jim Bowie, the sick man of the Alamo, who would pile dead
Mexicans about him in windrows before he himself was
killed. He shook the hand of William Barrett Travis, Ed
Burleson, David Crockett and others. They saw a tall, stern
giant of a man over six feet tall, who rarely smiled, but they
also saw the gleam of leadership in his eyes — whether they
liked him or not. So, they moved over to make room for
him in Texas and ever since people have been calling their
cities, their streets and their babies after Sam Houston.

He was a much more dominant personality than Austin,
older and more seasoned, and he dared more. Austin recognized his strength and gave Houston his confidence and respect. They never clashed although Houston overshadowed
the leader of the colony at every turn. Austin yielded grace-
fully as only a great man could.

It so happened that when the April 1 convention of Texans
at San Felipe drew up petitions to go to Mexico City telling
the authority there what they did not like about the new
laws and edicts, Stephen F. Austin had to carry them and
deliver them to President Santa Anna in person. When the
slender figure on horseback rode away to the south, disguised as a common *soldado,* for security's sake, Sam Houston
quietly took his place at the head of the Brazos colony.

All that time when Austin languished in Castle Pelote
prison in Mexico and the flames of revolution were slowly
gaining ground along the Brazos, Houston was practicing
law at Nacogdoches for a living and giving advice to serious-
faced Texans on the side. Sterling C. Robertson came to see
him and Smith of Brazoria journeyed to his office and laid
their plans before this taciturn giant of a man, who spoke as
one having authority.

It was late in 1835 when Sam Houston slammed shut his Blackstone, locked his law-office, sold his land-holdings and put the cash in his saddle-bags. "The Lawyer of Nacogdoches" was through with the woolsack and ready for the saddle. He who had followed Andy Jackson into battle was priming his pistols and sharpening his sword. He had been to Washington City and sounded out the men in power up there. They were apparently neutral, but Houston knew that they were for a free Texas.

Texas had seen some flare-ups. Over at Gonzales there had been a skirmish between the Texans and the Mexicans that had caused hard feeling and Barrett Travis, that impetuous South Carolinian gone Texan, had charged the forts of Anahuac, Velasco and Galveston. They had whispered to him to be careful how he flaunted Mexican authority.

"You can't get away with it, Barrett," said the wise heads.

"Who the Hell wants to?" was the dauntless reply.

With Austin slapped in a Mexican jail there was bitter resentment and powerful talk along the Brazos in these uncertain days.

Then came the September 1, 1835, news: *Austin is back from Mexican prison. He says: "War is our only recourse!"*

"What are we waiting for?" swelled from thousands of throats. Houston had already assumed the leadership. He called for volunteers to start drilling. He wrote numerous letters back to his friends in the old States. The New Orleans Grays were on their way to Texas and other volunteer organizations from Kentucky and Tennessee were forming.

"Let's meet at San Felipe and hold a conference!"

The word rang up and down the valley of the River and there they came for a "Consultation," as they called it, on November 3. Santa Anna's own brother-in-law, General Cos, with a superior force of Mexican Regulars was crossing the Rio Grande. Word of his advance came to the group gathered at San Felipe.

Austin rose in the assembly. "Gentlemen," he said quietly. "I am far from being a well man. I am not a military man as you know. I ask that you elect Sam Houston who is experienced in such matters as the Commander of our military effort."

One lone vote was cast against him. But it was easier to be elected than it was to assert the prerogatives of the command. The Brazos-land was full of ambitious "Commanders." Jim Bowie was leading ninety Texans to attack General Cos' four hundred at Mission Concepción without orders from anyone.

Jim Fannin — Walker was his name before he came to Texas, but who cared? — was a graduate of West Point and he was champing at the bits. He bellowed for action . . .

"To Hell with safety! We can take San Antonio by storm with two hundred picked men!"

Ben Milam, another hotspur, took him up.

"Who'll go to San Antonio with old Ben Milam?" he challenged. They came to him in droves, volunteering and eager to go.

Without a word of notice or a request for permission from Commander Houston, they charged on to attack Cos and his reinforced command of 1,400 men and claimed a victory. But how costly it was! Ben Milam fell in the first hour's fighting and Francis Johnson assumed command on his own responsibility.

Houston, meanwhile, was planning, organizing, scheming and issuing orders. He knew better than anyone that an army has to have supplies and ammunition to succeed. There must be discipline. Shot, powder, shoes, food, wagons, cannon, knapsacks, howitzers and above all — a single command — these were the elements that went to make a victory.

But, no, they had tasted first-blood and victory was sweet. They wanted more. They scoffed at Houston and Burleson for being delayers, did these Texans, spurred on by their initial successes. *"On to Matamoras and take the fight to the Mexican side of the Rio Grande!"* was the cry.

Finally, to appease them, Houston had to give his reluctant consent to Bowie's leading an expedition to Matamoras. It would allow time for cooling off and he could have a chance to assemble a Texas army. And, too, he thought he could trust Bowie . . .

But he had not reckoned with Dr. James Grant, an old fire-eater from down south of Bexar, who moved in, took over the Bowie Expedition and was soon running it full blast as head man. Houston had to leave what he was doing and hasten to Goliad to intercept the column by joining it.

It was hard on him, charged with being Commander-in-Chief, to find a swash-buckling old doctor signing himself as "Acting Commander", ignoring him (Houston) and leading the expedition himself. He had promised the men the spoils that they would take when they sacked the Mexican port-town. Houston rode in the column silently thinking.

Bad news began to arrive, much of it the inevitable rumor of campaign, but who could differentiate between which was true and which was false? Santa Anna was gathering a great army to come to Texas and put down the rebellion . . . Fannin was siding with Dr. Grant and the Irregulars . . . the promised supply-reserve was not at Refugio as promised . . . there was talk that Fannin had grabbed those reserves for his own force . . . the General Council at San Felipe had deposed Governor Smith, Houston's duly constituted chief . . . Houston was to be ordered to give way to Fannin . . . rumors!

Sam could stand it no longer. Wheeling his horse about and with only a handful of followers he rode hell-for-leather to Washington-on-the-Brazos to set his house in order. In his pocket he carried the credentials of a delegate from Refugio that would seat him in the new convention that had been called. Let them try now to force him out!

[127]

But when he got to the Brazos he found that many of the rumors were baseless. Smith was still at the head of the Provisional Government and he was waiting for Houston to tell him what to do next. Sam saw that the Indian situation was becoming acute. Agents from Santa Anna were among the tribes promising them much if they would turn on the Brazos settlers and massacre them. But the old Raven of the Cherokees knew his Indians. He turned his horse's head from Washington, splashed across the Brazos ford and rode to the wigwams of his friends.

Around their council-fires he smoked their pipes and reminded them of how the Mexicans and Spaniards had robbed and exploited Indians from the earliest day. Stand by him — the Raven — and they would not regret it.

Meanwhile back along the River there were questions: "Where is Houston? Was Santa Anna really coming? Was it safe to stay here or should a man take off for Louisiana with his family? Why would not Colonel Gray from New Orleans spend any of the money he had until he saw Houston? Where was Houston?" The man's name was on every tongue . . .

February 28th and there came a message from Barrett Travis at San Antonio, where, it seemed, he was still in the Alamo fort, just about hemmed in by Santa Anna's forces.

"I will not surrender. I will not retreat!"

He had barely one hundred and eighty men to defend against a force twenty times that large.

On the morning of March 1, Houston rode into Washington-on-the-Brazos and a cheer went up. *Houston's back!* It was his forty-third birthday and he celebrated it by scrawling his name on the Texas Declaration of Independence in letters that left no doubt as to where he stood.

Travis had disobeyed orders and was defending the Alamo. It was not unusual, the grim-faced man sighed and reflected.

On March 4th he heard himself elected Commander of the Texas Army and they read another message from Travis to the assembled delegates. It was his final plea. *"I call on you to come to our aid with all dispatch!"*

Up jumped Robert Potter in the little square frame blacksmith shop that did not even have glass window-lights, but cloth to keep out the cold winds of the Norther that was raging.

"I move you, Mr. Chairman," he shouted. "That we do now adjourn, arm ourselves and march to the relief of the brave defenders of the Alamo!"

Before the cheers had died down Houston was on his feet. "Mr. Chairman!"

"The Delegate from Refugio," said the presiding officer.

"This motion is a harmful one," he said deliberately. "We are all for Travis and his men. Some of my closest friends are trapped in that fort. But Texas, her future and her government are also close to our hearts. You stay here in session and formulate a government. I'll go as I should, as I am obliged to do and I'll throw a screen of troops between the advancing enemy and you men here building the government —"

"But what about the Alamo?" a voice interrupted.

"I'll do all I can," Houston went on doggedly, never once reminding them that Travis had his orders to evacuate the fort. "With the help of God and what troops I have I will send Travis help. If mortal power can do it, it will be done."

His calmness prevailed and he stalked out of the meeting, climbed on his horse and with a mere half-dozen in his company rode, as Marshal Ney once counseled, "to the sound of the guns." He had to form an army to stop Santa Anna, self-styled "Napoleon of the West" who had 7,000 crack Mexican Regulars, flushed with success, at his back.

Sam Houston rode directly to Gonzales to assume command. Moseley Baker had 374 men, two cannon and a few days' supplies.

"Start drilling!" Houston ordered. "Organize into companies. Send a courier to Fannin and tell him not to get himself trapped at Goliad. Tell him to fall back on us when the enemy approaches."

"A messenger, sir, from San Antonio!"

"Send him in," Houston's voice was troubled. It was a tragic story that the man had heard. Every one in the Alamo dead. It was not official. Perhaps a Mexican ruse. The men were ordered back to drilling.

Sherman and his men were eager for action. The Newport Kentuckians had come to Texas to "fight for their rights," not to drill for them.

Their chagrin was great when they heard: "We are falling back on the Colorado."

The discord grew. What! Quit before they got started? Run away from these cursed Mexicans? Suppose the Alamo rumor *was* true . . .

While Burleson and the others drilled their men, Houston tried to form a staff and lay his plan of strategy before them.

"We are in a country friendly to the Mexicans," he explained. "They have a lot of their own people here. Every native is a spy for Santa Anna. We've got to draw them up into our country on the Brazos and the Trinity. Divide their forces and then, when the time comes, let them have it!"

There were murmurs against this. Everyone wanted to be heard. They want to fight, General, we can't stall them with such talk.

In came Deaf Smith, Houston's chief scout and with him he brought bad news. Mrs. Dickinson, her baby, and Travis' slave-boy had just arrived in camp, acting, she said, as express messengers from General Santa Anna.

"There is not a survivor of the Alamo," the haughty Mexican had charged her to tell Sam Houston. "That will happen to every other rebellious Texan who persists in bearing arms."

Retreat!

"Are we going to run away from them, General?" they asked even in the ranks.

"Call it what you please," the leader looked them in the eye. "We are falling back on the Colorado. We will make a stand there. We've got to get these refugees here to safety and get some reinforcements for ourselves. We need artillery badly."

But the roads were hopelessly choked with refugees, wagons, ox-carts and impediments of all kinds. The sick, lame, aged, young and helpless were fleeing before the wrath of Santa Anna and it was impossible for the Texas army to maintain march-discipline. It had to help the fleeing people.

Houston felt that he could depend on Fannin joining up after he had held out at Goliad until the Mexican column was checked. The word was already in that Dr. Grant and his expedition to Matamoras had been routed and defeated by General Urrea's column.

General Houston left Gonzales on the 13th of March and reached Burnam's Crossing on the Colorado on the 17th. He promptly crossed and marched down the east bank to Beason's where he remained until the 25th. When the Mexicans under General Sesma showed up on the opposite bank with 800 men and two pieces of artillery, Houston faced him across the river with his men — every one of them resentful that he was not on the other side battling the Mexicans. They wanted to fight.

But the banks of the Colorado were clogged with fleeing civilians begging for a way to cross to safety. Houston had to become a ferryman for displaced persons. They looked to him and he did not fail them in their helplessness. But it played havoc with his military operations.

Noah Smithwick has a tale of how one of Houston's leaders, "General" Rohrer, they called him, was commandeering oxen, mules and horses for the Army's transportation when an old pioneer widow rode up. She had her guns strapped on and a rifle across her saddle. She was very angry. Rohrer referred her to General Sam about her oxen and she let him have it.

He stood it as long as he could and then throwing up his hands in despair, he said:

"Take them, my dear woman, for God Almighty's sake, take them!"

On the far side of the Colorado he counted his troops. From his "Authentic Memoir," one of his rare writings, we learn that he wrote the Provisional President of The Texas Republic and sent a courier with the message: "If only 300 men remain on this side of the Brazos, I will die with them or conquer."

Where was the new Texas government? Some of the leaders wanted to withdraw to Nacogdoches or even across the Sabine, but the others howled them down. The night before their final adjournment they framed a Constitution, made David Burnet Provisional President and Lorenzo de Zavala Vice President. At 4 A.M. on March 17, 1836 they swore in the new officials and Texas was born on St. Patrick's Day in the morning!

With attempted dignity the new Government withdrew to Harrisburg on Buffalo Bayou where present Houston is located. Tom Rusk was Secretary of War and Houston gave him a hiding for running away.

"Get me some equipment, supplies, artillery and reinforcements," the Commander of the Army sent him word. "Don't tell the people that our cause is hopeless or let anyone else do so. We are going to resist. If we don't, we are forever lost. Stand by us and we will win."

"We can send you 1,400 men," Rusk sent the word back.

"Not enough. Send more!"

Deaf Smith had scouted Sesma's column and reported that he had 725 men and two field guns. Houston decided that he could not attack but that he would make them think that he would. Meanwhile, he, himself, the General of the Army beat the men up at Reveille with the roll of his own drumsticks. And how he drilled them!

And then came the disheartening word that Fannin and his entire command had been wiped out at Goliad. Another futile stand and the sacrifice of men so sorely needed on the Colorado. There was no rear-guard now for Houston to depend upon.

"I'm sorry to tell you, Gin'l," said Deaf Smith, "but ole Sesma's been reinforced agin."

Break camp and fall back on the Brazos!

Bitter talk arose. He can't mean that! Where's the man's guts? He doesn't need me to help him run away. I'm quitting if he ain't going to fight. Near mutiny resulted and they talked about electing a new General.

But there was thirty miles to do. Sam Houston, overcoat and cape gone or given to a needy refugee, in a drizzling rain, needing a shave for many days now and without a distinctive uniform to his name, except a wide sash and a sword, drove his little band along. He had quit telling his plans. He was giving orders now and his few faithful officers were seeing to it that they were carried out.

He kept them marching and by that night he was encamped with what he had left within a mile of San Felipe in the haw thickets of the Brazos.

They had come all the way from the Colorado in one day.

But the rebellious spirit was at a new high. Lt. Colonel Sherman harangued his fellow-officers to refuse to march when Houston gave the next command to retreat. He was bitter in his denunciations.

Then up spoke George Hockley, Colonel and Inspector General of the Texas Army, who would command the Artillery at San Jacinto, "Alright, Sherman. If there is going to be any mutiny, the sooner we face it the better. Do you march or don't you?"

[133]

He got no answer.

When the order came to form columns and move out they all did except two companies and the sagacious Houston left them to guard the crossings at San Felipe and Fort Bend. There was rain continuously and much mud underfoot. The march-order was badly confused. They were at Groce's Crossing, and wondering how they would get across.

But for once luck was with Houston. The boat *Yellowstone* was unloading cotton bales at the landing and the owners put her at the disposal of the Texas Commander. The River was high from the spring rains and it took many a crossing of the packet to get the army and its belongings over, but they made it.

There was more marching. It took three days to make the next eighteen miles through the miry Brazos bottoms with only 900 left of the 1,300 who had crossed the Colorado five days before. They were as rebellious but none dared express it to the stern Commander. He was in charge of the situation, now.

When he got to Donahue's he turned toward Harrisburg and reached Buffalo Bayou on April 18th. Certainly, they grumbled, he will match battle here.

Meanwhile, Santa Anna was getting glowing word of how his forces were winning all of their encounters and he grew lax and careless. The *Yellowstone* had run an exciting gauntlet on the 15th of April down the Brazos. The River was more than half-bank full as Captain Ross and his cotton cargo came down from Groce's Landing under a full head of steam, rounding the curves with all the speed that he had, bouncing and bumping over the sand-bars. The Mexican soldiers stared in amazement. Many of them had never seen a steam-boat before and she was gone before they could take a pot-shot at her. The shrieks of the whistles startled them and the whole affair was a fascinating show.

There were no maps of this section of the Brazos and the

strange forests were perplexing to Santa Anna. It was as Houston had planned it. The Mexicans had no friends here to tell them where the enemies were or to give any intelligence reports. Santa Anna could have intercepted Houston by driving southwest, crossing Vince's Bayou in what is now South Houston and making union with his troops under General Urrea . . . but he did not know where he or his enemy was at the time.

Meanwhile, Deaf Smith had captured one of the Mexican couriers with papers that showed Santa Anna was marching on Lynche's Ferry on the tiny San Jacinto River. The Mexicans were everywhere, the scouts reported to General Houston. They had taken San Felipe, burned it, proceeded down to Fort Bend, then whipped back to Richmond. There had been a small skirmish on the east bank of the River where Captain Wiley Martin had engaged the Mexican troops at Moreton's.

Urrea was making for Brazoria by forced march with the right wing of Santa Anna's army. Filisola had the Fort Bend country in control with strong Mexican Regulars and here Santa Anna was thrusting across to Harrisburg to capture President Burnet and carrying a twelve-pounder along for distance fire.

But when he found that the Provisional President and his cabinet had escaped him, the Mexican President-General burned Harrisburg and headed for New Washington — Morgan's Point — where Colonel Almonte, his brilliant Chief of Staff, reported to him that he had fired shots at President Burnet as he was escaping in a flat-boat but the range was too long.

Santa Anna was winded by now and decided to make camp and rest until he could gather his columns, exterminate the balance of Houston's force and then move on to Galveston and take boats for Mexico. What a triumph it would be at Vera Cruz when they came home in victory!

He chose the banks of the San Jacinto and bivouacked there. He expected General Cos and his men to reinforce him on the night of April 20, arriving over Vince's Bridge.

Houston received a frantic message from President Burnet: "Sir, the enemy is laughing you to scorn. You must fight!"

No reply. To his faithful few staff officers Houston said shortly: "I hold no councils. If a mistake is made, blame it on me. History will."

Across the Brazos they had chanced upon a herd of beeves that did not seem to belong to anyone and Houston's men had a square meal for the first time in a week. He set the remnant of his once large force to drilling to keep their minds off their plight and to instill some discipline. Recruits were coming in slowly. Most of them were United States soldiers, AWOL from over in Louisiana. They wanted to be in at the fight, and then return to their barracks.

But Sam Houston had the ground he knew beneath his feet now, here on the banks of the Brazos. These people were his friends . . . or had been until lately. The going was hardest with his own people against him. The word had spread and persisted that the Indians would turn against the Texans now that they were running away from the Mexicans. The Tonks and the Caddos were flirting with Santa Anna's agents and the Comanches . . .

"I'm not worrying about the Indians," Sam Houston said.

He had made it plain that if there was any treason now against the Texas Republic, the army or him, its chosen commander, he would string the traitor up to the first tree. That stopped the loose talk. They were convinced that the old hellion would do it!

"General, we've just gotten two guns," said the Chief of Ordnance. "The people of Cincinnati have sent them to us!"

Houston's face lighted up for the first time in days.

"Start chipping scrap-iron. We've got something at last to throw at them!"

But when General Sam began his retreat from the banks of the Brazos the resentment reached its fullest culmination. Moseley Baker, who had exchanged shots with the enemy across the River at San Felipe, was white-hot.

He demanded to know — in writing — if General Houston was "going to take the road to Harrisburg and do battle or the one to Nacogdoches and complete his run out of Texas? If you do not intend to stand and fight then I propose to beat for volunteers."

The grim commander read Baker's letter.

"Tell him I said to go to Hell," he said shortly and tore the letter in two.

At the cross-roads he never hesitated. Riding at the fore of his depleted force, he led the way down the Harrisburg road to combat. They had their answer. Some of the soldiers under Wyley Martin went down the Nacogdoches Road to safety and it left Houston with about 750 effective men as he headed for where General Santa Anna lay encamped.

In the hearts of Houston's men spirit was high. They made fifty-two miles in less than three days. They lifted wagons out of the mud gladly now. They even sang as they marched. They knew the people along the way and exchanged cheers. Deaf Smith brought in another captured courier — and the rascal had Colonel Travis' own saddle-bags, too! — the messages showing that the Mexicans were not sure of just where they were. They had not a single map of the Brazos country.

Thereupon Houston held a council-of-war. "Now, on this map — absolute secrecy — follow plan without deviation — cross the Bayou here after dark — get rid of your sick and noncombatants — move up and over Vince's Bridge — proceed for two miles — be here at dawn without fail — sleep for one hour and rest animals — then press on — the enemy is here — yes, Cos will have joined him — can't be helped — besides we won't have to take two bites at the cherry — I hold unit commanders responsible — that is all!"

Just as they began eating breakfast they got the word to march.

"We camp where the river and the bayou meet. Don't let your men scatter, whatever you do," Houston warned them. "Form infantry and cavalry lines for attack before you bivouac. Get the guns to the edge of the woods to command the flat-ground. Don't break ranks. Rest on your arms and be alerted for instant orders."

In getting to the rendezvous they encountered a detachment of Santa Anna's force.

One of the "Twin Sisters" spoke and there was a rattle of musketry. The Mexican gun was hit and its retaliatory shot went wide. Each side drew off and went into camp. The Texans should have pressed the advantage and captured the enemy gun, some thought, Houston among them. But they had made contact with the enemy and night was coming on. They did not fight battles in those days at night.

April 21, 1836 . . .

Sam Houston, at home campaigning in the field, rose and shook himself. This was a day of battle. Only his men were nervous. The Brazos mud was on his boots and the heavy clothes that he wore had been soaked and dried a dozen times by the heavy spring rains of the bottoms.

Cos had joined his brother-in-law, Santa Anna, during the night and now, with less than 800 men, Houston faced at least 1,500 Mexican Regulars with General Filisola coming up under a forced march with his column.

"Send me Deaf Smith," Houston ordered and when the scout came he ordered him to take Karnes with him and destroy Vince's Bridge. "And hurry back, Smith, or you'll miss the fun!"

Then the General called a staff meeting. John Wharton was impatient, walking up and down. Moseley Baker had nothing to say. But they all aired their views. With his chin down in his dirty and worn old stock-collar that had not been changed for days, the pupil of Andrew Jackson of Lundy's Lane and New Orleans listened. When they had had their say he dismissed them without saying a word of his plans.

Time: 3:30 P.M. — *Form companies for the attack!*

They leaped to obey but wondered why he hadn't told them sooner. Using the woods for a screen to parade and form his troops, he divided his men into four divisions. Colonel Lamar commanded the cavalry on the extreme left. Sydney Sherman had commanded this arm until the afternoon before but he bungled the job on the Mexican gun and now he found himself commanding a regiment of foot on the left wing.

Millard came next with the infantry and Hockley rode with the Texas artillery. Colonel Burleson was in the center with foot-troops. On a white stallion, his shoulders back and a new sash about his waist, the grizzled Houston rode and gave orders. He was everywhere, in command of the situation, as he leveled his cannon point-blank at the Mexican camp and loaded with scrap-iron.

A nervous young Newport officer rode up and saluted. "General, sir, what are the standing orders of the day?" he asked.

"Give the sons-of-bitches the bayonet!" Old Sam returned the salute. "Remember what they did at the Alamo and Goliad!"

The men in the ranks heard it and took up the cry. It was to be the shibboleth of this bayou-battle. "Remember Goliad! Remember the Alamo!"

General Houston nodded to his two musicians who were at the head of the battle-line. To the piping quick-time the music began, *"Come to the bower I have shaded for you"* . . .

The commander waved his arm in a sweeping gesture toward the Mexican camp and moved his white horse before the line of advancing Texans. Deaf Smith came tearing up on horseback and announced: "Gin'l, Vince's Bridge is out!"

With Lamar's fifty horses prancing and snorting the line moved forward evenly. A few small arms fired down on the left and Houston spurred toward the noise.

"Hold that fire, goddammit, hold that fire!" he shouted.

From the Mexican camp a quick bugle blared. Maybe it was the same one that had played the *Deguello* — No quarter — at San Antonio on March 6. Now it shrilled an Assembly and from their tents the Mexicans came running. Santa Anna in lounging clothes and slippers stood in his tent door. *This could not be an attack. It was not done in modern warfare.*

The two Texas cannon spoke bravely and the men charged behind the smoke and noise. Yelling their curses, their battle-cries and warwhoops that they had learned from the Indians up and down the Brazos, they fell upon the disorganized enemy.

Firing, then clubbing their rifles, grabbing Mexican bayonets and arming themselves anew, using Bowie knives and their bare fists and feet, they laid about them with no semblance of quarter. No prisoners were taken that first few minutes. The Mexicans overcome by the fury of the attack broke and ran . . . it was all over in less than a half-hour.

There had been a few Mexican retaliatory shots and one of them had hit Houston's white stallion. He was down but up again at once and remounted.

Houston saw Almonte form up about four hundred men and try to make a counterattack. He rode toward them and directed the battle in that direction. The brave Mexican Colonel saw it was useless and surrendered his men. They were the first prisoners taken.

With his third horse under him and a boot full of blood, the General paused to say to one of his men near him, "They could whip Hell out of us if they had a hundred organized men, but they can't get together!"

And then it was over and the battle-field quieted down. The Mexicans had 630 dead, 208 wounded, 730 prisoners and a war-chest captured that contained $18,184, along with all of their baggage and impedimenta of the march. The Texans had lost two killed and seventeen wounded and Sam Houston, lying under a tree on an Indian blanket having his leg dressed, was one of them.

But he was still giving orders. One was to send a garland of flowers to a lady with his note of greeting, another was to begin a letter to Andrew Jackson in Washington and the third was to round up Santa Anna and Cos.

"You let them get away and join one of their columns and you will have all this to do over again," he warned his leaders again and again that afternoon and night.

But it was not until late the next afternoon that he got results. James A. Sylvester and Joel Robertson were scouting in the bushes around Vince's Bayou when they jumped a slender little Mexican wearing a fancy silk shirt with gold studs in it. They brought him in and when they approached a group of Mexican prisoners, the soldiers leaped up and saluted.

"*El Presidente!*" they shouted.

To the tree-headquarters they brought him. Robinson saluted. "Here he is, General, the old he-polecat hisself!"

The figure stiffened and bowed from the waist in Spanish fashion.

"That man," he said in his native Castilian, "may consider himself born to no common destiny who has conquered the Napoleon of the West. It now remains for him to be generous to the vanquished."

"What does he say?" growled Houston to Moses Austin Bryant.

He listened while they translated. "Ask him why he didn't think about that at Goliad and the Alamo. Why did he murder those men? Ask him!"

Santa Anna gulped and replied, "When a fort refuses to surrender, by the laws of war, the defenders are doomed to death."

"What about Goliad?"

"I had orders from my government to execute all who were taken with arms in their hands."

Old Sam leaned forward. "You're the government! I ought to hang you to this very tree!"

The Mexican General-President looked nervously about at the men in buckskin and homespun who were fingering their Bowie knives. He asked for an opiate and it was given to him.

There was a strong demand for the life of the hostage, but Houston was a trader. He knew that there were three other strong Mexican forces in Texas. Kill Santa Anna and they would move to avenge him. Filisola, Gaona and Urrea were not bad military men themselves . . .

"If you will order every Mexican soldier to quit Texas," Houston proposed, "I will spare your life and let you go back to Mexico. Refuse and we string you up first!"

Many were against the bargain but it went through and down at the Brazos' mouth, at Velasco, on May 14, they signed a treaty whereby Santa Anna ordered the Mexican troops out of Texas.

Lamar was made Secretary of War, Rusk took over command of the Texas army and Sam Houston went aboard a vessel for New Orleans to have his wound treated. The Government came back to the Brazos at San Felipe and Velasco and began functioning.

There were many sordid aftermaths to the battle that are not pleasant to relate, but they are part of the Brazos story. President Burnet, trying to recoup some of his lost dignity, came with his cabinet to scavenge over the spoils of the Mexican camp; Sherman, Baker and the others tried to rob Houston of the glory in their own favor; they even refused him a Texas Navy vessel to go to New Orleans to a doctor.

Santa Anna went home by way of Washington where Andrew Jackson gave him an interview. At home he began explaining away his defeat. There is an excellent compendium of the accounts of San Jacinto and its campaigns as seen from the eyes of the Mexican leaders gathered in a book by Dr. Carlos E. Casteñada, "The Mexican Side of the Texas Revolution."

The secretary to His Excellency, Ramon Martinez Caro, has his say and scores his chief for laying the blame on everyone but himself. Generals Vicente Filisola and José Urrea make their very logical explanations. The Mexican Secretary of War, José Maria Tornel y Mendevil, is perhaps the most brilliant and scathing of them all.

But it is Santa Anna's *apologia* that is fairly ludicrous. He tells why he destroyed the Alamo, massacred the Goliad garrison, divided his forces into three columns and why he was caught napping at San Jacinto that afternoon. It is a masterpiece of equivocation and alibi.

He mentions reading Mrs. Holley's letters and books and gathering much information from them and he speaks contemptuously of Houston and his men. He pardons his own lack of watchfulness by saying:

Let it suffice to say that it never crossed my mind that a moment of rest, now indispensable, should have been so disastrous, particularly after I had issued orders for strict vigilance to insure our safety. It was over-confidence that lulled the zeal of those in whom I trusted. My sleep was interrupted . . . In vain I tried to repair the evil . . . I exhausted all my efforts trying to turn the tide.

The Brazos was the strategic line, he explains, where he would have united his three columns. He blames everyone but himself for not obeying his orders . . . "if Gaona had not lost himself between Bastrop and the Brazos" . . . "if Urrea had only gotten to Columbia in time."

[143]

Then, in a perfect paradox, he blames his Generals for carrying out his orders to quit Texas. They should have known, he argues, that he was acting under duress. They should have come right on and delivered him. He says:

I offered nothing in the name of the nation, but only acts of my own that our government could have nullified.

The others in turn scored him for his tactical errors, for his allowing Houston to draw him on, extending his supply and communication-lines, leaving his reinforcements behind, dividing his forces and even allowing his flanks to go unprotected — the prime sin of a soldier.

Tornel, the Secretary of War, takes a fling at Austin and the Texans in general when he has his say:

We should have known that the United States plan and carry out their conquests quietly, without endangering the peace with the nation whose territory they intend to take . . . Ever to open the door to the Americans was a grave mistake, but it was continued until its consequences could no longer be ignored . . . After we had taken them to our bosom, they destroyed us.

There has always been a dispute as to where Santa Anna crossed the Brazos. Some claim at Richmond and that he went on to Harrisburg direct, crossing Oyster Creek near present-day Sugarland, but the Mexican diaries all show that it was by Thompson's Ferry. All of the maps were so farcical and inadequate at the time that the two forces were almost upon each other until that Mexican courier was captured on April 19 and Houston learned that his foe was on his way to Harrisburg.

Tom Rusk wrote from his position as Secretary of War and gave a graphic account of San Jacinto as an eye-witness. He extolled the valor of the Texas troops and had this to say of their leader:

Major General Houston acted with great gallantry, encouraging his men to attack and heroically charging in front of the infantry within a few yards of the enemy, receiving at the same time a wound in the leg.

This is the story in brief of the campaign of the Brazos, "The Runaway Scrape", when a smart fighter playing the cunctative role of the defeated, drew his enemy into the morasses and bottoms of the River of the Arms of God where he shattered an army's force by a single stroke of military genius. The sons of the Brazos fought in that battle.

> *They were the answer to grim Goliad,*
> *The phoenix from the pyre at Alamo,*
> *The single flickering hope the Texans had,*
> *The last thin line against advancing foe.*

Chapter VIII

UP THE TRAILS WITH THE HERDS

THIS WAS THE SONG THAT the cowboy sang to the herd in the dark of the Brazos moon in the old days of the late 1800's, when the railroads reached no farther than Kansas and the cattle of Texas had to be driven up the trail to meet the market:

> *Come along, boys, and listen to my tale,*
> *I'll tell you of my troubles on the Old Chisolm Trail,*
> *Come ti yi yuppy yuppy yay,*
> *Come ti yi yuppy yuppy yay!*

And up they went to the tune of ten million Longhorns and one million mustangs, bound for the rail-heads of Abilene and other Kansas towns. The fantasy of the Trail-Driver — the cowboy gone traveler — still haunts the Brazos memory and forms one of its most picturesque chapters.

The Brazos is, of course, a cowboy's river from source to mouth. You will find him up on the Staked Plain, a wind-tanned ranch-hand, whose daddy before him headed for Old Tascosa of a Saturday to make whoopee after living all week in a dirt dug-out with a dried hide for a door. Or he may be out fixing fences in the shinnery country in a modern jeep and only put on his gaudy pants and fancy shirt for the square-dance or the rodeo-under-the-lights.

He may be getting his registered Herefords ready for the Fat Stock Show down in the Cross Timbers or the Grand Prairie and polishing horns and hooves while he dreams of the blue ribbons they will take. You may even find him leaning over a fence and admiring his deep gray Brahmas grazing under moss-clinging oaks down in the lower Brazos-land with pardonable gloating.

Or he may be a dairy-inclined brand of cow-poke with more Jerseys than he and his milking-machines can take care of up around the Falls, or just a farmer-rancher with a lot of cotton and a herd of cattle, dividing his loyalty between what comes out of the ground and what grazes off of it, cutting wheat where his grand-daddy cut fences to discourage "nesters" from hemming this same country in.

But wherever you find him along the banks of the Brazos today, he will have a yen for cattle and powerful admiration for one breed or another. He will talk in the lingo of the pen and the range, have a western costume in the bureau-drawer at home, and nothing will delight him more than to see a rodeo or take part in one. The story of the spurs and the saddle is definitely a part of the Brazos saga. The *remuda* and the *riata*, the longhorn and the lasso are a part of its heritage.

This chapter is one of the cowboy who "come the Chisolm Trail with the buffalo wild and woolly", without benefit of clergy or help of haberdasher. He hired on to wrangle at $30-a-month-and-found, he nursed a thousand dogies up the trail to Kansas, come dust, storm, hail, hell, high-water or hostile Indians. If adversity showed up he fought his way out of it or swam his herd through it.

The valley of the Brazos with its grass and moisture has always been a cattle-land of sorts. In the last three decades of the past century almost every Brazonian owned cattle or went out and "hunted" some to own. There was profit in cattle in those days. Back as early as 1854, Shap Ross of Waco hung up a record by buying five hundred head of steers at $13 each in the Brazos-land, drove them to Missouri and sold them for $27 per head.

One had no fences to bother with then. The cowman just followed level ground, steered clear of settlements and Indians, forded the streams when he came to them, pastured his herd where he found grass, kept to the trails and made the fords of the rivers until he reached the market and got his price. Henry Caulfield followed that routine and brought a lot of range cattle to sell to the Quartermaster of the Southern Confederacy. These cattle raised themselves while the menfolk were off fighting with Lee in Virginia and Caulfield drove them overland to Louisiana and sold them on the hoof.

But that was only a drop in the bucket . . . when the Boys in Gray came marching home, they found their houses falling down, their fields and gardens in weeds, but their cattle wild and plentiful . . . it was a puzzle to know what to do with them.

Necessity is the mother of invention, so they invented something that want dictated to them. There were no harvests and families had to be fed before the crop could be planted and made. The outside world was hungry for red meat and would pay well for it if it could be delivered to where they could buy it. The question was one of delivery. . . .

The Spaniards had driven cattle to the Brazos in the early days of the 16th century when they toiled up El Camino Real building missions. Then, when the Anglo-Americans had come across the Sabine and the Red, they drove their European breeds of cattle into the pastures of the Brazos, where they mated them with the rangy Spanish-Mexican types. Of this union the Longhorn was born, fit for long drives with a hardy resistance all his own. He needed it.

They knew something about "cattle-driving" in the Brazos-land to start with. Joseph, Abner and Robert Kuykendall had driven from across the Sabine to the Brazos in 1821. The next year saw Dan Shipman of Brazoria drive a bunch of his stock to the River's valley. Allen and Pool in 1860, just before the War, had moved their herd to the Houston plain between the Brazos and the Trinity. All of these herds, together with those of the Mexican loyalists that they had abandoned after San Jacinto, ran the census of Brazos cattle to about 100,000 when the Texas flag went up at Washington-on-the-Brazos in 1836.

There had long been coastal "drives" from Texas to Louisiana. In 1846 there was one herd that went from the Brazos clear to the Ohio. Then, there was a herd that T. J. Trimmier drove in 1848 from the Brazos to the gold-fields of California, with their wide horns weaving; and the drivers brought back plenty of gold with them.

One might think that driving cattle out would deplete the herds in the Brazos-land, but actually it did not operate that way. By 1865, despite the Civil War, there were estimated to be three and a half-million cattle in Texas and more than half of them fed on Brazos grass or drank from the River and her tributaries.

But how to get them to market . . .

In the spring of 1867, Joseph McCoy and Will Suggs were leaning over a cattle-pen fence in a central Illinois town, haggling over the price of a herd that Suggs had gathered down on the Brazos grazing-ground, shaped up and driven to the Illinois market.

"How'd y'ever get them wild critters up here, Will?" Joe asked.

"Hunh! Last year there was more'n a quarter-million of them same kind what come across the Red lookin' for markets. They'd have brought more, but folks up in this country claimed they was afraid of Texas fever."

"Afraid of Texas competition, most likely."

"Yup," Will sighed. "Weren't fer thievin' Injuns, rustlers and herd-owners stealin' us blind when we pass through their land, we'd brung more."

"Pretty long ways," Joe suggested.

"That's cause we have to drive so fur east . . ."

That gave Joe McCoy an idea. Down at the sorting-yards he looked up Colonel J. J. Meyers of Lockhart, Texas who knew the west of old. He had marched with John C. Fremont when the General opened up the Kansas country and should know something about "driving" through that area.

Then McCoy started haunting the railroad yards, cattle-owners' offices and officials of Kansas towns. Salina and Solomon brushed him off. But a drab little settlement on the Kansas prairie, Abilene, with a half-dozen log huts decided it would not do any harm to try. So they did business with Joe McCoy. He himself put 35,000 hard dollars back of his hand-shake and they began building pens, yards, spurs and buildings in Abilene.

Suggs took off for Texas to carry the word to the herdsmen of the Brazos and before they knew it a man named Thompson stole a march on everybody and headed a herd out to Abilene. He guided by the North Star at night and laying his wagon-tongue on it, drove hard by day, checked again that night to see if he was right and got almost to Abilene.

On the edge of the Kansas town, Smith, McCord and Chandler bought him out for a good profit and had the honor of driving the first Texas herd into the streets of the cheering town. The Longhorns overran every place but the saloons, and the cowboys were in there celebrating in too great numbers.

Others were on the way and Wilson and Hicks drove the next herd all the distance with the water-marks of the Brazos on their saddle-leather. Up the trail that same year over 35,000 head of cattle were said to have plodded.

But Joe McCoy did not profit by it. Like many a discoverer, they forgot him. When the politicians and the railroads took over the market in Abilene and the other Kansas towns they thrust McCoy aside or froze him out and he went bankrupt. He had shown the light to the folk on the banks of the Brazos and the Kaw and they had found the way by themselves.

Thereafter, for many years, the Texas Longhorns would stamp out the grass and beat a swath across the prairie that would never disappear. The money that these drives brought to Texas rebuilt many a home, repaired depleted fortunes and furnished capital for new enterprises in the valley of the Brazos. The trails were many . . .

It was significant that practically all of them crossed the Brazos as they went from the grazing lands of Texas to the markets of the north. They drifted back and forth depending on the weather, the grass and the Indians, but it was up to the Trail-boss to know where he was fording the Brazos and hit it on the nose. Get his cattle and his chuck-wagon over, know the men whom he had to take along to wrangle his herd — that was what he was hired for and why he drew his one hundred bucks a month.

They had to be men who could ride, shoot, swim, sleep in the saddle, eat on the go, swear hard oaths, crack a bull-whip loudly and croon sweet songs to the night-herd. They had to be men unafraid to take a chance on dying in a mid-night stampede or of getting a twanging arrow between the shoulder-blades for their $30-and-keep.

It was a sight at the fords!

Cattle that had never seen so much water would shy away from swimming across a broad sheet of river even when it was low. But when she was up with flood-waters, then it was a real task. Myriad horn-tips and noses were in the russet tide with naked, swimming, yelling cowboys urging them on. Milling about, lashing frantically, feeling for the gravelly bank beneath their hooves, clambering up on the farther side, wet, dripping, bawling, mooing, complaining, but headed for Wyoming, Kansas or wherever the Boss said to go. Baptized they were in the muddy waters of the Brazos.

The Chisolm Trail . . .

A great deal has been written about this old highway of the herds. There are those who argue about how John C. Chisolm, a Cherokee cattletrader, who supplied the troops at Fort Scott, Kansas with his wagon-trains, spelled his name. Chism — Chissum — Chisolm. Anyhow, he drove many a time from Texas and Louisiana to Kansas and when the herds started up the trail they naturally took the way that he and his wagons had blazed. When one advised "Why don't you take the old Chisolm Trail?" one knew what they meant.

There were plenty of others. One went from the Pecos to Wyoming, another through Tascosa and the Panhandle to Dodge City and one ran from San Antonio — Waco — Mineral Wells — Santa Fé, along the upper Brazos Forks. From these and many others one could take his choice. The ones down near the coast crossed the lower Brazos at well-established fords.

W. D. H. Saunders drove often from Goliad to the Mississippi crossing the Brazos at Richmond. The outside world was a bit dubious about these driven-cattle, but when prices soared to $25 and $30 a head at the railhead the industry was established. By 1871 more than 600,000 steers went up the trail from Texas to Kansas.

But back to The Chisolm . . . it started at San Antonio and ended in Abilene, Kansas. It went through New Braunfels, crossed the San Marcos below that town, forded the Colorado three miles below Austin, passed to the right of Round Rock, Georgetown, Salado and Belton, to the left of Fort Graham in Hill County, over the Brazos at Kimball's Bend just to the left of Cleburne, then on to Fort Worth, crossing the Trinity below town, thence to Elizabeth, Bolivar where the trailed forked and at last reached the Red. There was an alternate route that led through Waco and crossed the Brazos there. That way ventured through a River town where the herd might stampede in the streets and where the cowboys might get "lickered-up" on the wet goods of Rat

Row or partake of too much amusement and entertainment on Second Street.

It is quite likely that Chisolm himself never drove a single herd up the trail that bore his name. The drives had three fixed Brazos crossings on the upper River — Waco, Kimball's Bend and, later on, Fort Griffin on the upper Fork. Richmond was the chief crossing on the lower Brazos.

Fort Griffin became a popular ford, the McCoy and the Dodge Trails both using it and the rivalry between it and some of the others became hot. In 1879 they had a big newspaper controversy as to whether more cattle went by the Chisolm and Fort Worth or by the Dodge and Fort Griffin. *The Fort Worth Democrat* and *The Fort Griffin Echo* bet $2,500 and Fort Griffin won, for almost half of the total drive that year went up through the Shackelford County crossing.

The Goodnight Trail to Colorado followed the Double Mountain Fork of the Brazos. The vagaries of the River's floods and shallows became an important factor to the trail-drivers. Also the water and supply-points cut a figure in the plans for the drive.

It was customary to gather a herd in a neighborhood, the various cattle-owners contributing to make it up to about two or three thousand head. They allowed about fifty horses for the drive, selected a road, trying to avoid settlements and the Indian country as much as possible. Every step was plotted like a battle-campaign. Twenty wranglers and the trail-boss went along with two cowboys riding point to keep the herd to the route. These jobs, hard ones, were alternated to share the work and the less experienced youngsters were put at the tail of the herd to take the dust, whip up the stragglers and yippee at the little dogies that wanted to stop and graze.

Night guard was a steady job. The herd usually grazed at dawn, again at eleven and then late in the afternoon at the rest-stop for the night. The men snatched their chow when the cattle did, for the chuck-wagon had raced on ahead to be there with a hot meal at sun-down. The speed of the drive was regulated by the distance to the next water. The width of the point was about twenty animals unless the terrain required narrowing it down more than that. The trail-boss rode well on ahead to spy out the land, locate trouble, likely causes for stampede and to change the direction if he thought wise. He had made the trip many times before along the same route.

The cattle were allowed to graze from sundown to dark when they were moved close together and bedded down for the night. Four men could night-watch 3,000 steers after they were used to the road, but at the start, or when there were Indian signs, a storm brewing, or a buffalo herd nearby, everybody was on his toes to keep the herd in hand. During the night the guards rode slowly about the cattle constantly, meeting at fixed points. They sang in soft tones to assure the cattle of their presence and were careful to watch for anything that might cause a stampede in the night. If a rattler buzzed, the guard marked the spot, for come daylight he would return and kill the varmint . . . he could not chance doing it in the dark, even if he saw the snake in the moon-light, lest the herd get alarmed and it was well-known that the reptile would not leave the vicinity until morning.

A stampede could come from the least little thing — a thunder-clap, a sudden flight of birds, an Indian war-whoop, a pistol-shot. A buffalo bull might come up to flirt with some of the domestic cows of the herd and when the cowboy approached take off at a run and start the herd running too. All that could be done was to try and ride hard, head the leaders, quiet them down and get the herd back into position. Old timers belled the leaders and got the herds used to following the sound of the bells.

These men had to be reliable, responsible and conscientious to make good trail-drivers. Of them Colonel Charlie Goodnight writes:

Taking them all in all, my life on the trail was the happiest part of it . . . Few of the younger generation realize that the western men, the cowboys, were as brave and chivalrous as it is possible to be. Bullies and tyrants were unknown . . . Timid men were not known among us. Many of the richest and greatest men of Texas today were cowboys. Of the hands I employed there are now at least three millionaires. Fewer cowboys have been tried for crimes than any other class of men.

There was a fast rule that if a man were caught offending on the trail he could be tried right then and there by his associates and dealt with accordingly. Nothing was said about it when the men arrived back home. Many who started for Abilene never came back to the Brazos.

Often the leading folk of the Brazos towns, seeing the value of cattle in those days, would go out "cow-hunting" in the thickets, brakes and bottoms to gather up wild strays and add them to their holdings. The range was full of unclaimed stock of this kind to be caught, penned, branded and tamed to bring money to the pockets of the "hunter." It is related that once staid old Dr. R. C. Burleson of Baylor University went out on such a "hunt" and met Governor. Ross likewise trying to enlarge his cattle-holdings in the bottoms of the Waco Brazos-land.

Henry Caulfield's name appears again and again in the accounts of the drives. One time he drove from the Brazos to New Mexico and brought back $75,000 in specie in his saddle-bags over a thousand miles of Indian country. It was not uncommon to see in the Brazos plain a herd of a couple of thousand Longhorns strung out for a mile or more, trudging along under the Texas sun, cowboys riding clouds of dust around them and heading them to the next river. Caulfield was an old-timer at this and drove many a herd.

One of the tricks was to bed cattle down thirsty before swimming them across the Brazos and then pushing them right on across in the morning. Using the best swimming-horses, holding them tight in the water, they were calculated not to get panicky. After they had crossed a few streams they got their "swimming-feet" and gave little trouble. But at first they were balky and refused to go into the water unless forced.

Of course, if the Brazos was up they had to drift the herd down-stream or up to find a shallow place to cross. Handlers of the chuck-wagon had to be careful not to let it over-turn or let the water get in to damage the food and the bedding. Then, too, if the herd got in the stream and drifted into a U-shaped formation they could get out of hand. But the naked cow-punchers handled them loosely in the water, broke up bunching and swam in to cuss them apart with yells and urgings. It was a busy time for the herd-guards when the River was up.

When they got across, the herd was watered and grazed. In that way they got the habit of looking forward to the reward for crossing the stream in order. "Falling-weather" which included rain, hail, snow, sleet, thunder or lightning, was hard going for the men. Cattle would not lie down and a stampede was easily started. A tired herd slept.

The farther you could move your cattle away from another herd the better, unless you decided to throw the two together, which was often done for convenience. Then they had to be divided again before reaching the market. But woe to the guards of two strange herds that got entangled on the drive . . . it might take two weeks to straighten them out and head them in the right direction again.

Indians, outlaws and "bad men" gave the drivers considerable concern. They would swoop down and make demands on the herd-boss for beef, bribes or "tax" for letting the herd go by unmolested. The owners allowed this graft for a time and then began hiring gunmen of proved ability to go along and shoot it out with the marauders. A "protected herd" was let alone on the trail.

One of the most terrible things that could happen to a herd on the drive was to lose its chuck-wagon by fire, accident or by overturning in a stream. Salt, staples, bedding and other essentials went by the board and there were times cited when a cowboy would have to boil his saddle-pad for the salt that his horse had sweated out.

The "drives" would begin to shape up in March or April so that they could make it up the trail during the mild summer months, let the cattle graze on the Kansas grass and be fat when they were driven into Abilene or Dodge City to be marketed. The shipping was done in the late summer or fall. When the cowboys were paid off they headed straight for the bright lights of Ogalalla, Abilene, Wichita or Dodge City where amusement, wheels of chance, wine and women were to be had and where a lonely herder could get quick action for his hard cash.

When he had his fill of diversion or was broke, he headed back for the banks of the Brazos ready for a return-trip and with a lot of breeze to shoot for the boys in the bunk-house during the coming winter. It would lure younger and less-traveled cow-punchers to take the trail the next spring. The supply was ample.

It was said to have cost about fifty cents a head to get the cattle up the trail to market and it would average about fifty days to the drive, bar accident, disease, prairie-fire, Indians, outlaws, predatory animals and stampedes. The losses were kept to between five and ten percent. It was only when the railroads, the nesters and barbed wire came along that the cattlemen found these percentages failing to stand up.

Waco and other supply-points on the trail made an industry of supplying the outfits with necessaries for their chuck-wagons to stock up with as they went along. It became quite an item of commerce. Farmers in the bottoms of the Brazos caught and killed wild hogs, salted down the hams and shoulders and sold them to the outfits. At one time there was a bill in the Federal Congress to fence a trail a mile wide from Texas to Kansas following the Chisolm, over the Brazos at Waco, for cattle outfits exclusively. The U. S. Army would patrol it against Indians and outlaws and there would be feeding-stations en route. It never passed.

They had regular watering-stations on the trail and the trail-boss had to know where they were and set his course accordingly. Water, like shelter and grass, could change the course or the fortune of the herd and it was often the difference between profit and loss. George W. Littlefield ran his cattle in central Texas around Austin, but once he sent a big herd to Kansas — said to be the biggest that ever crossed the Brazos at Waco — and found the market glutted. That was in 1877, at the hey-day of the drives, so the trail-boss drifted his herd south to the Texas Plains for the winter. In the canyons and arroyos he found good shelter against the "Northers" and in the spring he had 3,500 cattle in excellent flesh ready for market. The LIT brand stayed in the Panhandle and Plains thereafter for many years to come.

A code of honor existed among these trail-drivers that was abiding and fast. The man engineering the drives might line up as many as ten thousand cattle at a time and not give or take a single note or bill of sale. There would be a tally of number, class, brands and markings. The men who contributed their stock knew they would be dealt with honestly and that the collector would account for the last dollar due. If he said that he lost so many cattle in a blizzard, to the Indians or in a stampede, that was right. They settled on a cowman's word in the Brazos country in the 1870's.

Of course, there were unprincipled "accumulators" but they were soon weeded out. They hunted other men's strays, stragglers and isolated herds. They pilfered at water-holes and beat the mesquite for calves that had wandered off from their mammies; and then they would show up with a good-sized herd.

There was a vernacular of the herd that was its peculiar own. You "worked" calves by finding and branding them while still running with their mammies; a "cutting-horse" was one that was skilled in darting in and separating a particular critter from the herd; "flanking" was where a cowboy reached across a calf's rump and grabbed a handful of skin to throw it for branding; "bull-dogging" was grabbing an animal by the neck or tail and twisting it down with a sudden jerk, although rodeo-parlance of today has amplified it some; a "running-iron" was one heated for branding; "jungle-bob" was where the ear was split and allowed to flop for identification; "dewlap" was a cut in the fleshy part of the throat; "hog-tie" was to get three feet together and tie the animal, while "side-line" was to tie two feet, and "boppled" was to tie both back legs; "tooths" was to examine a mouth for age. The terms Big-Boss, Straw-Boss, Line-Riders, Trail-boss, Waddy, Screw, Buckaroo, Stray and Fence-Rider were all trail-terms and for the most part self-explanatory.

The cabin was a "hooden" and "come 'n' git it" was chow-call. "Forking a horse" was to mount him and "loco" was crazy after the weed that made cattle that way when they ate it.

Names of great old trail-drivers parallel those of the famed ranches. The Slaughters — William, John and C. C. — were all sons of Rev. G. G. Slaughter and began driving herds north from the Palo Pinto range to Kansas with the "Lazy-S" and the "U-Lazy-S" brand on them in the early days of the drives. Oliver Loving was a pioneer to Illinois in 1858 on the up-trail, to Colorado in 1860, and he hit many another trail. But he ventured among the Comanches in 1867, driving from Fort Sumner in New Mexico and he stopped an Indian arrow. They named a trail for him after his untimely end.

The XIT, 10-A, Cross-C and many of the other brands of the Brazos Forks country drove their herds north and west. Colonel Dillard R. Fant came from South Carolina and settled on the Brazos in 1852. He drove in all, it is claimed, over 200,000 cattle up the trail with his brand on them in his day.

M. A. Withers, a famous Brazos cattleman and trail-driver drove a herd to Lockhart in 1862 and on to Shreveport Depot of the Confederate Army, but the cattle got there so poor that he had to drive them back to the Brazos and fatten them up again. He said he paid drivers $2 a day and board — the latter being straight cornbread, coffee and bacon — and he admitted that sometimes the boys did not get their $2 if the returns were bad. He did a hitch in the 36th Texas Cavalry during the Civil War and in 1868, when the fighting was over, he went up the trail with 600 wild Longhorns to Wichita, Kansas, crossing the Brazos at Waco. The next year he drove 4,500 steers to the Dobie Walls in the Texas Panhandle and made the crossing of the River at Fort Griffin.

The old timers will tell you a story with trimmings . . . of how a herd went up by Waco in 1869 headed for Montana. The Longhorns were stout old fellows, five to fifteen years old, branded on the horns so that all the new owner had to do was to saw off the tips and pay on that basis. They came to the Chisolm and found every last river on the rise, so they just added a boat to their equipment and ferried over at every stream. A boat as standard equipment of a trail-drive made history.

They tell another story of a Gonzales herd in the spring of 1870. The steers were from four to twelve years old and when they got to Waco they found the Brazos high and raging. They finally got across and the chuck-wagon safe on its wheels on the farther side. Thinking they were doing very well by now they were disappointed when they ran into a Comanche war-party in Hill County. These redskins, in full war-paint, stampeded the herd for the sheer deviltry of it and demanded twenty-five beeves for "tax."

There was naught to do but comply and the four hundred Comanches ate of the raw meat and daubed themselves with blood. The drivers stood by and watched disgustedly, but dispatched one of their number to carry the word to the Tonkawas where the Comanches were. Glutted and gorged from their feast, the marauders were set upon by the wily Tonks and over half of them killed. Thereby the cowboys got some of their vengeance.

Then, there was a trail that went up by Abilene, Texas, not far from the Brazos Forks . . . "a town that set a pace that left the wayfarer purseless and breathless, to say naught of headaches" . . . on over the Clear Fork into the range beyond. If the River was up they drifted the herds, usually, to the Round Timber Crossing.

Now and then there was trouble en route, for the cowboys were a rough and ready crew. In April, 1871 two herds were moving up the Chisolm from around Lampasas. They crossed the Bosque at Clifton where a drunken Mexican let his oxen run into the tail-end of one of the herds. A rear-guard cowboy beat up the hapless *cartero,* who, on sobering up, got his gun and went looking for his assailant.

The coroner's verdict was that the Mexican came to his death at the hands of unknown parties who threw his body in a prickly-pear patch. The jury strongly suspected the outfits that were passing through on the way North with the herds. The Sheriff went out and tried to arrest every cowboy, but there was a stampede on and he had to wait until the herds were under control again. He took all but a few guards to town and lodged them in jail, but the two guilty suspects had skipped out and over the Brazos. On the farther side they joined up again with the herds, but never again did they sign on to come this way. Texas Sheriffs remembered . . .

Jerry Nance took over 200,000 cattle up the trail in a period of fifteen years, using all of the Brazos crossings at one time or another, but preferring the one at Fort Griffin.

He tells a tale of driving from his home town of Kyle, south of Austin, with 2,100 cattle, 40 ponies and his chuck-wagon, ox-drawn. When he got to the Brazos, he says, it was so high he had to pay to have his oxen and wagon ferried over.

"All the cattle were in the river," he related, "swimming at the same time and it looked as if there were no cattle at all, just tips of horns and noses."

They drove the other way, too. From north Texas they had to ford the Brazos to get south to Mexico. Captain E. C. McAdams, who fought under Zachary Taylor in Mexico and served with Captain Jack Hays Ranger Company, settled in Palo Pinto. In 1863, he assembled a Brazos herd and drove south to Mexico where he knew the country well. There he traded his cattle for staples and brought them back to sell to his Brazos neighbors. He tells of trouble down there in the rainy season, however, in the river-fogs around Fort Griffin. The cattle stampeded and he went three weeks without unrolling his bedding-roll. He got one hour's sleep a night and that in the saddle.

There was a peer of all trail-drivers — Colonel Ike T. Pryor — who lived out his long and useful life in San Antonio. He claims that when he drove fifteen herds in 1884 across the Brazos to the northwest, he never lost over three per cent of them, making a profit of over $4 a head from start to finish. He always kept 165 men and 1,000 saddle horses ready for his drives — six horses per man allowed for the trip North with eleven men and a herd-boss for every 3,000 head of cattle.

The odds were high against the man who drove the dogies up the trail and they took many chances with Indians, floods and stampede. W. E. Cureton of Meridian says:

We camped near the Brazos the night before and tried to cross in the early morning. The River was high and muddy and the cattle refused to enter it. We just backed out and grazed them until the sun got up and they could see the far bank. They wanted water so they went on across. You couldn't swim across as big a stream going east in the morning or going west late in the evening with the sun in the cattle's faces.

They had facilities and toll-charges at certain places. There was a corral and chute at Kimball's Bend in Johnson County that is still visible in the banks of the Brazos today.

Here one cent per head was considered reasonable and there was a ferry for the chuck-wagon and for the horses that refused to swim. The price for the wagon was 75c and 25c for each horse. At John Payne's house nearby there were accommodations for the refreshment of the drivers and a place to buy supplies. But the herds coming up through Bosque County usually stocked up at Valley Mills, which was a famous rendezvous point for trail-drivers in that day.

It is recorded that the ranchers in through the Brazos valley had a way of keeping their ranch-hands armed and lying behind cover when these herds came driving through. Some of them had the idea of supplementing their losses on the drive from local herds. By the same token the herd-boss would keep his men alerted at certain stages of the drive lest the local folk prey on his herds as they passed.

The cow pony on the trail was a cross between the wild mustang and the bigger horses from the old States. He had to be broken and trained to handle strays, cut a herd and give his all in a stampede. The sentimental tie between him and his master was a fast one and a good trail-driver brought his own mount, usually, when joining up. Others took theirs from the ranch's *remuda* and got used to him.

Not many of the old trail-drivers are left. They still hold their conventions, but their memories are becoming hazy. They had to be very young then to be chipper now but the hard life has preserved many of them remarkably well and they still tell their stories. Many books have been written about them, monuments and statuary perpetuate their deeds and their place is fixed in the saga of the Brazos.

Many of the olders ones in those days smelled gun-powder in the Civil War and many of their comrades are buried beside the rivers up and down the trail. They experimented with a fancy and built it into an industry. That industry saved their country from the depression that dealt such a severe blow to almost all of the old South. Theirs is a colorful tradition.

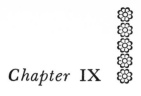

Chapter IX

THE LAW OF THE WHITE MAN

 "I ESTABLISHED LAW AND JUSTICE IN THE LAND!"

These words were ascribed to Hammurabi, King of Babylon, in about 2250 B.C. The Anglo-Saxon settler on the Brazos might well have them inscribed upon his monument as an epitaph. Until he came to the banks of the River and established Law and Order, enforcement and respect for authority, men lived by the arrow and rifle; they went armed and the survivor was the one who could shoot the quickest on sight. If crimes were committed, a posse formed, a hemp-rope was shaken out and a tree-limb sighted for use. But the Law of The White Man changed all that.

If the Brazos Basket-makers and Mound-builders had codes and laws outside of their tribal customs, they left nothing to indicate it. Their artifacts deal with things and people, solely, never with ideas and ideals. Were they that primitive and shallow a people? Were they eager to show what they had and what they did rather than what they thought and believed?

The red tribesmen whom Cabeza de Vaca and Coronado found along the course of the stream that was to be called the Brazos were ruled by a Chief and the laws of the particular tribe. There was no appeal. The council of the elders might advise but the word of the Chieftain was law. That is, until a more powerful Chieftain arose from about the council-fires.

Beyond those within his own compound or mission-wall the Spaniard had little inclination to govern. He lived by an ecclesiastico-civil code of his own, but he did not impose it on the Indians of the Brazos-land for three hundred years after he claimed it for his king. It was two hundred years almost — 1691 — before the Spanish Viceroy in Mexico City even prescribed that *alcaldes* and *ayuntamientos* for local government should be named or empowered along the Brazos.

Neither did the French care to impose their law or government upon the dark-skinned tribesmen who flitted before them in the forest or worked for them at Garcitas Bay to build their fort under pressure of slavery. Gold and silver, rather than empire and conquest, were the ambitions of La Salle and his men. They brought the sword to the Brazos-land and by it they perished.

The outposts and mission-presidios satisfied the Dons of Spain during the 1700's and they kept to the coast and the wide rivers where they had a few colonies contained in forts. There was a form of taxation and extortion practiced by the Spaniards, a slavery imposed and a penalty for violation of the Spanish-masters' law. But no fixed and prescribed code governed in the valley of San Xavier, as they called the River in some of their writings.

But when the 1700's waned and England was losing her colonies in North America, when France saw her hold slipping there until finally Napoleon would put a price in gold upon the rich Louisiana country, when Spain was hearing unpleasant rumblings from Mexico about a patriot-priest inciting his followers to rebel . . . the people who dwelt in the new Tejas began to think in terms of *our* country, *our* laws and *our* rights. These strange thoughts were in the consciousness of the first Anglo-American that crossed the Sabine or put into the mouth of the Brazos down at old Quintana.

The Filibusters and their brief attempts at regulation,

rule and control are hardly worth the name. They were short-lived and their skyrocket dreams of conquest were fancies to pass with the breaking of a new day. It took the 1820's and their momentous decisions, their ground-breakings and their home-buildings, their steadfast men and determined women with "Here we build!" in their hearts to make of the wilderness a garden-spot and of the barren plain a field of growing grain. After Magee, Nolan, Lafitte, Long and all the others had tried, it remained for a reasoning man out of Missouri by the name of Stephen F. Austin to begin in the 1820's a regime that would last.

When Moses Austin was pleading with the Governor at San Antonio for his franchise, they had no law on the Brazos save that which the Spanish guns dictated . . . and it could be bought or traded for with gold. When Austin finally wrung the permission to found the colony it was more contract than law that he signed. "They shall all be Catholics . . . they shall pay tribute to Mexico City . . . their grants shall be from and subject to the Spanish Crown" . . . it did not sit well upon the stomachs of freemen as they swung their axes in the valley of the Brazos.

They wanted morals enacted into law, manners into codes, ways of dealing into precepts that all could understand and live by. He who violated them must be punished or perish. Thus only would peace and prosperity be in the new land. Austin and his leaders tried to live up to their bargain, despite what their Mexican biographers and traducers may write in the history-books against them. Those who came on the *Lively* or drove in their wagons across the Sabine would have been willing to meet Mexico City in a fair way . . . but "Taxation without representation" was as repugnant on the Brazos as it was on the Potomac, the Ashley or the Susquehanna and liberty stirred the hearts of the River's men from the first day they arrived.

When, in 1830 Mexico declared that no more Anglo-

Americans could come to Texas, that the kinsfolk and friends of those already there were barred, it added fuel to the flame.

Three years later a new law: the Legislature down in Monclova set up three Judicial Districts — Nacogdoches, Brazos and Bexar — with a Judge to be named from Mexico to each and a Superior Judge of Appeals over these three; and the bonds galled all the more.

But Tejas was never a State to the Mexico City conception. A wild wilderness, inhabited by savages, exploited by a few greedy Anglo-Americans and coveted by the United States . . . it was something to be regarded with concern, to be taxed and "reduced" but hardly to be settled and governed as one would an ordinary State of the new Mexican Republic. They would attend to that later . . . tomorrow . . .

The *mañana* never came.

True, they allowed Stephen F. Austin to sit in at the sessions of the Legislature at Saltillo, but he represented outlanders and foreigners and he dared not lift his voice.

If they found no Law in the Brazos-land, it can not be said that the settlers allowed this condition to last very long. Consultations, Conferences and Assemblies were called on the banks of the Brazos at San Felipe, at Washington, Richmond and Columbia. Decorum prevailed and parliamentary procedure governed. Each of the settlements was recognized and delegates were seated. They would have a declaration of principles and a constitution to which free men could adhere. There would be legislative bodies, representatively elected, executives to carry out their laws and judicial bodies to interpret them. Justice was to come to the land of the River.

After San Jacinto, almost immediately came the Texas Courts. By 1837, the learned Chief Justice James W. Collingsworth had them functioning and lawyers from the old States who had been busy at other tasks, got out their Blackstone and Coke and began practicing their profession. Due process of law was not an idle phrase any longer.

Up until then there had been courts of sorts that the Brazos folk tried to operate without much sanction of the Mexican authority. Sufferance rather than right was the rule. In 1834 an accused on the Brazos was charged with "branding a neighbor's calf with his own mark." Alcalde John W. Moore of Harrisburg came with Judge David G. Burnet to hear the case. William Barrett Travis was the defense attorney and Robert M. (Peg-Leg Willie) Williamson was for the prosecution. They had a trial at Fort Bend and Court convened under a great oak tree. The trial lasted all day and the man was sentenced, on his guilt being determined, by the Court and Jury to be sent to Mexico to work in the mines.

Travis filed a motion for new trial setting forth that the man had a wife and five small children who would be a charge on the colony . . . so the Court re-considered and gave a suspended sentence and the man stayed on.

The Indians could never understand why they had to obey the white man's law and why he never obeyed theirs. Guns, horses, rum, superior attitude — these were the things that the Indian could never reconcile with the offers of friendship and the professions of religion. Stealing, pillaging, killing were none of them crimes to the red men. If he were strong enough to get by with them, he accepted that as right and law. When he found that even in his own homeland he had to bow to a rule-of-conduct not of his own making, his heart rebelled and his feet gave ground. He would not stay.

The Indian resented the white man's law and the Anglo-American resented the Spanish-Mexican edict and statute . . . they wanted their own way and their own say in this free Brazos-land . . . gunpowder decided finally who should have his own will respected.

Once, the story goes, the Comanches showed their disdain

for the law of these invaders by riding into San Antonio de Bexar and forcing the *rurales* or Mexican policemen to hold their ponies while they rifled the stores in broad daylight. If the Mexican authorities could get the Indians and the Anglo-Saxon settlers to fighting, they considered it good diplomacy. The three different ethnological concepts could not very well exist in the same River valley in harmony when each demanded his own law.

Law as such came with the dawning of the Texas Republic's era. It was established and throve. It was violated by the border-ruffians and the Rangers punished them and drove them away. Then the Civil War and the days of "Reconstruction" followed, and Law stook a holiday, while tyranny and power ruled. Desperados and outlaws flaunted the cause of justice in the Brazos bottoms and plains until 1874 when law came back to stay.

If there was one name that was synonymous with Law in the valley it was the word "Ranger." He was a symbol to the lawless — red men, white men and black men.

Whence came the Texas Ranger?

Stephen F. Austin mentions him in his letters of 1823, although Bancroft contends that his advent was not until 1838. He did not know his Texas for the Council in 1835 authorized a Ranger force as part of the Provisional Government. Three companies of twenty-five men each were provided — one to range east of the Trinity, another between the Trinity and the Brazos, and the third from the Brazos to the Colorado. Pay was $1.25 per day.

Theirs was a varied task, patrolling the woods and plains, fighting and destroying bad-men, outlaws and Indians wherever they found them. Many of the Rangers were waylaid and killed; and, in turn, they disposed of many a bandit — "shot-trying-to-escape." No questions were ever asked.

The Ranger had grown up with the land and knew the Mexican and the Indian. Expert with a gun and a horse, he had a quicker draw and a bit more courage than his adversary. Colonel John S. Ford said of them: "He must ride like a Mexican, trail like an Indian, shoot like a Tennessean and fight like the devil."

Hays — McCulloch — Ross — Ford — Erath — East — Stephen — Hall — Armstrong. The Ranger Hall of Fame in the early days claimed those among its great, but the deeds of the men who went into the shinnery and the bottoms and sought to bring in a bandit-band will never be fully known.

Never distinctively dressed — big hat, usually black in the old days, white in later times — with cowboy boots, a brace of six-shooters, a buckskin suit, or a corduroy later on, or maybe a gabardine in modern times—you could pick him out in a crowd . . . he looked like a Ranger.

A Texas Ranger helped Samuel Colt perfect the six-shooter after the United States Army had laughed at Colt's idea for a repeating-pistol. Sam H. Walker went to New England for the Texas Republic, perked Colt up, suggested a few changes and the "Walker-Colt Pistol" came into being. It made war-on-horseback possible and when the Texas Rangers went against the Comanches armed with a gun that would repeat without loading . . . it was the "difference."

Before the Texas Rangers would go from the banks of the Brazos to the Mexican War as Uncle Sam's army scouts, Sam Walker went to New England and brought back 1,000 six-shooters for the Rangers to carry along. After watching them in action, the United States Ordnance Department warmed up to them.

With its peculiar penchant for the unusual, the War Department ruled at one time after Annexation that the Rangers should be armed with sabers. Sam Houston, then Governor, opined: "The damned things ought to come in handy in the rattlesnake country!"

Generals Zachary Taylor and Winfield Scott swore by

the Rangers down in Mexico and once, it is said, a Ranger was killed in a Mexico City street-brawl. His comrades rounded up the eighty Mexicans "guilty of the offense" and strung every last one of them up as a warning to those who harmed Rangers thereafter.

When the U. S. Cavalrymen went to the Brazos forts, the Rangers were officially disbanded, but the Inspector-General of the U. S. Army said: "General Harney from San Antonio Military Department Headquarters can have his dragoons, but what he needs for his light work is Texas Rangers. Without them he will get nowheres."

Sam Houston plead with the War Department to use Rangers rather than troopers against the Indians, but he got no place. So, he stormed in the Senate: "Give us a thousand Rangers and we'll be responsible for the defense of the frontier . . . We ask for no regular troops, withdraw them if you wish. I ask this through no unkindness to them but because they have not the efficiency for frontier service."

They sent the Rangers to supplement the cavalry and Houston won his point. And when Governor Coke took over from the Carpetbaggers in 1874, the first thing he did was to form six companies of Rangers of seventy-five men each. Whether against Lone Wolf and his Comanches, Mexican bandits, train-robbers like Sam Bass or cleaning out a Robbers' Roost, their guns were out and ready, blazing a little earlier than their foes.

Working in pairs and detachments, they rarely went out alone. Their high days were from 1854-60 and from 1874-80. In the 1864-74 interim, the corrupt State Police were the only force that operated to enforce Law, and they did more harm than good the Rangers found out when they returned.

The Rangers were sent on many varied missions. When a feud arose the Rangers had to go in and prize the enemies apart. If a bad man came to town shooting it up, they sent for the Ranger . . . he and his padlock came. Today they

[172]

may be armed with modern two-way radios and tommy-guns, but once they had only a pair of six-guns and a padlock. When they caught a culprit they chained him to a tree in the center of town and went off looking for his gang. In that way the entire town helped watch the prisoner.

Recruiting for the Rangers had its fine points. Joe Minear tells of how he was recruited in 1870 by Captain John Sansom for his Ranger company.

"We're headin' up for Fort Griffin, Joe," the Captain said to him in Waco. "The Indians hev druv four hunnerd Negro soldiers into that fort and they got 'em penned up. We're ordered to go there and scare them Comanches off. Want to go?"

Joe writes that they only found two Indians when they got there, for the word was out that "The Rangers are coming." He seems a bit sour over the smallness of the bag, but notes that one Comanche had a lance with many notches in it and the other had a white woman's hair braided into his own top-knot. Neither braiding nor notch-carving were indulged by the two any more, Joe states with finality.

When the big Sutton-Taylor feud flared up in DeWitt County, the order went to Captain Lee Hall and his Brazos patrol of Rangers to go over and prize them apart. The Captain went alone. One riot — one Ranger.

When Sam Bass got so bad down in the central Brazos country they told off a Ranger company to put a stop to him. They did.

When John Wesley Hardin left a trail of blood up and down the valley of the River and then ran off to Florida, they sent a Ranger after him and no extradition papers with orders to bring him back alive. He did.

When Clyde Barrow and Bonnie Parker,· Public Enemy No. 1 and his moll . . . but that is told elsewhere in this narrative.

The Texas Ranger, born on the Brazos in the midst of

storm, had his time and passed. "The Men in the White Hats", as Douglas calls them in his book, became prohibition-agents, strike-breakers, vice-campaigners and finally slot-machine raiders.

In 1935 they went under the Texas Department of Public Safety with the Highway Patrol and today they number about fifty men in six companies. Their importance has been diluted by the number of "honorary" commissions that the Texas Governors have issued through the years to celebrities. The old-time Ranger has gone down the trail with the Indian and the buffalo, the trail-driver and the cowboy . . .

But the tales of him survive and always will.

Noah Smithwick relates how he served in the Rangers and got 1,280 acres of public land for two years duty. Each Ranger furnished his own horse and the State paid him $100 if the horse was "killed in action." Since he could buy a new one for $40, it was an inducement to pad his expense-account, but a dangerous way — to anyone but a Ranger.

It was Captain Jack Hays with a bunch of Brazos Rangers who stormed the famous Bishop's Palace in Monterrey during the Mexican War. High up on the hill outside of the town, where many tourists visit today, the Rangers won the point and gave the advantage of battle to the Americans. Richard Addison Gillespie, after whom the county in Texas was named, captured ten Mexican cannon in that assault but he found a bullet with his name on it. He had a great record as an Indian-fighter in the Rangers.

Walter Prescott Webb in his book *The Texas Rangers* gives this pen picture of them:

Their uniforms were an outlandish assortment of long-tailed blue coats and bob-tailed black ones, slouched felt hats, dirty pajamas and black leather caps. Most of them wore long, bushy beards. They carried a rifle and four pistols . . . and everything else they could tie to their saddles.

The Rangers fought at sea once and got the name of "Horse

Marines". On June 2, 1836 there was a Mexican ship bound for Velasco on the Brazos. It was lying in the Bay of Copano, Lafitte's favorite hang-out after he was driven off Galveston Island. The Rangers slipped aboard and captured the vessel. Then their leader, Major Isaac W. Burton, forced the Captain to lure the Captains of two sister ships aboard and they, too were captured. They brought the three prize vessels into Velasco safely and the supplies were used by the Texas patriots to advantage.

The Rangers were prominent in the Plum Creek Fight, when General Felix Huston and several Ranger companies under his command pursued a Comanche war-party that had come boldly down into the Coastal Plain. Sacking Victoria and Linville, brutally murdering the settlers, pillaging ruthlessly, killing small children, they were making their way toward the Brazos with their spoils. The Rangers took out after them.

Ed Burleson commanded one Ranger company and Old Paint Caldwell another. Ben and Henry McCulloch were in the ranks that day as was Jack Hays, Alsey Miller and Monroe Hardman. The Rangers never fought harder or more cruelly than they did that day against the marauders at Plum Creek. Seven Rangers were killed, but the Comanches lost almost every one of their warriors and it was the last of their war-parties ever to come that far east and south. Ranger Frank Childress was killed in that battle. His brother wrote the Texas Declaration of Independence with his own quill.

Mirabeau B. Lamar was strong for the Rangers and got the Texas Congress in 1839 to write them into the Defense Plan. It was Lamar who got the Consultation at the very beginning to establish Rangers on the frontier and with his own hand he signed the commissions that sent young Burleson, Erath, Coryell and others to the Falls of the Brazos as Rangers. Sterling C. Robertson in January 1836 commanded the Viesca Ranger company on the midlands of the Brazos and kept a wary eye on 5,000 Mexicans and Indians who were consorting together on the South Bosque. There were companies always at Fort Bend and Fort Milam and whenever an Indian outrage occurred they took the field.

When they took over in 1874 they found things so bad that they declared war on the *comancheros* who were trading with the Indians for stolen goods looted from the settlements. The Rangers penetrated even to the Reservations to hunt out culprits. Appeals to the Indian Office in Washington by the whites went unheeded. The Indian was always right. But to the Ranger he was just another law-breaker and dealt with as such.

Big Foot Wallace was one of the most noted of the Ranger characters and his record of exploits on the Brazos and the Neches, ranging as far west as the Llano, was one of such prowess that Duval wrote a biography of him that sang his praises to the sky.

The Rangers worked with the troops, but preferred to work with their own kind. Once, in later days when a famous old Ranger was at the White House conferring with President Woodrow Wilson about Villa, he said:

"Sir, give me a thousand Rangers. Let me pick them and I'll get Villa and clean up the Border for you besides."

"Why can't you use the soldiers, too, Captain?" the President asked.

"Mr. President, confidentially, I ain't for blowing a bugle before I shoot."

The Rangers blamed Albert Sydney Johnston for the Council House Fight perfidy of the white men in killing the Comanche Chiefs who had come in under a flag-of-truce. It was the Ranger and the settler who paid for that.

Here is a typical page from a Ranger's diary. J. M. Stephens with eleven other Rangers went out on a patrol:

On Hubbard Creek we came on a party of Indians driving 25 or 30 head of horses — Indians had eaten buffalo and were stuffed full — Questioned them and let them go — We kilt a buffalo calf and had a feed, too — Legs of a man found kilt a good while back. Reckon he's a Regular AWOL from one of the forts. Gave bones burial. Named this creek where we found him 'Dead Man's Creek.' Marked it on map. — Going is hard on Double Mountain Fork. Game and horse-feed scarce — Kilt deer and cooked it — Saw bunch of Indians crost the canyon. Swapt a few shots and a few sassy words with them. Nobody hurt — Returned to headquarters.

These were the men who kept the channel of the law clear along the Brazos in the old days. When they left the banks of the River, driven away by the exigencies of war or the Carpetbaggers' rule, the citizens had to team up into Vigilantes and attend to justice themselves.

Possibly there were some mistakes made when irate cattlemen found a rustler in a compromising position, with a branding-iron hot and a neighbor's calf under his knee, and let him have Cottonwood Justice at the end of a lariat. There was no appeal from such a sentence, and it was highly effective to suppress rustling.

In 1875 the "Regulators" were organized among the little cattlemen and sheepmen to take care of the big fellows with their paid gunmen who tried to drive the smaller operators out. Claiming that they were "nesters" or interfering with the range, the big operators poisoned sheep and drove off the small-fry's cattle to add to the bigger herds. If the little man came complaining, they pushed him around.

The Regulators were smart. They secured partners from the next county to come in and do their work for them while they paraded their alibis on the main square of the county-seat. The next day they would be over paying the debt back by aiding their friends in the next county.

Many times the lawyers and judges were men who had served in the Rangers. Major Charles B. Pearre of Waco, who was the District Attorney of a wide region — McLennan, San

Saba, Falls, Coryell, Comanche, Hamilton, Lampasas, Brown, Palo Pinto and Bosque Counties; the 19th Judicial District — in 1866, was a Civil War veteran, a lawyer, and on top of it all a Ranger.

The first Court of law to be held under the aegis of the new Republic was convened on May 21, 1836 with Benjamin C. Franklin, Judge of the District of the Brazos, presiding. His first decision was a disposition of the treasure-chest captured at San Jacinto.

As the country became more settled, great cases shaped up in the valley and noted court-trials were held. Outstanding lawyers, giants of oratory, forensic warriors battled for the life and freedom of their clients or over their property-rights. History was made in the tall-ceilinged court-rooms with the long windows and recounted over barbecued ribs, under the sycamores on the creek-banks.

Judge R. E. B. Baylor, a Baptist preacher (the man who gave his name to the University) was Judge of the Third Judicial District in the new Texas and held the first sessions of court in many of the Brazos counties. He had been a Congressman from Alabama and was later a member of the Supreme Court of Texas. He was succeeded as Judge of the Third District by N. W. Battle, a classmate at William and Mary College, Virginia, of Richard Coke, another illustrious Waco advocate and a Governor of Texas.

There have been many noted trials on the Brazos banks. A few find a place here . . .

At Jacksboro the trial of the Indian Chiefs held attention because it was the first time that prominent Indians were tried in a white man's court. With Satank shot-trying-to-escape on the way down from Fort Sill, Satanta and Big Tree plead to the charge on July 5, 1871 with Judge Charles Soward of the 13th Judicial District Court presiding. S. W. T. Lanham of Weatherford, later a Texas Governor, was the prosecutor and J. A. Woolfolk conducted the defense.

It was a noted trial, filled with brilliant repartee, bitter invective and weighty summations. Much of the account has been preserved in court reports, copious notes and incorporated into novels. It was a dramatic occasion. Satanta talked compromise with his enemies rather than beg for mercy. If they would release him he would kill the others who had escaped the white man's vengeance.

"If you will let me go back to my people, I will withdraw my warriors for all time from Tehanna. I will take them back across the Red River and that shall be a line between us and the palefaces hereafter . . . But if you kill me it will be a spark on the prairie . . . Make big fire, burn heap!"

Verdict: Murder in the First Degree. Sentenced to hang, Sept. 1, 1871.

But the Indian Agent at Fort Sill, Lowrie Tatum, begged for commutation to life imprisonment for fear of reprisals by the Indians. The trial judge joined in the recommendation and Governor E. J. Davis, the Carpetbagger head of the State, granted it. Three years later, just before he went out of office, Davis opened the doors of Huntsville prison and let the two Indians go free.

But General Phil Sheridan, on duty up at "Sheridan's Roost" on the North Canadian, caught Satanta up to his old tricks and revoked his parole on October 30, 1874 and sent him to jail. Big Tree broke his parole but escaped into the Territory and was never caught.

There was a big case on the high Plains . . . in the spring of 1886, Ed King, Frank Valley, Fred Chilton and John Lang, cowboys, rode in from the LS Ranch to see what was doing in Tascosa on a Saturday night. Ed went to see his girl, Sallie Emery, and as they were strolling by Jenkin's Saloon, King heard some remarks. He sent her on and stepped up on the porch "to make something of it." A shot rang out and Ed was Corpse No. 1 that night.

The word spread quickly around the saloons and soon the

[179]

air was thick with bullets. Lem Woodruff who had shot Ed
got two in his middle, while Charlie Emory got one in the
leg. But Woodruff had enough life in him to plug Frank
Valley in the eye as he came in the door. Then Jesse Sheets
showed up in his night-clothes to find out what the shooting
was about and got what innocent bystanders proverbially
get. Chilton's bullet cut him down, but furnished a target
for two hits on Chilton. Four dead, three wounded, Woodruff badly hurt.

The Law came running up about that time and The Catfish Kid, trying to beat it, stopped one from Sheriff Pierce's
gun. Next afternoon there were four graves on Boot-Hill
and the Sheriff had a posse organized to keep order. He had
a tip that the fifty-five cowboys from the LS were coming in
to shoot up the ceremonies. Murder charges were filed against
Woodruff, Bousman, Emory, Lang and The Catfish Kid before the dirt was packed down on the graves.

The first trial was at Clarendon in Donley County with
Charlie Jenkins, the top defender of the High Plains, for
the defense. It was he who had maneuvered to save John
Wesley Hardin's neck from the rope when he was brought
back from Florida to be tried. He got a hung jury.

They tried the case next at Mobeetie where Bousman
turned state's evidence. Jenkins and Presiding Judge Frank
Willis had some bitter encounters during the trial and Jenkins swore he would get Willis impeached. The judge was
actually tried, but it resulted as did the Mobeetie case in an
acquittal.

Then, on the middle-Brazos . . . Judge J. W. Oliver was
the Carpetbagger District Judge at Waco and on one occasion put the entire Commissioners' Court and the County
Judge in jail. They then filed a lunacy complaint against
Oliver. The County Judge had exclusive jurisdiction of that
hearing. Oliver came off his high horse when the Sheriff
locked him up. A compromise was effected quickly.

Later, when this same Judge Oliver stationed Negro soldiers at the polls in Marlin, a delegation of lawyers of Marlin waited on him.

"Judge," said the spokesman, "if you persist in keeping them there, somebody is going to get hurt, perhaps killed. We don't know who will be the first one, but you'll damned sure be the second!"

The soldiers were withdrawn.

Down on the lower Brazos they also fought great court-battles . . . Dr. John Lockhart, that pleasing raconteur of events in the Coastal Plain of the River, tells of a case in Brazoria County where an orphan boy, bound out to a farmer, was beaten unmercifully by the farmer.

Phil Claborn heard of it, went over, called the farmer out, and whipped him soundly. An assault and battery charge was filed against Claborn. W. J. Jones and Jones Rivers, noted advocates of the Brazos country, appeared for the defense. It was a bitterly fought case.

". . . a father to the fatherless . . . My client did what he was commanded by the Almighty to do . . . What father would not resent this outrage?"

The jury was out only a few minutes and returned with the sage verdict: *Not guilty and we recommend that he thrash hell out of him again.*"

There was another case down in the Fort Bend area that involved the killing of a prominent citizen, J. M. Shamblin. William Caldwell, a Negro, was suspect. It was claimed that he had left a note on Shamblin's fence after the latter had caught him and another Negro stealing a bale of cotton and gotten them indicted.

The other witness was poisoned and if Shamblin could be disposed of, a conviction would have been impossible. The bloodhounds tracked to Caldwell's house but the two Negroes had fled into the Brazos bottoms. Bill-heads similar to the ones posted on Shamblin's fence were found at the house and the wadding of his gun matched that found near Shamblin's body. Caldwell's rifle had been recently fired and reloaded. They caught Caldwell in the woods and came near lynching him.

The case was transferred to Houston where a conviction was secured. It went to the Supreme Court of the United States where James Stephen Hogg, the Attorney General of Texas in 1891, argued for the State while J. Randolph Burns appeared for the defense. Relief was refused and Caldwell hanged.

Another case on the lower Brazos concerned Henry Frost who was shot from ambush while going home. Neighbors rushed to his house and when H. F. Randal, Deputy Tax Assessor, entered the room, Frost rose on his elbow, told him to get out and used strong language.

Randal was a very respectable citizen but was arrested next day for murder. The dogs followed a trail to a lonely Negro cabin where John Ewing, his son Mitchell, and a Negro school-teacher by the name of John Donovan was found. They were jailed and a mob formed that demanded they be tortured to force the truth from them. This was averted and when the Grand Jury met it did not have enough on the Negroes to indict them. Randal, out on bail, skipped to Mexico and never came back. Feeling ran high on the River.

Up at Waco was the Satterwhite case.

The elder Satterwhite was a prominent citizen whose son went to school to a young lawyer named Jackson, who thrashed him in the course of his scholastic routine. The father was irate and had a violent quarrel with the young man and shot him down. A mob gathered to take Satterwhite but he barricaded himself in and stood them off. A big trial was in prospect and everyone in the Brazos midlands was keyed up about it.

But young Jackson recovered from his wounds enough to

call old Satterwhite out and shoot it out with him in fair fight. The older man received a mortal wound and the decision was that both sides had their inning and that Jackson had prevailed. No trial of Jackson was ever held.

They fought a big case at the old McLennan Court-house in 1899. Judge Sam R. Scott, a noted jurist, was presiding over the trial of a doctor, charged with murder in an abortion case. The defense was carried out by James E. Ferguson, later Governor, and James E. Yantis, whom Ferguson named to the Supreme Court when he got into power.

They called the brother of the dead woman to the stand and as he came down the aisle he drew his pistol and shot the doctor. Trying to escape from the wild bullets of the accused's kin, the brother ran for the door. The doctor on trial jerked out a pistol and attempted to fire it, but Judge Scott scrambled down, disarmed him and rapped on the bench with the six-shooter for order, expressing himself in salty language at what he thought of all this contempt of his court.

Sheriff Baker finally managed to restore order and the only casualty was that the accused doctor was paralyzed from his hips down from the brother's shot. He was never brought to trial again.

It was Judge Scott who tried in 1894 the first case filed to "bust the trusts." The Grand Jury indicted the Waters-Pierce Oil Company and all of its big names from John D. Rockefeller on down. A test-case was made of one of the minor officials who appealed his conviction to the higher courts from Judge Scott's decision. He had to remain in jail, so his cell in the old brick bastile back of the court-house was made into a bower of luxury by the oil companies for many a week.

The main issue was not settled, however, until 1907 and in that year the oil trust paid a whacking big penalty judgment to the Attorney-General of Texas for violations of the anti-trust laws. It was paid in cash — $1,808,483.30 — and paraded down Congress Avenue in Austin where the Waters-Pierce lawyers delivered it to the State Treasurer in one lump sum.

Law has been respected in the valley of the Brazos since the days when the Lone Star flag went up to the top of the pole at old Washington. They tell a story of how a case was transferred from McLennan County to Coryell in 1911, when a woman accused of murder had much of the popular opinion against her.

Chief Justice W. L. Davidson came from the Court of Criminal Appeals to hear the application for bail. She had received life imprisonment on the first trial and a new hearing was granted. Friends of the Judge advised him that feeling was high and there would be a strong sentiment against the granting of bail.

He replied: "I shall follow the law, as I see it. If the woman is entitled to bail I shall grant it . . . otherwise the liberty of a citizen can not be safe. A wave of popular feeling, like a wave of the sea, passes and is gone, leaving no trace, but the evil which results from the failure of a judge to do his duty or the failure of a Court to follow the law is permanent."

He granted the bail and on her second trial she was acquitted.

"Judge Lynch" was not unknown even in the earlier decades of the 1900's along the course of the River. There was one mob-hanging in Waco in 1916.

A Negro ranch-hand had killed a prominent white rancher out from Waco and the trial was being held in Judge Richard I. Monroe's court in the old gray court-house amid the trees. The halls were crowded the first day of the trial with relatives and friends of the deceased from the ranching country. The judge ordered the Sheriff to search everyone who entered the courtroom for guns. Some stayed out in the hall.

When the Negro entered his plea of "Guilty," someone shouted: "Get him!" The crowd surged forward. They hauled him out into the street and made for the "Square," back of the city hall toward the Suspension Bridge, where a prior lynching had taken place. But this time the subject was strung up to a tree and his body riddled with bullets. Then they set fire to a pile of wood beneath it and burned it to a crisp.

It was the last lynching of record in the Brazos valley.

Not many months later in that same court-room there was called for trial one of the really great criminal trials in the history of Brazos jurisprudence. Over in nearby Freestone County, at the little town of Teague, the chief banker had killed a State Bank Examiner who was in the act of posting a notice closing old man Watson's bank.

It happened at noon or shortly thereafter as the accused and his sons were returning from noon-dinner. Patterson, the young Examiner, was killed instantly by the elder Watson's bullet. He came from Waco originally and there was much interest in the trial. Watson was an elderly man, heavily mustached, and he and his family hired a staff of skilled defenders.

Pat M. Neff, later to be Governor for two terms and President of Baylor University thereafter, led the defense staff. He was assisted by Cullen F. Thomas of Dallas, formerly County Attorney of McLennan County, an able lawyer and leading Baptist layman. He was a brother-in-law of Senator Morris Sheppard of the 18th Amendment fame. There were several other defense attorneys.

To assist County Attorney John B. McNamara, there had been retained by the dead Bank Examiner's family Lud Williams of the Waco Bar, a skilled prosecutor and a relentless cross-examiner. Jed Adams of Dallas, prominent lawyer, advocate and orator likewise assisted and several others.

The trial lasted for several weeks and night sessions were

marked by the summations which were classics of court-room oratory. The climax was reached while Pat Neff was making his closing plea to the jury for an acquittal. He had been speaking for hours in what was, perhaps, his most impassioned speech. His adversaries referred to him on one occasion as "The Tall Sycamore of the Brazos." He was a fine figure of a man, over six feet tall, heavy hair roached back, with a wing collar and black tie that he always wore with his black suit.

Suddenly and without warning a figure rose in the court-room. Throwing back her heavy widow's veil, a slender, frail little woman said in an accusing voice: "You carried his body to the grave and now you defend his murderer!"

There was a moment's hush and Neff then went on with his point. After he had finished with that part of his speech he bowed toward the lady and expressed his regret at what had happened. He had been named as an honorary pall-bearer along with other members of the Waco Bar, he explained, but had been away from the city and had not been able to attend the funeral. Now he was but carrying out his duty as a lawyer retained to represent an accused at the bar of Justice and doing his duty as he saw it. Perhaps no other lawyer could have done as polished a job of avoiding a delicate situation as he did on that occasion.

The verdict was life imprisonment, but Governor James E. Ferguson saw fit to pardon the elderly defendant before he had served much of his time. There have been few trials in all the Brazos valley that have attracted as much attention in recent years as this.

Back in the days when the Justice of the Brazos was in the making, Judge Peg-Leg Willie Williamson, noted soldier at San Jacinto, lawyer, patriot and jurist (who knelt on his wooden peg and made it look as if he had three legs as he walked), was going over one day to hold the first session of Court in Shelby County.

A meeting of the citizens decided there would not be a

Court held there. They sent a burly Chairman and his committee to tell the Judge from the Brazos bottoms about it.

"Jedge," said the big chairman, when Peg-Leg Willie rapped for order, "we ain't a calculatin' to have any cote meet here."

"What's your law for it?" the peppery little Judge demanded.

The chairman snapped his big Bowie knife on the desk before His Honor, "Bowie on Knives, Jedge, that's law in this county!"

Whipping out his big hoss-pistols and laying them on the desk, the Judge snapped back: "Colt on Revolvers over-rules that law! Mr. Sheriff, call the list of the Grand Jury!"

In the interest of law-enforcement there was a meeting held in February 1877 of forty Texas cattlemen on the Brazos Fork in Young County, under an oak tree near Graham, that had a significant effect. The Stock Raisers Association of Northwest Texas was organized there that day and grew through years of steady service into The Texas and Southwestern Cattle Raisers Association of today. It is powerful in the Brazos cattle country.

Committed to honesty and fair-dealing in and with the cattle industry, today there are 8,000 members, 28 field inspectors and 60 market-inspectors, all busy checking brands, running down crooks and thieves and suppressing fraud against the men who run cattle on the range or in their pastures. The name and reputation of the "Cattle Raisers" is known throughout the Brazos valley and The Plains. Its inspectors and attorneys are there to protect the members and few dare meddle with or harm a member's herd.

But what of the law on the upper Brazos?

Judge Charles E. Coombes in his book "The Prairie Dog Lawyer" has taken care of the history of the men on the Grand Prairie, the Cross Timbers, the Plains and the Panhandle, who follow the law. He has done for this section what Judge C. A. Oltorf of Marlin did for the middle Brazos and what Judge Clarence R. Wharton did for the lower Brazos and the Fort Bend country.

Up in the high *mesa* they called them "Prairie Dog Lawyers" in the early days. Judge R. W. Hall of Amarillo has an after-dinner speech on this subject that is not only classic but history. He tells of the exploits and experiences of Law and Justice in the feuding days of the Landjumpers, the Fence-Cutters and the Cattle-rustlers. Says the Judge:

The Prairie Dog Lawyer was a powerful advocate. He was sorter weak on the law occasionally, but strong, long and awful loud on the facts. He didn't need much written law in his business, though he frequently had to appeal to the unwritten law in behalf of his client.

It seems that back in the old days on the Plains of the Brazos Forks there were two unpardonable sins — horse-stealing and cattle-rustling. The Judge recalls that:

If a fellow stole a horse and the evidence was sufficient to convict, the case was not justiciable. Why waste time and money trying a proven thief? If the evidence was weak and there was danger of an acquittal, the culprit was hanged to the first cottonwood limb and there was no case to try.

The Prairie Dog Lawyer came into being when folks began to think in terms of arbitration and fairness instead of by the rule of the six-shooter that hung at every hip.

The lawyers, the Judge and the Court officials traveled together up on the Plains in parties — a peripatetic Bench and Bar — meeting the parties to the case at the Court-house at the County-seat and going into action at once. At night they would gather in the little hotel or boarding-house and have a talk-fest as if there had not been a hard scrap that day in the court-house. Court finished in that county, they would move as a caravan over to the next county-seat and set up there.

[188]

In his saddle-bags or in the back of his buggy, the traveling lawyer of the shinnery carried an extra pair of socks, an old Cap-and-Ball edition of the Texas statutes and a form book. He might carry a few worn copies of Texas Supreme Court reports if the case was a "white horse one on all four feet," fitting the case at bar. But he relied more on oratory and argument than he did on precedent and book-law. Substantial Justice was his goal.

The lawyers attached little importance to getting rich or even to the orderly collection of their fees. They gloried in a fight and rejoiced in a jury verdict in their favor. There were comparatively few appeals. If they could not win before a jury, they lost the case.

And so the Law of The White Man came to the Brazos, low, high and midland.

Dwellers in the valley set up a code by which the honest lived and to which the righteous adhered. Others who tarried in their midst were forced to respect and abide by the law, move on, go to jail or feel for ground beneath their feet. The Brazos legislators made the law, the Brazos judges interpreted it and the Rangers and peace officers enforced it.

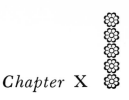

Chapter X

FROM STAGE-COACH TO STREAM-LINER

"WAGON-WHEELS, WAGON-wheels, keep on rollin' . . . wagon-wheels."

Next to fire, perhaps, the single most contributive agency to the progress of the Brazos people throughout the years has been the wheel. During four centuries of recorded history the sons of the Brazos have moved as fast and only as fast as their means of transportation has permitted them.

The early Indian used a sled. It consisted of a load between two shafts with a squaw hitched-in. When the pony came, the squaw was relieved for other duties as the tribe trekked to a hunting-ground, sought warmer climate or followed the water in the River. After the Spaniard brought both the horse and the wheel, the Indian was mobile and was able to move quickly and easily toward new horizons and to establish new frontiers.

It was probably 1541 when the first horse came to the Brazos. After that followed a procession of horses, mustangs, mules, ponies, burros, oxen and draft-animals that were hitched to carts, wagons, buggies and sleds of various kinds. The horse was the Indian's greatest advance. He cherished and used that gift more than any other that the white man brought. He earned the title "The Centaur of The Plains" for his riding and used the mustangs as well for eating and trading. The settler, needing his farm animals or ranch *remuda,* had to contend with Indian horse-thieves, or with wild mustang stallions enticing the mares of his herd to the prairies.

[190]

Before the horse the Indian had used forest-trails or the shimmering surface of the River itself. In scooped-out logs for *bateaux,* he poled himself along, or made a raft by tying many logs together with hide-thongs. When the bottoms were miry, he went by river-craft.

Almost every kind of transportation was tried in the Brazos-land until Jefferson Davis, Secretary of War at Washington in 1856, experimented with camels and for a time those queer beasts from North Africa tried to supply the forts of the Brazos and become accustomed to Texas weather. They did not last and were soon abandoned.

When the settlements increased, the wagon-trains became popular. Later, when longer distances must be covered in quicker time, the stage-lines were installed. Mail, passengers and freight went from St. Louis to San Diego. Down through the wild Indian country, the stage-coach rolled over the desert wastes of the Plains. It stopped at the forts of the Brazos, daring the outlaws, bandits and hostile Indians. Across the Pecos, on to New Mexico and California it used a fixed schedule and made it remarkably often.

The railroads, when they came, built slowly up the valley of the Brazos. It was not until 1851 that the Buffalo Bayou, Brazos and Colorado Railway came into being and then it took nine years to get anywheres . . . The Houston and Texas Central was the only road to survive the Civil War. It was 1872 before the Missouri, Kansas and Texas came in across the Red River to Denison . . . 1886 saw the Fort Worth and Denver come down out of the Northwest . . . while the early 1870's had seen the Texas and Pacific toiling against many adversities to reach the Brazos.

Once in, the railroads were to know a half-century of no competition before the busses, truck-lines and airplanes would challenge their supremacy as modes of travel. In a magic century — 1850-1950 — the Brazos pioneer went from ox-carts to wagons; from bad roads and no bridges to ribbons of paved roads and networks of super-highways; from boggy trails and snail-speed to all-weather farm-roads and surfaced secondary thoroughfares. He saw the laborious old wagon-trains, many of them ox-drawn, give way to fleets of huge vans that would do dock-to-dock and even door-to-door service; from rude time-speculation depending on feeding the stock to hourly schedule in air-conditioned busses; from three or four cotton barges when the River was favorably high to refrigerator and tank trucks; from buggies to super-speed automobiles and from wood-burning engines to stream-lined Diesels; while above the airplane liners would fill the sky with schedules and bring the whole earth to the Brazos door within a matter of hours.

On that day in 1845 when Texas became the twenty-eighth State in the American union, a stage took an hour to cover two miles on the run between Houston and Washington-on-the-Brazos at a fare of ten cents a mile. The railroads wrote their own terms and if they were rejected they could make or break a man or a town. If the required bonus was not forthcoming or the concessions given, the railroads marked a town off the map and it stayed marked off. A mile of track, Texas, for sixteen sections of State land — sign here! And Texas signed.

Today a State Railroad Commission sits in judgment on the rights of public, railroad and citizen. Every form of transportation, communication, travel and natural resource is guarded zealously by the controls allowed the Commission under the law. It was a far advance in a half-century from the creaking Conestaga wagons, using the roads when the weather permitted; ox carts hauling cotton to Galveston from the banks of the Brazos; wood-burning locomotives sending out the smoke of pine-knots; to the modern choice of transportation at almost any and every hour of the day.

Roads . . . Few wheels may turn in a miry bottom or in a blackland bog. The network and maze of highways and subsidiary roads that interlace the Brazos valley represent the taxes, tribute, planning, and toil of people of vision who saw that progress would never move unless it moved on passable roads.

The Brazos built roads, highways and railroads within her own domain. They were not dependent upon other States. When the Butterfield Stage Line was seeking a way through Texas to California it found roads already built in Texas, and the United States, after Annexation, had only to connect up with the roads of Texas. When the railroads ventured into the Brazos valley from other states after the Civil War, Texas was struggling with her own local rail system.

Up from Mexico through the eastern part to the Brazos had come El Camino Real in the early day . . . the *padres* worked out paths of their own as they went about their mission-building. The explorers and gold-seekers wore their trails bare. Later the trail-drivers burned their routes into the grass with the hooves of their Longhorns. And the Brazos had roads and trade routes along which the railroads and the stage-coaches could travel.

Captain R. B. Marcy laid out his "California Trail" in 1849 when people caught the gold-fever. The wagons of the 49ers wanted to come the southern route through Texas. They crossed the Red River at Preston's Crossing, picking up the old cattle trail down through Cooke County, by Barrel Springs in Montague, through Young by Fort Belknap, passed the Comanche Reservation — where the Indians were supposed to remain — whipped on down the Brazos Fork through Haskell and by Fort Phantom Hill into Jones, by Fort Chadbourne and then on to Pecos and El Paso. The Texas part of the road was waiting.

After El Camino Real there was the Atascocita Road along the coast, passing over the Brazos down near her mouth. The La Bahia Road crossed the River at Washington and the old

Butterfield came over at the Fort Griffin crossing, which was famous. The San Angelo-San Antonio Stage Line followed the latter road for the greater part of the way. The Connelly Trail came over the Brazos in Baylor County, through from Throckmorton and connected up with many well-known routes. A military road started at Fort Martin Scott in south central Texas, crossed the Brazos at Fort Graham in Hill County and ran on to Fort Richardson in Jack, over to Belknap in Young. It was used to connect up the forts. The Preston Trail went up from Austin, over the Brazos at Waco and on to Preston's Crossing on the Red from which it took its name.

"The Old San Antonio Road" was the pioneer of North-South travel until Texas became a state. It connected infant Texas up with Mexico. Caldwell and Bastrop were stations on it. The north line of present Brazos County down near Texas A&M followed the old highway for a great distance and the Mexican fort of Tenoxtitlan was on this highway. When the steamboats navigated the Brazos as far as old Washington this latter road was where water and highway met. It made of Washington an important center of trade, the newspapers of that day claim. It had a population in the late 1940's of 1,500 people.

But they would not choose between the water-transportation and the rails and when the Houston and Texas Central levied a bonus on Washington-on-the-Brazos to get the rail-line by that town, the business men voted to make no choice. The railroads went the other side of the River and Washington is a deserted village now with only a shrine to the place "Where a nation was born."

Everyone who wrote about Texas in those days of the middle 1800's commented on the roads and the availability of easy travel. Roemar, the noted German writer, back in 1847 spent quite a time on the Brazos visiting the German settlements and preparing his book that he would publish when he returned to his homeland. He was bitter in his criticism of the roads between San Felipe and Houston since it was a matter of days in the wet weather when no travel except on foot was possible.

This affected the freight rates and as late as 1880 the charge for carrying 100 pounds from one Brazos point to another was $1.25 minimum, with $1.40 the raised tariff for every additional 100 miles. The postal rates were high also. The Texas Republic's Postmaster General published the rates. For a single letter going 200 miles, 6½c and over 200 miles 37½c. Extra pages were charged for at the same rates.

Mail Route No. 1 went weekly from San Felipe to Whitesides in Cole's Settlement, through Washington, Fantharp's and Sims' to Robbins' Store on the Trinity, 118 miles. It left San Felipe every Sunday at 7 A.M. and got to Robbins' Store on Tuesday night at 7. It returned Wednesday morning at 7 and was supposed to be back in San Felipe by 7 P.M. Friday. Another route ran: San Felipe — Fort Bend — Orozimbo — Columbia — Brazoria — Velasco. There were several others.

Ox-drawn carts were the standard equipment for freight in the Texas Republic days and freight-rates depended on whether you shipped by "fed oxen or grazing oxen." The latter stopped oftener and longer and the cost was less. It was hard to raise the tax money for good roads. In 1839 the Texas Congress passed a law to build a road to Nacogdoches from San Antonio through the Brazos bottoms, but unfortunately left out the appropriation clause.

When there were not good roads the people stayed at home, traded at home and the communication was limited between even the nearest towns. For the prior century to 1850 the crossings of the Brazos and the other rivers were the important road-controls. If there was a bridge, a ford or a crossing it was charted on the meager maps and the traveler, wagoner or trail-driver would set out in that general direction, guiding on the sun by day and the polar star by night trying to hit that crossing. He might have to come or go up or down the River but he had to make it to the right place to get across.

Dr. D. Rose says in his diary of the Texas Revolutionary days that there were three kind of folk — "the upper class had wagons, the middle class had carts and the lower class had sleds."

Near the River's mouth the farmers on both sides of the Brazos collected their cotton at William Little's plantation where the *Yellowstone* — Sam Houston's army-ferry in "The Runaway Scrape" — stopped to pick it up. At times they would ferry the bales down on rafts.

Another reference by Dr. Rose in his account of the times:

In the spring of 1836, just after the fall of the Alamo, when the news reached the Brazos and Oyster Creek, a vast herd of about 4,000 buffalo crossed the Brazos above Fort Bend and came into the open prairie at Stafford's Point going toward the coast. The land that they traversed looked as if it had been plowed up, the roads destroyed and this was the last great herd that was to cross the lower Brazos.

It is interesting to note that down in this country they *destroyed* the roads while farther up the River the Indians sought to follow the roads that the buffalo left to efface their tracks from the whites.

In January 1844, *The Houston Telegraph* stated that from Hodges Bend on the Brazos the people were promoting a wagon-road to Houston eighteen feet wide at a cost of $50 a mile. A year later that paper was censuring the Houston people for not being alert, pointing out that the Galvestonians were raising money to drag the snags out of the Brazos below Richmond so that boats could more easily ply the River. The paper pounded for a wagon-road to Houston from the Brazos to hold the trade for that city.

The editor commented sagely that in his opinion the Brazos would eventually go dry. But a few years later he had to retract his words, when, in January 1850, four steamboats were running regularly on the Brazos from Washington to Velasco.

Up in the Brazos Cross Timbers in 1859, which was the farthest up the River that colonization had spread to any great degree, a mounted mail-service or Pony Express was running once a week, the weather, the roads and the Indians permitting. It ran from Burnet County — Comanche — Torrey's Trading Post on the Brazos — through Hill — Johnson — Parker — Palo Pinto — on into Fort Belknap in Young. It became a standard route for travelers and wagon-trains.

Walter Timms of Kimball's Bend in the Brazos on the edge of Bosque and Johnson Counties made a fair living hauling cotton and other crops for the outlying settlers in the 1850's. But the Indians got so bad and he lost so many loads to their depredating that he gave up freighting and joined the Rangers "so's he could get a free shot at 'em without being bothered with a team."

Ruts, chug-holes, arroyos and waxy blackland made travel slow down to where five miles a day was good time to make in the 1840's. Judge John Lockhart writes of travel along the Brazos:

The roads were in the worst of condition. If we traveled five miles a day from Houston to Washington-on-the-Brazos we did well. But there was abundant game on the prairie. Geese and ducks innumerable, deer by the thousands, large covies of partridge, wild turkey and occasionally a drove of wolves . . . Only a few houses or settlements did we see after leaving Houston, but large droves of wild horses came into view and we had fine hunting to pass off what would have been a tedious trip.

Stage-coach lines had to have good roads to make their schedules, so they began to barter with counties. No stop or passing through that county to serve the people with mail, passenger or freight traffic unless there were roads provided. Then, in, order for the local people to reach church, school or town, they would agree to give so many hands, teams and days of "working the roads," thereby eliminating the worst places. Convict labor was used in the building of passable roads, both state and county chain-gangs being frequently employed.

The cities had all they could do to keep up their streets. Again the question of bonded indebtedness was a serious one and taxes became prohibitive when bonds were voted. The City Fathers were sorely perplexed for a way to keep the city streets in order. *The Waco Daily Examiner* in 1874 had this to say:

Condition of the streets in Waco is simply outrageous. The public health is quite in as much danger as the public morals, at least it seems so to a man up in a tree where he goes to get out of the mud. The stench of Austin Street arising from an accumulation of mud and other filth is, under the warm rays of spring sun, fast becoming a nuisance. The attention of the City Fathers is invited to that odorous locality.

There is an allied enterprise to the roads. The Brazos had much to do with the cosmopolitan wagon-yard of the old days. Every town of any size where the farmers and country people came to trade, shop or tarry for the night had a wagon-yard. There the stock was fed, watered and bedded down for the night. The family used it as a base after visiting stores. Many of them slept the night in their wagons, safely stationed in the yard.

Old friends were greeted, gossip and news were exchanged, the travelers from the East going West had to be told about what they might expect and the dejected failures giving up and going back to the old States had to air their disappointments for the local people. The creek-banks were used when a wagon-yard could not be afforded but for the most part it was hotel and hostelry for animals and family.

Kirkpatrick's Wagon-yard in Waco was just opposite The Live Oak House and was a famous stopping-place for wagons coming north or going south of the River. The social life of the average wagon-yard deserves a treatment of its own. Many reunions of friends, along with the making of new friendships were attributable to the propinquity of the wagon-yard.

From the day when Cabeza de Vaca forced a landing at the Quintana beach and went on to establish a beach-head for the white explorers, the Brazos has known the value of water-travel.

"Alo, compadres, esta el rio!" shouted the shipwrecked mariner to his men as he saw the russet tide of the Brazos meet the green waters of the Gulf that morning.

He had not discovered a great seaport by any means. The Brazos has been her own worst enemy in respect to navigation. Washing the clay of her banks and the soil of her alluvial deposits into sand-bars all along her course and down into her delta, the passage on the River is today limited to only a very few miles upstream and then only at seasonal intervals.

The records in old newspapers and the story passed from generation to generation tells of how the old *Columbia* plied up stream to Washington in 1830 before it was wrecked on a sand-bar. The *Mustang* ascended the Brazos to Fort Sullivan on schedule in the 1840's. The *Sam Houston* was a sister ship and frequently mentioned in the papers. They were stern-wheelers, loaded for the most part with cotton, coming down to the Gulf to meet the ocean-going vessels.

Passenger ships went up the Brazos, steaming along between the scenic glories of the trees and flowers of the low country with people on the decks to admire the sights. In her 1836 book, Mrs. Holley says:

Though there are many rivers navigable for steamboats, the Brazos alone is visited by them; several steam vessels regularly

[199]

navigate its waters for the purpose of commerce. Unfortunately, notwithstanding the precautions taken to avoid accidents, serious injury sometimes happens to vessels in passing the bar at the mouth of the river. This obstacle, however, we are assured, will not long exist and had it not been for the occurrence of the present war, would probably have been removed by this time.

The lady's optimism was not justified, for the authorities have never gotten around to removing the obstructions to Brazos navigation. In fact, it was many years after she wrote that before the true sources of the Brazos were known. At the time of Annexation, informed writers and cartographers stated with positiveness that the Brazos rose in the Rockies and the Cross Timbers was "way out west" to the people of Brazoria. They murmured vaguely about how the "corn crop farther up the river has to be gathered in boats by wading slaves."

In September 1851, *The Galveston Weekly News* said this about Brazos shipping:

The Brazos has been so low that there has been no navigation for about two months. Both steamboats have been laid up. The boat *Brazos* is at Lyncheburg for repairs and the *Washington* on a bar of the River at Cuney Plantation.

The Brazos had many ferries. At San Felipe the old ferry is still visible. Captain Shapley D. Ross started the one at Waco and operated it for twelve years until the Suspension Bridge went in.

The Texas Gulf coast has few good sites for harbors. While Quintana and Velasco were capable of taking sailing vessels and some steam in the early days, their usefulness as ports has long since passed. But as long as Quintana was a Mexican port-of-call people of importance lived there and now, upon its site, Freeport, a thriving sulphur town, has sprung up in recent years.

"Here comes the stage-coach!"

That was the shout at the finale of Buffalo Bill's Wild

West Show. Likewise it was the cry in the valley of the Brazos for many a day as the great event of the little town or fort took place . . . in came the stage, whirling a cloud of dust behind it.

In 1858 the only stage-line coming up the Brazos had this route: Houston, Washington, Booneville in Brazos County, Wheelock, Franklin in Robertson County, Alta Springs in Falls, Springfield in Limestone, Marlin, Waco.

Beginning as hacks to take a passenger to another town and then gradually getting onto a schedule, increasing the size of the accommodation and adding mail and freight, the stage-lines "grew." By 1860 there were thirty-one stage-lines in Texas and most of them crossed and re-crossed the Brazos. Two things they relied upon— roads and security — so that the coastal territory appealed more to the operators than farther west up the course of the River.

As the frontier and the settlements moved west and up the stream, the stages crept along with them and the railroads, when they came, followed the routes of the stages. The Southern Pacific tracked one, mile by mile. They drove four to six horses with frequent changes at relay-stations and it was not uncommon for the passengers to get out, help work the roads around a bad place that was holding them up, or put a shoulder to the wheel to get it out of the mud. The toll was ten cents a mile and baggage was not encouraged.

Sawyer, Rusher and Hall owned most of the early stage-lines on the Brazos. Mail contracts and subsidies helped tide them over their losses. It was 1850 before the Butterfield, backed by Eastern capital, came down from St. Louis running on a regular schedule. It made a stop at the Brazos fort towns of Belknap, Phantom Hill and Griffin as they grew big enough to warrant a stop. By 1857 the Butterfield had a government contract that called for almost a half-million dollars a year subsidy to carry the mail to California from St.

Louis and the East, twice a week. It took twenty days from the Brazos to the Pacific coast.

And then one day the railroads came. How the Brazos eight hundred miles of valley called out for them! They were to bring the people of the River-land close to the rest of the country and to each other. Progress was humming on every inch of rail that was laid. The Latin-American never envisioned it. All he had a yearning for was a highway — an El Camino Real — but the Anglo-Saxon wanted a system of railroads that would get him quickly where he wanted to go and get his products to market while there was still a demand.

President Houston signed a resolution in December 1836, that the Texas Congress passed, which chartered the Texas Railroad, Navigation and Banking Company, organized by Branch T. Archer, James Collingsworth, T. J. Green, T. F. McKinney, A. C. Horton, A. C. Allen and Moseley Baker. They asked for privileges to operate financial institutions, issue money, conduct internal navigation, run railroads, dig canals and own real estate.

A protest went up immediately. Down in Brazoria Anson Jones took the stump and ran for the Senate in opposition to this octopus.

"How will we ever get rid of this devouring monster?" he demanded and they elected him.

It fell of its own weight in the panic of 1837. The promoters had asked for too much and public sentiment was outraged.

In 1840 the work on the Galveston, Harrisburg and San Antonio Railroad began, but it was not until 1851 that the Harrisburg and Brazos began as the Harrisburg Railroad and Trading Company . . . the first real operating railroad in Texas was the Buffalo Bayou, Brazos and Colorado, now a link of the Southern Pacific.

General Sydney Sherman's group in 1851 were laying track and they called their first little wood-burning engine "General Sherman." By August 1, 1853 twenty miles of rails had been laid and a barbecue was held at Stafford's Point to celebrate. It took two more years to make the thirty-two miles to Richmond and by 1860 it had reached to Alleyton within ten miles of Columbia.

In 1856, the Washington County Railroad started building from Hempstead on the Brazos to Brenham and by 1858 eleven miles were open, reaching Brenham in 1860. Meanwhile, the Galveston and Red River Company had its line reaching Hempstead by 1858. To Columbia on the Brazos came the Houston Tap and Brazoria, fifty miles out of Houston, and in 1861 it hauled sugar and cotton. It is now a part of the International and Great Northern system. These were essentially and alone Brazos railroads.

The whole valley prospered and flourished as the railroads advanced. Brazoria County subscribed $100,000 to the Houston Tap and Brazoria. But came the Civil War and a severe set-back was suffered by the rails until 1872 when railroad capital came out of hiding. But in that year there were not over one hundred fifty miles of railroad in all Texas. Galveston-Houston, Houston-Brazoria, Harrisburg-Alleyton were the operating lines.

But the State of Texas had plenty of acreage to trade for rails. Sam Houston had seen to that when he was horse-trading on Annexation with Washington. In the last three decades of the 1800's there would be 36,000,000 acres of public lands traded for steel rails in Texas.

Backed by The Grange, a farmers' organization, in 1889 there was a constitutional amendment passed authorizing the Railroad Commission of Texas. Governor James Stephen Hogg appointed John H. Reagan, William P. McLean and L. L. Foster as the first members of the new body that the Supreme Court said could regulate the transportation system in full legal form.

They had to have a railroad bridge over the Brazos and

the first one ever to cross any Texas stream of any size was the Buffalo Bayou, Brazos and Colorado bridge in 1855 over the River. It was six feet above water at low stage and the middle section was on a barge so that boats could pass when it was not in use. If the train came along and the River was up or down, the barge would not fit and they had to wait until it did. The passengers would not trust crossing on it however, but were ferried across and took the train on the other side. The uncertainty of *whether* and *when* the train would run was a serious matter in the schedules of those days.

The early railroads used second-hand street-cars, purchased back east, four-wheeled vehicles. With a number of freight cars it made up an "Accommodation" train that stopped at every flag-station and many times in between. The schedules were highly elastic.

On September 18, 1872, the Waco and Northwestern brought the first train into Waco. There was a big fiesta to celebrate. They called it "The Waco Tap" and *The Galveston News* reported that 3,000 people watched George Barnard as a final gesture drive the golden spike that connected up the line. Now the rich north and west territory of the Brazos valley could come to Waco by wagon-train and meet the rails. Said the *News*:

Waco is in a good humor. She extends her iron arms across the State and into the sea to clasp hands with the metropolis of the Southern empire. Her future is assured. The coming capital greets the world. The first passenger train arrived all right at 8:30 P.M.

Waco had led in traffic-control with her Suspension Bridge opened on January 8, 1870 at a cost of $130,000. The people came from far and wide to see it and pay the toll by which the promoters hoped to liquidate their investment. But one day the circus came to town and the elephants and the promoters of the bridge both balked at the elephants essaying to cross it. Finally the great pachyderms splashed across the ford — with evident relief to all. It was built by Thomas M. Griffith who later built Brooklyn Bridge.

July 4, 1853 had brought the rails to the Brazos valley at Stafford's Point with a great barbecue and jubilation but the actual River was not reached until two years later. It was in answer to the problem of the boggy bottoms and transportation over them in the rainy season. Barges to Velasco with sugar and cotton were supplanted by rails.

With the coming of the railroads and advanced stages of transportation, the limited triangle — Nacogdoches, Goliad, San Antonio — over which the Spaniards and Mexicans had exercised their principal domain — grew to embrace the State of Texas and new population-centers sprang up and began to increase.

Country that had been charged off as barren plain, desert-waste, impenetrable woodland, dark morass and impassable wilderness was now open to exploration. Tremendous distances vanished overnight and waterless prairies became picturesque scenery from the car-window of a fast-moving train.

Sam Houston's argument that the Texas capital should be removed to the coast from inland Austin because of transportation difficulties was exploded. He was not alive to see the day when the rails would carry more cattle north than the drivers had taken up the trails, but it happened thirteen years after he died at Huntsville. In 1879, 275,000 head of cattle went overland and 245,000 were shipped by rail and water.

It is a far cry and a long call from the *padre* on his little mule toiling up the long El Camino Real, fingering his beads lest an arrow out of the forest deal him his death-blow, to the air-liners that cover the distance in a few hours from the Rio Grande to the Brazos. Spain, itself, is overnight from San

Felipe. Instead of the vague, grotesque maps of Cabeza de Vaca and Coronado of the Brazos-land, today every gasoline station has a complete map of the elaborate network of roads in color.

PART THREE

The Stalwart People

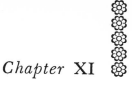

Chapter XI

THE BRAZOS MELTING-POT

MANY AND VARIED HAVE
been the races, the nationalities and the temper of the people
who have come to settle and dwell upon the Brazos in the
years of history that we know. A babel of tongues, beliefs,
loyalties, affiliations, colors and causes have been theirs. In
this day we call them one — Brazonian.

At times they have resented each other; have come to blows
over convictions or prejudices; but now they dwell together
as brethren. There is little antagonism today over race, creed
or culture. Tolerance is prevalent in the land of the River.

But in the early days there were deep lines of cleavage.
People who came from foreign lands across the sea wished to
be with their own kind. They held to their societies and
churches, their foreign-language newspapers; and the ways
and customs of the fatherland or motherland were inherently
theirs. Fraternal orders, clannish and sectarian, jealous of
their prestige and power, drew the garments of mysteries
about them and glorified their isolation.

It has been estimated that now over ninety percent of the
people who dwell within the valley watered by the Brazos
and its tributaries are America-born; a goodly number of
these Texas-born and a fair proportion Brazonian natives.
Today they have no loyalty along the River to any flag but
The Stars and Stripes and no division of their allegiance.

During World War II there were few draft evasions, except
for a few Conscientious-Objectors; no treason trials and no one

discovered any subversive activities among the people. Communists or their sympathizers would today be regarded with aversion. There is a two-party system in the state, but historically it has not been a strong one. Efforts of the Republicans, through the years, have not been very successful, but there is no lessening of their energy and determination.

No longer do groups as such come to the valley of the Brazos, but individuals who seek no affiliation with sect or clan, creed or clique.

In the little church-yards along its course, in the family-burying grounds on the high hills of the Brazos farmlands one may pause and read the history on the head-stones of the pioneers of common ancestry, faith and speech who emigrated here and clustered with their own kind because it pleased them.

That was in the day of primitive-living, when the coffee-pot and spinning-wheel were the tools of the woman, the axe and the rifle the mainstay of the man. Wild game and potatoes were "food" and "coffee" was made from whatever berries, wheat or corn that was available. Folk journeyed to Grand Saline or the Salt Fork of the Brazos for precious salt. Homespun was the only cloth and was made on spinning-wheel and loom in the unpainted cabin of the pioneer. One tanned his own shoe-leather and pegged his own soles.

Many who came in that early day did not entirely leave the intolerance of the old country or of New England and the old South behind. They brought some of it with them. Hatred of Indians, Negroes, Chinese, Catholics, Jews, Baptists, Wesleyans, Campbellites, Germans, Yankees, Latins and many other groups, just because they were such, blazed often along the Brazos in the years between its settlement and now. But few of these groups have any sort of mass-antagonism directed against them today and there is no marked persecution of them for the "sin" of their nationality, belief or pigment of skin in the valley of the River.

As to groups, the Indian was the first of whose existence we know and much has already been said of him and his clannishness. He was inclined to cleave unto his own. Together they dwelt and together they left. The American Indian did not assimilate well in the Brazos melting-pot.

There were groups of Indians here not entirely related. The Cave-dwellers from the Rio Grande country, the Mound-builders from the Mississippi, who came to dwell here on the banks of the Brazos, the Shoshonis from Wyoming and the many tribes from across the Father-of-Waters, pushed westward by the white man, Jumanes from New Mexico — these made of the early Brazos a sort of Indian melting-pot, but even then, they had their own fixed lines of demarcation.

It was not entirely the fault of the white man that the Indian and he did not mix and mingle in more happy accord. While a few were friendly at first, and some continued to be allied to new-comers who treated them fairly, for the most part the Indian was a model of reserve and taciturnity, repelling advances, refusing to share religion or social benefits with the whites and moving on westward before he would agree to conform to the prevailing Brazos norm.

When the Spanish group came and a new ethnic personality presented itself in the valley, it was different. The Spaniard and the Mexican mingled and married freely with others, mixed readily and was agreeable to serving where he could not command. A very definite imprint of the Spanish art and architecture, speech and tradition is imbedded in the Brazos way-of-living. A great deal of gentleness and refinement may be attributed to this contribution.

"Mexican food" is on the diet of the Brazos-folk today while in chapel, residence and public building the architecture of the Moor, the Spaniard and the Aztec has a prevalent influence. Listen to the favorite music of the River and you will hear the haunting melodies of Mexico and the soft, caressing speech of the folk of Oaxaca, Guadalajara or even of old Castile in the concerts or records that the Brazos-folk prefer.

Spanish is a language requirement in most of the schools and colleges of the Brazos and Mexico is a vacation spot for its people. Many of its citizens are bi-lingual in Spanish although not as pronouncedly as along the Rio Grande, the San Antonio or the Guadalupe.

Many Mexican-Americans dwell along the River that is called Brazos. They are second and third generation citizens, many of whom have never been outside of the United States. They still know and talk in the home the language which Charles V claimed to use when he talked to God. But they are educated in the schools of the Brazos valley and they have their interests and fortunes here. That they are not in high places of importance in politics and business is due to their own reticence. That is gradually being overcome.

There are many of the *peon* type who work as cotton-pickers, section-hands on the railroads or servants in domestic positions. However, the War experiences have gone far, along with education and opportunity, to elevate the ambitions of bright young Mexican-American men and women.

They have been more backward in the Brazos valley than they have on the Rio Grande "Border" or in the counties of South Texas. But the change is noticeable. More and more they are taking their places in stores and offices, schools and churches and finding that the part is theirs if only they will claim it.

On a Saturday afternoon in the small towns of the River the names of "Ruiz", "Dominguez" or "Garcia" are shouted with cheers as some tall, dark-complected lad catches a pass or gets off a punt. The Melting-Pot is doing its work.

Naturally, these people of Mexican derivation do not delight in the stories of the Alamo and San Jacinto which are on the tip of Texans' tongues. It was not a Mexican triumph that took place back in 1836. But the change is apparent in these post-World War II days. It has been a long time since San Jacinto and both Mexican and Brazos youth have had much to do with history-making at Iwo Jima and in the Ardennes. The new generation is having less trouble with its prejudices, discriminations and historical differences.

Of the French group-influence, as such, there is little to remark. La Salle and his settlers did not leave much of an imprint in the valley of the River, but there have been settlers from the Louisiana French families who have left their names and their cultural contributions here and there.

During Governor Houston's administration, Henry Castro brought six hundred Alsatian families to Texas and settled most of them in Castroville near San Antonio, but many strayed away and came to the Brazos. Their influence has been felt here and there along the course.

The predominant settler from over the waters has been the German. Not the Prussian of the Kaiser's day or the Nazi of Hitler's regime, but the farm-type — the simple folk of the Rhineland, the substantial landsman of Brunswick and Westphalia and the quiet mountaineer of scenic Bavaria.

They are people for the most part who delight in solitude and peace. Having left their fatherland because of the domination of their leaders, the tyranny of their systems, and the crowdedness of their country, they and their children have taken delight in the tranquility of the Brazos-land.

It reminded them of the gentle hills of the Ahr and the Mosel, the wide wheat fields of Nassau, the sweeping grandeur of the Hessian plain, and they have come to settle it in great numbers through the years. They have built huddled little villages; quaint *kirches* to worship in and stone houses in which to dwell. They sang the songs of the old country in this new land across the seas and the welkin has rung with the voices of the *saengerbunds*.

Their movement of settling Texas was not an haphazard one. Back in the 1840's there was a careful investigation made by about twenty Princes, Counts and Barons of the small German states. "The Association for the Protection of German Immigrants in Texas" was formed in June 1843 at Bieberick with Prince Frederick of Prussia as its head and the Duke of Nassau and Count Castell as directors.

Prince Carl von Solms-Braunfels in his lovely castle atop a high, imposing hill in the state of Braunfels not far from the Rhine — where an American Infantry Division billetted in 1945 — came to Texas as the High Commissioner of the Association. He explored the valleys of the Brazos, the Colorado and the Guadalupe Rivers and found them strikingly akin to his German land.

The emigrants came, landing at Galveston, toiling overland to the country about San Antonio, Waco and Brenham; founding their little settlements that today are Seguin, Fredericksburg, Fayette, Schulenberg and many smaller towns in the valleys of these rivers. From the Brazos to the Colorado in the early days they called it "Little Germany" and from the Colorado to the Rio Grande, "Greater Germany."

German writers such as Roemar came and studied the settlements and land and went home to write accounts of what they saw. Others took courage and came to join their compatriots in the Brazos-land and throughout Texas' south region.

They were clannish for a long time with their societies, newspapers, language and customs. They lived to themselves and their kind for the greater part. When the Civil War came and many hot-heads wanted to sell out and leave Texas because the South was defeated, these German-Texans bought their lands from them at bargains and stayed on.

Their *vereins, bunds* and *fests* continued dear to them for the second and third generations and when there was a war between their new and their old lands, they were distressed and perplexed. But they kept faith and remained loyal to this land that had given them haven. No finger of accusation has been pointed at the disloyalty of the Brazos folk of German descent. Their boys have marched in the ranks of American patriots to both conflicts.

While others were *heil*ing Hitler, they kept quiet, whatever they thought. When others started cursing Hitler, they kept quiet again and rode out the storm. Perhaps, they hurt inwardly and grieved in secret that enmity should be between the two peoples that they loved, but never by act or word did they evince any disloyalty to the land of their adoption.

They still love the old *lieds* and *sangs,* the old customs and memories . . . that is, the elders do. The newer generation, the product of the Brazos Melting-Pot, have little time for German tradition. To them it is attic-and-album stuff. This is their land, all the land that they know, or that they want, and it suits them.

Many cities and towns upon the Brazos, all along its course, have their contingent of German-ancestried folk. Waco and Brenham are two examples of this influence. In 1877 a grand *Maifest* was held in Waco in which all the community joined. *The Waco Daily Examiner* tells of how 20,000 people stood and viewed the parade "sweep into Austin Avenue at 8th Street with Luke Moore as Grand Marshal." A delegation of Tonkawa Indians came from Fort Griffin to march. They had Comanche scalps hanging at their belts in gruesome reminder of the time when here on this very spot, where once the Indians dwelt, scalping was regarded as a worthwhile activity.

The Germans still hold their feasts and shooting-matches here and there in the valley and keep their religious festivals and observances. For the most part they are Lutheran and Evangelical although there are many of the Catholic faith. The Hermann Sons is their favorite organization of a fraternal nature. There is still much German spoken in the Brazos valley.

There have been Danes. A colony of them settled a Utopia

in the Cordova Bend of the Brazos in Hood County a decade or so ago. It was committed to a commune similar to those in Denmark, with all of the old customs and language-dialects, ways of farming and barter, that originated in the old country across the seas. But it did not last. The people wandered away to nearby cities and towns. The influence of the Brazos Melting-Pot was too strong.

> *Where is my home? Where is my home?*
> *Offspring grand of dear Bohemia . . .*
> *Thou art my home, my fatherland!*

There have been many Czechs. Good citizens have these Bohemians, Croats, Poles and Wends made, who came from a little section in central Europe where persecution has been the rule rather than the exception through long ages.

At first they were inclined to be clannish but as the years have passed they have taken other peoples in and others have assimilated them. There is a Czech settlement near the founding-place of the Brazos story. Frydek is near to old San Felipe's site. If you go to West Station, not far from Waco you will find many names ending in -*cek* and -*ski*. They are substantial farming people, and it has been said of them: "A Czech can get rich cultivating land on which a German can barely make a living and on which an American will starve."

They have their old traditions and their organizations, their patriotic festivals and *sokols*. A picturesque people with the pathos of persecution written deep into their souls.

The Irish came, too. A colony of them were led by two Scotsmen. McMullen and McGloin brought them to the Brazos in the early days by promising them much lush "cowgrass" as green as in their native isle. But they did not stay to themselves for long. Somehow or other, in a peculiar fashion, they mated with Spanish types. Many is the dark-complected "Mexican" along the Brazos today with an O' before

[216]

his surname. It was a fanciful alliance — the breezy Irishman with the soft-voiced, gentle Mexican. The Irish colony broke up and permeated the entire valley with its people in fashion typical of their kind.

Then the English came. The English Immigration Company sent thirty families from England in the 1840's to 27,000 acres in the midlands of the Brazos led by Lieutenant Charles Finch Mackenzie to found the town of Trent. It was a sort of physical culture group and they proposed to regiment their living by army bugles and commands, but it did not work out. By 1852 they were scattered up and down the River.

But what of that first little group on the *Lively?* They really started (under Stephen F. Austin) this actual settlement of the Brazos valley and their descendants continued it in the next hundred years. It required a supreme effort.

It was a lonely venture on the banks of New Year's Creek. It was winter-time and the colonists of that First Three Hundred had only what they had brought along. No place to trade, no friends to visit, no store from which to buy, nor a neighbor from whom to borrow. Only the solitude of the River and the forest, a stillness that was haunted with fear and uncertainty. Even Austin hurried off to San Antonio to see the Mexican Governor.

They had to set in and hew down trees, dig wells, hunt game, and exist. It is said that only three of those who came on the *Lively* stayed on and survived to the taking of the land-grants — William Little, James Beard and James Nelson, the latter a New York engineer.

Others came and it was easier for them. The pioneer had already felled the first tree, braved the first winter and could cushion the shock of loneliness. Additions to the colony were persistent. They made it to the seed-time and they stuck with it to the harvest.

Austin sent a census-taker out once in the early days to see how many people he had on the banks of the Brazos.

"I went to a log cabin, General Austin," the census-taker reported. "I asked who lived there and a woman said: 'Me and my old man.' I told her I was counting the people and she told me to go ahead. How many children? I asked her. 'Plenty of them,' she said. 'Isaiah, Tom, Bill, Jake, Ed, Bud and I liked to have forgot Joe, who's gone right smart.' What about girls? I asked. She shook her head. 'Naw, boys is trouble enough, but arter a while they kin look after theirselves.' General, they're too rough to live with, those people."

"That's the kind I want," said the head of the colony. "Here on this frontier we want them hardy, honest and brave. When the settlements fill up, they'll move farther on. Wish I had more like her."

To the Melting-Pot came strange new friends to the early *empresarios*. One was a huge man, seven feet tall, astride a great mule, and he was bewhiskered and evidently of German-Mexican derivation — Baron de Bastrop — assigned by the Governor to make the two hundred ninety-seven grants and sign them with his name. The colonists chose him to be their spokesman in the *Congreso* at Saltillo.

In the National Assembly in Mexico City Don Erasmus Seguin was their representative and these two men remained fast friends of the colonists throughout. Two Texas cities bear their names today.

Few if any towns or even villages along the Brazos can be pointed out today and said to be "Little Germany" or "Little Mexico" or any similar designation. They may have a German, Norse or Swedish flavor to their ways and customs. The names on the drug-stores and garages may be tinctured with a foreign sound, but you will find that the pride is rather in how American the community is than how it harks back to ancient connections.

The Melting-Pot has come upon some strange dregs at times that did not assimilate and those it cast forth. It was not unusual in the early days for people who had failed, gotten into trouble or who sought to evade their duties in the old States to hie to the banks of the Brazos to seek a new start. Others thought that by their wits or by their tricks they could get rich on the River by preying on others.

They became desperados, bandits, robbers, outlaws and border-ruffians. At times they congregated into bands and gave considerable trouble. But they were in the minority and when the Melting-Pot spewed them forth they went on further west, were carried back in chains to their old residence to stand trial, or sought for footing beneath a stout oak tree while dangling from a length of hemp-rope.

The Melting-Pot of the Brazos has brought forth no individual speech, mannerism or cultural characteristic that is solely Brazonian in its century of working. It is far too long a River . . . eight hundred miles and more if it were strung out . . . a distance that would reach from Boston to Charleston, from Des Moines to New Orleans, from Los Angeles to Salem, Oregon if it were situated elsewhere.

The Brazonian of the Plains wears a sand-colored Stetson, spool-heel boots and speaks with a nasal twang in an open and hearty manner; while his fellow-Brazonian of the midlands is inclined to the effeteness of the large cities of Texas, culturally-disposed and very conventional in his speech; and the lower-country Brazonian is a typical coastal provincialist, speaking the lush language of the Gulf perimeter and contented with the customs and ways of his own little area. But there is a kinship and a similitude that is underlying from Bailey to Brazoria . . . the Brazos-land is the heartland of Texas and her people are all akin.

Not only at the start but throughout the years they seek for this "Land of Beginning Again." They still come from other places in the Americas and from abroad to try and mold their lives "closer to the heart's desire." They stay, build their homes and rear their children. Two days after they arrive they are bragging on the country and claiming it for their own. A new confidence, a new loyalty and earnestness seems to possess these folk in the valley of the Brazos. Of it they have built and are continuing to build their idea of peace in the forest and plain of the River's land.

Perhaps it is the newness of this ever-new land that appealed first to the settlers from Kentucky, Tennessee, Missouri and Mississippi. They came, stayed, and they wrought. Out of those basic determinations and from the primitive origins that were theirs they succeeded in hewing a new freedom and engendering a new spirit to accompany it.

To appreciate the determination of the settling fathers of this Brazos-land one must go into the farming-country and seek an old stone house and live in it until he finds its spirit. Perhaps old ghosts come with pride to show him these things . . . how did these stones come together? Tugged by the settler and his family from where they lay in the field and in the river-bed . . . and the mortar? The man and his wife and son mixed it with River-mud and put in the gravel found near the rock-piles . . . on the floor, only some flag-stones . . . and those beams up there, every axe-mark was a bit of the colonist's strength, lovingly dedicated to home-building.

The fire-place, half-way up . . . about waist-high to a man . . . the smoke that blackened that chimney was a pine-knot of ninety years ago. It was crude and primitive, but it was stout and strong as the hearts of those who builded it. Now it may be a corn-crib or storage-house, but the grand-father of the land-owner was likely born in this very room . . . they heated the water in that chimney-place.

They came and after they settled they went back or sent back and induced others to come. In the little Norse cemetery in Bosque County today there sleeps a tired old Norwegian by the name of Cleng Peerson. He came from Norway in 1821 and he wandered over New York, Wisconsin, Iowa,

Minnesota, Michigan, Illinois and Indiana seeking a "little Norway." Finally, in Texas, on the Brazos he found it.

One day he said to a group of his people living over in Henderson and Kaufman Counties:

"A few hundred miles and you will be along streams and rivers as near to your own homeland as you will find."

So they packed their goods and followed after Cleng Peerson to the valley of the Brazos, green and wooded, and here they found what they had sought. Their Swedish brethren had found a place up on the Forks near Clairemont that they thought was like their homeland; and now the Norse have come into their own. They have been sturdy ingredients for the Brazos Melting-Pot.

Another who brought people to the Brazos was Robert Leftwich, a Tennessean from Nashville. He set out to bring eight hundred families to the mid-Brazos. He did not live to see his dream come true, but stalwart Sterling C. Robertson took over his contract with the Mexican authorities and drummed for people to settle on the pleasant slopes of the Brazos valley's little hills and swales. Back in Tennessee he waxed eloquent. Even Sam Houston listened to his story, but it was a big job just then being Governor of Tennessee and Sam shook his head . . . he would come some day . . . and he did.

At the Falls of the Brazos Robertson set up his Viesca, named for the Governor of Coahuila-Tejas. Alas, he argued and bickered with Stephen F. Austin over land-titles and encroachments and the fortunes of the Upper Colony were not happy ones.

Viesca District had a delegate at the San Felipe Convention and there is a brave plat of the Viesca Township. Robertson named the capital of it "Sarahville" after his own mother, but by 1835 they were calling it "Fort Milam" and by 1852 it was gone.

Philip Nolan came to the Brazos in July 1797 with ideas

of colonization in his mind. Many claimed — and still do — that he was sent by Aaron Burr to spy out the land. Burr was in New Orleans dreaming up an empire out of the dregs of an absinthe glass and talking Tejas to anyone who would listen to him.

Nolan was a young blade out of Natchez and he came with a letter from Baron Carondelet, Governor of Louisiana, recommending him to "hunt wild mustangs" on the Brazos plain. He ranged with his band of twenty-five swarthy, bearded men in present Johnson and Bosque Counties and rounded up some thirteen hundred wild horses.

Then, the Spanish Governor got an anonymous letter from New Orleans. It read: "He is a hypocrite and a sacrilegious man, who professes to be a Catholic among Spaniards and laughs at their religion when among Americans on the Brazos."

His Excellency, always suspicious, sent out an expedition from Fort Nacogdoches to wipe out the Nolan party. Lieutenant Musquiz, on March 17, 1801 — St. Patrick's Day was not propitious for Nolan — with his Spanish soldiers fell on Nolan's little party near where Cleburne is now located. After a sharp fight in which Nolan fell at the first volley, the expedition — fourteen Americans, seven Spanish-Americans, one Creole and two Negro slaves — was captured by the Spanish soldiers. Nolan's ears were sent to the Governor as proof of his demise.

The prisoners fared badly. The Spanish Judge Galindo de Navarro at Nacogdoches wanted to release them and let them go back to their native New Orleans, but the Military General in command, overruled him and appealed to the Spanish Crown.

In February 1807, the royal decree came removing the Judge from office and ordering one of the prisoners hanged. The Judge had died and so missed his part of the punishment.

There were nine prisoners left. It was decided to throw

dice to see who the ill-fated one should be. A drum, a crystal tumbler and a pair of dice . . . the low man losing. No. 1, trey-ace; No. 2, trey-four; No. 3, six-five; No. 4, five-trey; No. 5, six-five; No. 6, six-ace; No. 7, four-trey; No. 8, four-ace; No. 9 — how excited he must have been as he shook the tumbler! — five-deuce.

It was Ephriam Blackburn, the oldest of the group and the first to cast, who was low man and was hanged in the plaza at Chihuahua on November 11, 1807. He had been a Quaker, but it was said that he embraced the Catholic faith before he died.

In 1879 a group of Quakers from Indiana bought eighty-two sections of land in Lubbock and Crosby Counties and launched an all-Quaker colony. They founded the town of Marietta and went ahead hopefully to build a town with a college and other institutions. But it was not a friendly country for too-peaceful folk who did not believe in the use of fire-arms. By 1890 they were fully "convinced that the Good Lord did not wish for them to stay here in this benighted place" and so the colony fell apart.

In 1896 a colony of Mennonites settled at Big Creek at what is now Fairchilds and fifty families made it their home. However, the malaria and general hardships were too much for them and they soon scattered and found places in other towns.

Special groups of nationals, religionists and fraternalists have not flourished in late years in the Brazos valley, but there is one exception. In Johnson County, where the Brazos "deep and wide, washes its wall on the southern side," the Seventh Day Adventists built a town for their own religious group and it thrives mightily. Keene is a place at which one should stop. The rule, the law, the religion and the custom of Keene is Seventh Day Adventist and you do your Sunday-ing on Saturday and the tenets of their faith is the governing factor of their town.

The Brazos people have never been over-modest as to the virtues and advantages of their land. When it was seen that the future fortunes of Texas would lie with the Anglo-American rather than the Mexican, a wave of emigration began westward and southwestward that never ceased.

This campaign for population along the Brazos began in 1870. The McLennan Immigration Society sang of the greatness of Waco and the central Brazos region. Climate, land-grants, opportunity for wealth, pasture, wild horses and free cattle for the hunting . . . these were some of the verses. In the Eastern papers the statistics and figures were printed, ending with glowing peroration:

Such is the county and the town to which we invite the attention of the immigrant. Are you a capitalist? We want you. Your money will net you a good percent anyway in which you invest it. Are you a farmer? We want you to develope our wild prairie lands into magnificent fields of corn, wheat and cotton . . . Are you lawyers, doctors, teachers or divines? We want you to settle our personal and pecuniary rights, heal our diseases, teach our children, mend our morals and last, though not least, secure yourselves wealth and honor!

But the Republic of Texas had started advertising back in an earlier day for more ingredients for its Melting-Pot. Congress commissioned and chartered "The Texas Immigration and Land Company" to bring settlers from Kentucky, Tennessee, Missouri and Arkansas. Many came and located on grants in the Parker and Palo Pinto County region along the Brazos. Ships were used by this company to bring emigrants from Europe, and the name of the concern appears on surveys and title-papers of the River country to this day.

To the Melting-Pot of the Brazos, not of his own volition, came the Negro. He has been and is an important factor.

His first representative was Estevan, the Moorish slave with Cabeza de Vaca, who washed up on the shore with that hapless party near the Brazos mouth. The Negro race does not stand sponsor for the statements of this charlatan, who led many Spaniards astray with his wild tales of the Gran Quivera that proved totally unfounded.

The next Negroes who came were those that Lafitte and his pirates stole in mid-ocean from slavers that were plying the Middle Passage. These were sold at $1 a pound to do the work of the farmer and laborer.

His next advent was with his plantation-master emigrating from the old Southern states and coming to found planta-tion-estates on the lower Brazos. He knew cotton-growing and when Jared Groce and others came they brought their slaves with them. Texas would not enter the Union without her slave-status as a State assured her.

Then, abruptly, the Negro was given his freedom and told that he must fend for himself. It was bad enough that he was so unprepared for emancipation, but of a sudden there came the Carpetbagger to the Brazos to ill-advise, counsel him badly and exploit him. Hampered rather than helped he stumbled through the next half-century, uneducated and ignorant, buffeted about by adverse circumstances. He was the grist for the mill-stones of hatred that existed between the Southern white man and the Yankee Carpetbagger. It was a hard position to occupy.

He became, in consequence, a pawn to be pushed about and imposed upon until the white man started educating him in the schools of the Brazos-land and sending his children to intelligent teachers who taught them to read and write.

It has not been easy for the two races to live together on the banks of this River and yet be so widely apart. The buga-boo of "Social Equality" has gripped the heart of the whites and "Discrimination in Opportunity" has embittered the Negro. Education is but slowly bringing about a better un-derstanding between the two.

The main rock upon which contention has broken with

fury has been segregation. The War has done much to bring about a changed situation. The Negro was admitted to the dining-car, the Pullman, the airplane-seat and the hospital as a "war measure."

The law has said that he may vote even in the Democratic Primary, that he may not be excluded from juries and that he may be admitted to State colleges under certain circumstances. There is violent protest, but little open rebellion talk.

Education is transforming the Negro youth from cotton-pickers, field-hands and laborers — "hewers of stone and drawers of water" — into clerks and business people, merchants and teachers, professional men and contractors.

There are still bitter resentments in the minds of some older folk. They look with disfavor upon Northern football teams coming to play in Bowl games at New Year's and bringing Negro players to compete on the gridiron with the Texas colleges. But there is no stir about it and it has come to be accepted after a fashion.

The younger generation shrugs and accepts complacently the Supreme Court decision that Negro voters shall go to the polls, sit on the juries, ride in the planes and Pullman cars . . . what of it? they ask.

The Old-Uncle-Ned type of "darky," as well as the Florian Slappey type of bombastic, over-important Negro, is passing and in a few years will be gone from the River as surely as the Indian and the buffalo, the Ranger and cowboy of old have gone. Slum clearance, better wages, economic betterment, higher education and cultural advancement are having their effect. The spectre of racial bitterness that hung like a cloud above the River of the Arms of God for a century is being laid.

There have been some fraternal, political, religious and business groups along the Brazos that have had processes of the Melting-Pot suffuse and change them until today they are hardly recognizable. There were in the earlier day along the valley the Grange — the Populist Party — the Ku Klux Klan — the Woman's Christian Temperance Union — the Anti-Saloon League — the Liquor Dealers Association — the Masons — the Knights of Columbus — the Hermann Sons — these have all been storm-centers at one time or another. Their battles made Brazonian history. But today there is little of feeling or resentment when they are encountered.

One mentioned because of its long history, so closely associated with the Brazos and its people, is the Masons. In 1834 the first Masonic Lodge in Texas was organized at Brazoria and John A. Wharton secured a dispensation from the Louisiana Grand Lodge for it to meet. There is an old oak in a stately grove just outside of Old Brazoria which marks the spot where the meeting was held.

In February 1851 the Masonic Lodge in Waco met in a two-story log hut and such distinguished names as George Erath, N. W. Battle, Shapley P. Ross and Joseph W. Speight were on the rolls. Today the Grand Lodge of Texas meets on the banks of the Brazos in a fine temple at Waco in annual session.

In 1837, Texas Masons gathered in the Senate Chamber at Austin to organize the Grand Lodge which was presided over by President Sam Houston. Anson Jones, who carried the first Masonic Lodge charter in his saddle-bags at San Jacinto, was elected first Grand Master and Edward Burleson was named Grand Junior Deacon.

There are many Masonic tales told along the Brazos . . . it was claimed that Santa Anna gave Houston the Grand Hailing Sign of Masonic Distress and, because of it, his life was spared . . . Shapley P. Ross carved up a Yankee soldier during Reconstruction times, but the Masonic sign managed to let him escape his guards and he got to California in safety. At Pepper Creek not far from Waco in 1838, some white men got away from some Indians by giving a Masonic sign that Anadarko Chief José Maria recognized and honored. He was a member of a French Lodge in Canada and a relative of Tecumseh, the famed Indian Chief of the North.

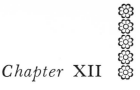

Chapter XII

FAIR WOMEN AND BRAVE MEN

 "HISTORY," SAID THOMAS
Carlyle, "is the essence of innumerable biographies."

For four centuries we know that Man has walked the paths of the Brazos valley and Woman has been at his side. Together they have left glittering stories of achievements and there are a myriad more that have never been written or told.

They were great people in the sense that they invested their devotions in their home-region. Some became great in their nation, in their state and in their local communities — Governors, Statesmen, Orators, Warriors, Tycoons of Wealth — but the dignified sublimity of their lives as they lived them out in and for their homeland, amid friends and neighbors, transcends their acclaim in other places.

Some were great only in the cities of the River and in the towns along her course. But they were content.

A few can be mentioned with no attempt at order to their procession, or effort to grade them in the rank of their importance. Each gave his life and his part, like tiny coral creatures, adding to the atoll to make the composite whole a lasting structure of infinite beauty.

There were great Indian men . . . we do not know their names except in so far as they were Chiefs and left some tale of conquest and defiance behind them. We have paraded the stern old sachems and chieftains of the tribes and told of their exploits. It is tragic that we may not as well refer to their poets, their artists, their humanitarians and their learned . . . but they did not choose to leave us that record and none of their enemies saw fit to preserve it.

Of the white men who were entitled to the guerdon of being called "The Brazos Great," their name is legion for they are many.

There have been fair and brave women on the Brazos. Stalwart and strong were the women who made homes in the wilderness of the River for their men and children. With hoe, rifle and skinning-knife she took her place at the side of her man. If he were not at the cabin when danger came, she stood and fought at the loop-hole for her children's safety.

The Brazos woman could help raise a cabin, born a baby, clear a field, milk a cow, bind up a wound, weave a garment, teach a child to read, lay out the dead and encourage a despondent husband back to faith again.

The widows of the Alamo, Goliad and the early days of the Revolution have a high place in Texas and Brazos history. They had families to keep going when word came of the death of the heroes of 1836 who had given their lives for Texas' freedom.

The messenger of the Alamo's disaster was Mrs. Dickinson. There in the little churchyard on the Brazos in Hood is a monument to the woman whom David Crockett last called "wife." Because of the fate that every Brazos woman knew would be hers in the Indian village if she were captured, or if her children fell into the redskin's hands, she became a tigress when the night air was filled with warwhoops, or when an Indian lurked in the shinnery near her cabin. The weaklings did not come to the valley in those days and if they did, they became strong or did not survive.

A typical Brazos mother was to be known as "The Mother of Texas."

Mrs. Jane Wilkinson Long was the favorite of the Brazos great in the days of the Revolution. Born in Maryland in 1798 she became the wife of Dr. James H. Long when she was seventeen. When Mexico was freeing herself from Spain, Dr. Long was thinking in terms of how Texas should be free from Mexico. The Longs lived in Natchez, but the urge was great, so the physician with star-dust in his eyes and a wife and baby beside him in the wagon, set forth for Texas.

At that time Nacogdoches had 500 people, Goliad, 1,000, and San Antonio de Bexar about 2,000. But the intrepid Mississippian raised the new flag that his wife had made for him, made a speech at Nacogdoches, and declared Texas free. He then set up at Bolivar Point on Galveston Island, armed his "fort" with a single cannon and taught Jane to shoot it.

She was his ambassador to Jean Lafitte but that gentleman-pirate was having no more to do with filibustering and turned a deaf-ear to her. Leaving Jane and the baby at Bolivar, the Doctor, with fifty-one Americans and one lone Spaniard, marched on La Bahia del Esperitu. He took the post by storm and drove on to San Antonio to complete his victory. But by now the Mexican garrison had sent out an expedition to dispose of him. They did.

When Ben Milam brought Jane back the clothes of her husband, whose foolhardiness had led to a firing-squad in Mexico, Jane packed up and left Bolivar Point with her two children. One was born after she got the news. She had fought off the hostile Cronks with her single cannon, borned her baby and gathered driftwood the same day, it is recorded. When the *Lively* went by she flew a red flannel petticoat at the flagpole of Bolivar Point and they set ashore a barrel of flour for her before going on to found San Felipe and Texas.

After her husband's death she too went to San Felipe and opened a boarding-house to which the elect of the colony adhered.

"She was tall," the account reads, "forming a beautiful figure, moving with a grace that is truly and wholly feminine. Her eyes were sparkling, her features regular, her aspect smiling . . . she fascinates her auditor by her ease and fluency."

Rumor had her often engaged to illustrious Brazonians. They linked her name with Ben Milam and Sam Houston. She entertained the New Orleans Grays on their way to fight for Texas in the autumn of 1835. Lamar boarded at her house when he was Vice-President of the Texas Republic and wrote a poem to "Bonnie Jane":

> *O Bonnie Jane, thou art to me,*
> *Whatever in both is best,*
> *Thou art the moonbeam to my eye,*
> *The Sunbeam to my breast.*

Later, he wrote a tribute-sketch to her and when she jilted him, he is said to have changed the "Jane" to "Anna" and sent it off to a Brooklyn lady. She died in December 1880 and is buried in Richmond beside the Brazos among the noted folk of her day.

There was another Jane whom the banks of the River knew. In Troy, New York, in 1813 the lady who was to become Jane McManus Storms Cazneau was born. Her father was a Congressman and her first marriage to William F. Storms ended in separation. When she met Aaron Burr in New Orleans he still had the light of larceny in his eyes about Texas.

"You should go to Texas," he advised her. "It is a place where you would fit."

"What is there in Texas?" she asked, intrigued.

"A place to build an empire," he said gazing dreamily out of his porch of iron filigree, "if one has the courage."

"Why don't *you* go?"

He sighed. "No, mine is an empire of politics, intrigues, conspiracies, moving to a sudden fulmination, my dear. It will take time to hew an empire out on that river in Texas. I am impatient," he got up to pace, "it's later for me than you think."

Jane and her brother went to Texas in 1832 and secured

an eleven league grant of land from the Mexican government, and located on the Brazos. A year later they brought a shipload of German emigrants to it.

Then began for her a fast and furious political career. She knew presidents, senators, ambassadors and statesmen of many nations. She wrote with a flashing pen. When she went to Washington they left what they were doing and rushed to greet her. She was strong for Texas Annexation to the United States and in 1847 President Buchanan did an unheard of thing — he sent a woman to Mexico to help with the treaty-making. Jane McManus was that woman. Then she married Cazneau and lived in Eagle Pass on the Rio Grande for a time, but she always retained a home at Matagorda and one at Washington-on-the-Brazos.

"God intended her for a filibusterer," wrote old Henry Watterson of her in his *Louisville Courier-Journal*. She went to Jamaica and dabbled in Caribbean politics and through her influence her husband was tendered important governmental posts. He served on Governor Thomas J. Chambers' staff and was given the commission to inter the heroes of the Alamo in proper manner. José Garcia calls him "the tenacious adventurer."

Once a duel was almost fought over Jane. Colonel I. R. Lewis of Matagorda resented the fact that she, a kinswoman of his, had not been invited to an important ball. He sent a challenge to every one of the members of the invitations committee — individually and collectively. It took a lot of mollification to quiet the Colonel's umbrage.

These were women of the lower Brazos, but one of the middle-River was "Grandma Moffett." She knew Houston, Austin, Wharton and Burleson well and the historian Brown wrote about her. She packed her family and her goods and refugeed ahead of Houston's army in "The Runaway Scrape." Born in Kentucky in 1812 she came out to San Felipe when she was thirteen. She married Andrew Roberts at sixteen and when he stopped an Indian arrow in 1847 she carried on the family business just the same from her lonely cabin. In 1849 she married Moffett and they moved to Blue Ridge up at the Falls of the Brazos where she became a factor in the life of the community. She was consulted just as the men were about policy.

Noah Smithwick was speaking of her when he used his famous line: "Texas is heaven for men and dogs, but hell for women and oxen."

These women of the middle lands of the Brazos were not always of the hardy, peasant type, but, like Grandma Moffett, were well-educated and cultured. One of these was Catherine Ross. Born to luxury and wealth back in Iowa she came with her husband, Shapley Ross, and her two sons, Peter and Sullivan, to the Brazos where there was much primitive living to be endured.

Her husband had to be away a great deal with his Indian agent duties up at Fort Belknap and she had to attend to everything about the Waco home from milking the cow to building the big house. In addition, she wrote lovely prose and was a community leader. She was a striking type of pioneer woman.

A doughty damsel of early Texas was Julia Trask. She could ride and shoot and travel the Indian country alone back in the 1830's. When her brother fell at San Jacinto she went on to found a girl's school at Independence that was to be the start of Baylor University. This act incurred the following criticism of Dr. Francis Moore, Jr. in *The Telegraph and Texas Register:*

The girls, we will not say young ladies, will grow up like mere patriots, accomplished in nothing but the art of "killing time" ... making themselves instead of objects of love and admiration, the mere toys to be trifled with for an hour and then cast aside with disgust and contempt.

The indignation of the redoubtable Julia when she read

this can be imagined for she boasted of the feat of "shooting off a chicken's head at an incredible number of rods." The school still lives, but the editor's name would be forgotten if it had not been for that comment. His paper is a musty library-archive.

On the upper Brazos, Meg Cook was a typical feminine prototype of the Plains country in the early days. She and Sam, her husband, came in the early 1870's to the Clear Fork. She had married at eighteen and 1872 saw the two with their household goods in a great Conestaga wagon rolling west with stock tied to the tail-gate.

In the wagon were the necessities. Staples, utensils and a bell-tongued plow. The herds were going up the trail and she was going with Sam to raise cattle on which they would get rich. Settlers were few beyond the Cross Timbers, but the land was free and open and a lot of wild cattle could be "hunted" there to make a herd.

One morning, they tell of her, Sam had gone off to help a neighbor who was having trouble with prowling Indians. Meg saw a wisp of smoke and knew that the redskins were starting a prairie-fire to burn her home. Quickly, she hitched up the plow and ran furrows around the house and barns. Then she started a backfire and dragged a wet cow-hide over the embers to save her place.

Lightning, Indians, nesters and incendiaries were the bugaboos of the prairie-folk in those days. Once when Sam was on a trip to the settlements with the team getting supplies in 1874, Meg, locked in for the night with the dogs, heard hoot-owls — too many! The calves were bawling for dear life and her own riding-horse was tied to a post right in the middle of a patch of moonlight. She trained her rifle on it, waiting for an Indian to come and try the bait. But they did not come. They knew the bead that Meg drew.

In 1876 the grasshoppers cleaned Meg and Sam out of a crop, the prairie-dogs got the garden and the loafer-wolves raided the stock. Sam loaded carcasses with strychnine to kill the wolves. Meg went through with Sam . . . helping him tail up the herd, ride the range, tend the young cattle, doctor the sick, water the horses, and when there was a blizzard get feed to the stock. She outlived Sam. In 1927 she was still alive, with her daughter in Erath County, not too far from the Brazos on one of its tributary streams.

Trust Mrs. Holley to glorify the woman she found on the Brazos when she came to visit Stephen F. Austin, her kinsman, and went home to write her books. She mentions Mrs. M — of Kentucky who killed eighty deer and a buffalo with her rifle, while supporting her children and a shiftless husband at their home on Chocolate Bayou. This woman taught herself to read and write so that she could, in turn, teach her children. She was too poor to pay for their schooling. Mrs. Holley marvelled at her ingenuity and her "not yet thirty."

Mrs. Holley also paid tribute to Mrs. Dust, grandmother of Daniel Boone, who lived with her large family on a mound between Brazoria and San Felipe. The children, Mrs. Holley relates, were wholly unlettered, wild and rude, fleeing at a stranger's approach; all except one daughter "who married an intellectual and industrious Yankee."

Noah Smithwick tells of a noted member of the First Three Hundred, Joe Kuykendall, who had a rugged pioneer wife, Anna. One day a visitor expressed concern that it was near sundown and Annie had not returned from following a cow into the brush to locate a lost calf.

"Don't worry about Annie, Colonel Knight," said Joe. "Annie'll not git lost. Iff'n it don't git cloudy and a snake don't bite her, I'll be damned if Annie won't come home and show that cow the way."

There are monuments to the great and illustrious of the River's valley . . . from Austin, "the perfectly unblemished, that moral and industrious man, absolutely free from the vice of intoxication," as one writer extolled him . . . on through the gamut of the heroes of the Brazos-land.

Austin was said to have picked his leaders for "their morality and sturdiness of character, the women for their ability to cook wild hog-meat, stir hominy and use a rifle." He needed builders, for, when he stood on the Brazos in 1821 there was only a single group of settlers' houses between the Sabine and the San Antonio Rivers and that was at Nacogdoches.

They listened to Austin even when he tried to hold them fast to the Mexican line. When he released them from their pledge they gladly went to battle behind Sam Houston against the Mexican over-lords. Stephen did his best . . . he conceived the way to carry out his father's idea . . . he led the leaders in . . . he gave his health and finally his life for his colony and then, at the fulminating point he went to lie beneath the moss-draperies of the oaks at Peach Point. The Father of Texas, and the First Citizen of the Brazos.

Other giants lived in those days — Edward Lovelace, Neil Gaspar, H. Holstein, William Little, Joseph Polly, James Beard, William Wilson, Dr. Hewitson, Bellew, Marple, Irwine, Smithers, Barre. These were the men who held the line for Austin when he was off at Saltillo, San Antonio, Mexico City and elsewhere seeing to the titles and security for his colonists, wearing himself out in the service of others. He always left Josiah H. Bell in charge.

It is a commentary on the times that when the distinguished head of the colony ventured down the Royal Road to Mexico he had to go disguised as a mendicant Mexican *soldado* lest the bandits set upon him.

There were other distinguished contemporaries of Austin. One was of similar name but no kin — John Austin of Connecticut. He and his brother William had intended to go to Mexico but were attracted by one of their name adventuring in Texas so they stopped off and joined up. They had grants along Big Creek on the Lower Brazos in 1831 and William feuded with John A. Wharton considerably. At one time they met in a duel and shot it out. Austin won but when Wharton recovered from his wound, they became fast friends thereafter.

Dr. Robert Peebles was entrusted with the records of the Colony by Austin and well did he keep them. He stood fast in "The Runaway Scrape" until Santa Anna's army was almost at San Felipe. Then he packed up the title-books and took off for Nacogdoches where he stayed until after San Jacinto. In 1836 he brought them back to Columbia and delivered them to Austin at Peach Point Plantation. When Land Commissioner Borden checked them not a one was missing.

Ben Milam sojourned for a time on the Brazos, but he was primarily of Goliad. Don Lorenzo de Zavala, the brilliant Mexican patriot of the Texas cause, native of the Yucatan resided at Harrisburg. He broke with Santa Anna and was proscribed by the Mexicans, but he stood fast by Houston and became Vice President of the Texas Republic.

Gail Borden, whose name appears again and again in the Brazos story published *The Telegraph and Texas Register*. He was another who stood by his presses until the Mexican Army was almost upon San Felipe. They found the last edition of his paper in his shop, burned the whole thing; but his most valuable presses, Borden had packed on his mules and taken to safety.

He got something for posterity out of the flight from Santa Anna. Observing the wise pioneer mothers putting sugar in the milk to preserve it for their children, Borden conceived the idea for Borden's Condensed Milk. He likewise invented a food-biscuit for the army, but it never became as popular as his milk.

Jim Bowie was primarily a Brazos man and teamed up with Noah Smithwick, the blacksmith-historian to make

Bowie knives with which Jim had disembowelled two adversaries in duels back in Mississippi. The knives sold for as high as $20 each.

William Barrett Travis came from South Carolina to cast his fortunes on the Brazos. He would have gone far and accomplished much in the new Texas if he had not had a fault of which his fellow-Carolinian, General Barnard E. Bee, who named "Stonewall" Jackson at Manassas, accused him:

Travis was a great commander if only he had taken Sam Houston's advice and not gotten penned up. Like Santa Anna he despised his enemy and it is a very dangerous thing to do to despise your enemy.

One of the Brazos' most colorful and brilliant characters was a young Kentuckian who listened to Colonel Sterling C. Robertson's speech while recruiting colonists for Texas:

We want settlers in Texas. All we offer you is a chance at your own land where you can grow up and be somebody. To every farmer who will come and bring his family we'll give 177 acres of farm land — good bottom land along the Brazos River — land that can be irrigated and that will yield good crops. You can get 4,428 acres of pasture-land for the same price if you'll promise to raise stock, six years free of taxes and whatever you can haul, duty-free. Plenty of wild game, wild cattle, wild mustangs. Buffalo-hides for clothes and all the bear-skins you can take.

There was much more to his effective speech and it brought these folk of Kentucky with their families, their household goods, working tools, farm-implements, forges and guns. There was not a single rail laid then in the land. So Noah Smithwick loaded up in Hopkinsville, Kentucky, by stagecoach and got to the Mississippi. There he hoped to get a ride on some sort of river-craft down the river to New Orleans from whence he could wangle a boat-trip to Texas. When he finally got to the Brazos, Smithwick with his dual arts — blacksmithing and letters — became the favorite of the Texas great — Austin, Bowie, Houston and others.

[239]

He writes of what he saw with a vivid pen. Missing San Jacinto by a fluke and going off with another detachment of troops, he arrived at the battle-field next day to add his gripping account of the struggle to history. He proved a most facile war-correspondent.

Samuel M. Williams was a Brazos-man and Austin's first scribe. He was against Santa Anna from the first and along with de Zavala was proscribed bitterly by the Mexicans. With McKinney he opened a store at Quintana and outfitted two ships of the Texas Navy. He was the first banker in Galveston and one of the commissioners to negotiate the peace for the new Republic.

Francis W. Johnson, who took over at San Antonio when Ben Milam fell, was from the Brazos as was Godwin B. Cotton, who founded in 1829 at San Felipe *The Texas Republic,* a newspaper that influenced politics sharply in the early days along the River.

Padre Muldoon was a noted Brazos priest of the early days of whom Noah Smithwick writes:

He is a bigoted old Irishman with an unlimited capacity for drinking and marrying people.

Down at Fort Bend, Walter C. White was a leading citizen, kept a trading-post and a general store. Along with Colonel Knight, he operated a cargo-schooner on the Brazos. Thomas J. Pilgrim was an itinerant Baptist preacher who cast his fortunes early with the colony, but Austin warned him against his exhortations due to the Catholic clause in the colony-grant. So he became a dominie instead and taught school until the season closed on Protestants in the Brazos valley.

In those early days the strangers came to the Brazos settlements first and got their bearings before going on. Ben Harrison, son of the President of the United States, came in 1835, a doctor of sorts, trading on his important name.

[240]

He lived along the lower River with uncertain success and reputation . . . "a big, tall Yankee with a Lord's Prayer face."

Thomas H. Borden was Gail's brother and quite a Brazos land-owner in his own right. He shot Jesse Thompson in a duel, which was the first killing recorded in the lower Bend, but he was never tried because the only witness was a Negro slave and his testimony was not admissible in Court.

Borden wrote a friend in Iowa of the incident: "He came at me with a pistol and I drew and fired at the old hellion. He fired at the same time and missed me. Then a running-fight occurred. I'm glad that I gut-shot him so that he might have the pangs of as hard a death as possible."

Borden was released on $2,500 bond but never came to trial. The Borden plantation was known as "Louisville" and they shipped their yield by steamboat to West Columbia, or Marian, as it was sometimes called. They would raise eighty-four bales of cotton in a single year and cleared over $3,000 on a single crop, which was a small fortune in those days. Santa Anna took delight in burning their gins and warehouse but they quickly rebuilt them.

"Don't bring a wife to Texas," Tom Borden wrote to Moses Lapham up in Iowa. "Wait and find one here. Then she'll be used to the climate."

On the *Lively* came William Morton who built a fine place on the lower Brazos. There is a story about him . . . he was entertaining a stranger from Alabama who was passing through — Robert Gillespie — who died suddenly. Morton buried him and since they were both Masons, he put the square-and-compass emblem on the grave-stone. When the Mexican soldiers came by his place on the way to San Jacinto, they began defacing the stone but Colonel Juan Almonte, Santa Anna's aide rode up and, being a Mason in Mexico, bade them cease.

Back in December 1839 a tall, bewhiskered man descended

[241]

from the Houston stage and announced that he was Dr. George A. Feris and henceforth would be the leading doctor of Richmond. After a few drinks to irrigate his throat of the dust of the journey, he went to the office of the newspaper, *The Telescope and Literary Register,* and inserted an ad:

To all whom it may concern: I want money, must have it and will get it. Dr. George A. Feris, Dec. 21, 1839.

Mrs. Holley writes of an early character out of Kentucky whom she covers by the name of "B——". He came to Texas for a new start with his family and was doing well until his past caught up with him. Word was tattled to General Austin that the man had served a term in the Kentucky State penitentiary. He was ordered promptly to leave the colony.

But old B went to Austin and stood manfully up to him.

"Yes, I served in the pen," he said, "but I also served in the Kentucky Legislature, where I made it so hot for the banks that they set a trap to get me in a small act of technical forgery, which banks do on a large scale every day. I've paid my debt to society and I claim the right to stay."

He stayed. But, alas, not for long. The cholera epidemic in 1832 got him and of his end, Mrs. Holley adds: "It can not be said that he lies interred, for he was buried erect and in full dress, with his rifle on his shoulder, facing west, according to his desire."

Wylie Martin, after whom they name Martin County, came to the Brazos in 1825 after a career in the United States Army where he served General Harrison as a scout, fought with Andy Jackson at Horseshoe Bend and was a Captain of Regulars. He became Alcalde of the San Felipe District, political chief of the Department of the Brazos and was set to guarding the Brazos Crossing at Fort Bend with a company of volunteers in "The Runaway Scrape." He served in the Texas Congress later and died in 1842.

Up at the Falls of the Brazos and around Waco there were

some substantial citizens in that early day. James Coryell of Ohio, friend of the Bowie brothers, Indian fighter and Ranger, operated out of old Viesca and with Andrew Cavitt helped to guard the settlement against the Indians along the middle River. They named a county for him.

The big men of Waco's beginning . . . George Barnard who came in 1844 and set up a trading-post . . . Neil Mc-Lennan who brought the first family to live here on the Brazos . . . George Erath, who surveyed the land and laid out the tracts and lots on which the first settlers built their homes . . . Shapley P. Ross, who came as the first leader of the community and its top citizen . . . Caleb Hubby, who opened the first store and mill at the site of the old Indian village.

The biographies of these men and others is the history of the early days of this section of the Riverland.

Jacob de Cordova, elsewhere mentioned, was a tireless believer in the fortunes of the midlands and went over all of the known United States as well as Europe preaching the gospel of emigrating to the Brazos lands. Strong for industrialization and the harnessing of the River's power, he controlled over a million acres at one time in central Texas and helped to found Waco town.

The name of Harrison was one to conjure with in Mc-Lennan County in the old days. Coming from Mississippi the family furnished three Generals for the Confederacy, besides many illustrious lawyers, doctors and clergymen. G. B. Gerald was a noted editor, lawyer, Confederate leader, post-master and office-holder. Once when County Judge he ordered the Sheriff to close a gambling-joint in Waco. Finding that he had not been obeyed he went there, single-handed, and tossed the equipment out onto South Fourth Street and smashed what he did not throw out. He then telephoned the newspaper to print that as a warning to other places of similar ilk.

Back in 1836 there came to the banks of the Brazos a distinguished foreigner, Count de Posse, a warm adherent and close associate of the first Napoleon. He mourned his master's fate until at last one day he called a small lad to him, gave him the medals that the French Emperor had bestowed upon him and committed suicide by drowning himself in the River.

The Ferguson family that was to play such an important part in Texas political history was originally a Brazos clan. The first Ferguson came from Alabama and fell at Goliad. His kin came to claim the land-bounty that was their due as relatives of the veteran and remained. Some of them were Methodist preachers.

James E. Ferguson, a preacher, first of the famous name, came to Victoria County and married Anne Fitzpatrick. In 1857 he moved to Richmond on the Brazos where he lived until Civil War times. He stayed in 1860 at John Schaefer's boarding-house and received from his congregation a big Bible that made news. Somehow or other, he accumulated $30,000 in land and $15,000 in personal property, which was considered remarkable in that day.

The naturalist Audubon tarried for a time on the Brazos banks studying its wild life and meeting its people. He called on President Houston in 1837 while Sam was enjoying the fruits of office. In his diary Audubon says:

We first caught sight of President Houston as he walked from one of the grog-shops, where he said he had been to stop the sale of ardent spirits. We reached his abode before him, but he soon came and we were presented to His Excellency. He was dressed in fancy velvet coat and trousers trimmed with broad gold lace . . . We were introduced by him to members of his cabinet and Staff and at once asked to drink grog with him, which we did, wishing success to the new Republic . . . Himself, his officers and the place of his abode can never be forgotten.

Of Houston himself much has been said in this narrative;

[244]

and there is much that can be added of his experiences and exploits along the Brazos. Many biographies of him exist. There was never a more diversified character, shining with alternate brilliance and admitting to many a fault. Queer contrast of saint and sinner, up and down in his popularity, a man of severe disappointments and high successes, we may say as Andrew Jackson, his great and good friend, did: *"History will take good care of Sam Houston."*

Back in 1824 the Brown brothers came to the banks of the River. Captain Henry Brown had stocked an outfit for trading with the Indians and Mexicans up the Brazos as far as Washington, which was as far as the settlements extended. John — "Waco Brown" — traded up that way while Henry headed out for Monterrey, Mexico, down El Camino Real.

But John got too ambitious and pressed on with three men and his pack-mules to the Clear Fork Country of the Brazos where he accumulated about 1,000 head of horses. He got safely back as far as the Bosque river in the Brazos midlands when the Indians set upon him and took everything that he had. His companions escaped but he was held prisoner. He began studying the ways of the Indians.

Henry, learning of his brother's fate, raised a company of forty-two men and went to war with the Wacos in the attempt to deliver him. He won the fight but the Indians had John hidden across the River at where East Waco now is situated and he was not rescued. A year later they took him on a raid down into present Fayette County and he managed to escape at Cumming's Creek. He got back to San Felipe and joined his brother. They raised a party and overtook the Wacos' war-party, killing every one of them.

Thereafter the Indians respected the Brown Brothers' trading-parties. Captain Henry commanded a company of eighty Texans at the Battle of Velasco and had an illustrious record, dying in Columbia and being buried on the banks of the River where he first pitched his camp.

William Davis Redd and Lysander Wells were two Brazonian hotspurs, who on May 9, 1840 met on the Field-of-Honor in a duel. Redd served in Lamar's Cavalry at San Jacinto, and was a citizen of Velasco. Wells, a New Englander, served in Sydney Sherman's Texas volunteers and at San Jacinto "was elegantly dressed and mounted on a gaily-caparisoned Mexican horse with silver-mounted saddle and bridle."

During an Indian campaign on the Brazos, Redd chided Wells for refusing to wage war against the Comanches and there were hot words. Wells had something to say about "the petticoat-command of the regiment," alluding to a young Georgia woman suspected of sharing the Colonel's quarters. Redd challenged Wells to a duel and the challenger was killed instantly, while Wells was so badly wounded that he died twenty days later.

The tragic part was that in Redd's uniform jacket was found a license, duly recorded, showing a ceremonial marriage with the young woman in question.

Many of the old States shared their distinguished sons with the Brazos-land. James Wright Simmons came from Charleston, after being schooled at Harvard and Oxford, at Mirabeau B. Lamar's invitation. When Lamar became President he made the South Carolinian his Comptroller of the Treasury. Also from that state along with Travis, came Generals Hamilton and Barnard E. Bee, Indian-fighters and Confederate great, to find glory and fame in Texas.

A gallant Alabamian, James Decatur Cooke, sojourned on the Brazos for a time and then went back to his old home. But when the drums of Revolution rolled he packed up and came back to Brazoria to found a paper and plug for Lamar. The opposition press dubbed him "The Fighting Cocke" and he served under Captain Ewen Cameron in the Mier Expedition and in the Comanche fighting. But he drew a black bead at Salado in March 1843, when the ill-fated Mier prisoners were drawing lots to see who would die for their aborted attempt at a Mexican invasion and that was the end of him.

The Brazos sent many of its fool-hardy sons to participate in that expedition which was supposed to be in retaliation for attacks made by the Mexicans on Texas after the disastrous defeat at San Jacinto. Gideon K. Lewis, a Brazonian, was "the boy prisoner of the Mier," drew a white bean, was imprisoned at Castle Pelote in September 1844, and later served in the Mexican War with the United States in the Texas Rangers. He was a founder of the King Ranch in later years, ran for Congress, but was killed in a duel with J. T. Yarrington in a controversy over the latter's wife.

Noah Smithwick mentions the names of some of his Brazos contemporaries of whom he was fond . . . William Christy and Adolphus Sterne, men of Velasco, who outfitted the New Orleans Grays with uniforms in 1835 . . . Charles Falenash and John Cummings . . . Bob Mathews who ran a tin-shop at San Felipe . . . who had a song that he sang to the tune of "The Widow's Lament," according to Noah:

The U. S., as we understand,
Vomited up the dregs of its land,
Murderers, bankrupts, rogues you see
All congregated in San Felipe.

Noah had to explain why he was not at San Jacinto but with Colonel John H. Moore and his LaGrange Company that got diverted from Houston's force and wound up at Tenoxtitlan, high on the mid-River . . . he never got over it in his writings. His account tells of dead Mexicans lying about and their prisoner-comrades never bothering to bury them . . . of buzzards and coyotes prowling the battle-field and preferring horse-flesh to Mexicans, because of the pepper the latter contained . . . of how the Texans had to bury the dead Mexicans in sanitary self-defense . . . the Mexican prisoners swearing that Houston's men were drunk on corn whiskey, which explained their courage and wild yelling . . . he lampooned President Burnet's "triumphal entry" after the battle when the danger was over . . . the setting afire of the pile of Mexican rifles and the popping of bullets that sent the politicians looking for cover.

He says that when Santa Anna's horse was taken it was found to be a fine black stallion with a $600 gold-mounted saddle. Houston took the saddle for his own but when he found that "The Napoleon of the West" had stolen the horse from Allen Vince, he sent the steed back to its owner.

Smithwick refers often to Big Foot Wallace, a Brazonian of note, about whom this story is told . . . in October 1837 he was hunting in the Palo Pinto country of the Brazos when the Indians captured him and decided to burn him at the stake.

He told Noah: "I thought my time had come and decided to meet my fate like a man. I don't know how long I would have succeeded but an old squaw, who had taken a liking to me in the lodge, rushed through the painted warriors and began throwing the wood away from me . . . a number of women rushed in and untied me . . . she had lost her son in a fight with the whites, claiming me as a substitute for her son."

He settled down and studied their ways and they took him on raids to Mexico. They wished him to marry into the tribe and be one of them, but he chose to escape with the help of his foster-mother, his friend, Black Wolf, and accompanied by his faithful dog, Comanche. When he got back to the white settlements he was a valuable Indian scout.

Once in 1849 when he was riding guard on the mail-coach on Devil's River he saw Indian smoke-signals. He noted with his practised eye a running horse, a frightened deer and alerted his comrades against Indians. When they encountered twenty-three Indians he led the attack and four of the redskins were killed. On the second attack the whites got five and the mail-coach got away safely.

But the smoke-signals to another Indian party brought more trouble and Wallace had to talk them out of a fight until California Springs could be reached. Outwitting them, he cut across country and by the time his coach got to the springs he had an escort of soldiers from a near-by fort.

Many of the Texas leaders took part in the Santa Fé Expedition that Lamar intended should add New Mexico to his domain. In 1841 he thought all that he had to do was to give the New Mexico settlers the chance and they would revolt as the Texans had done. The party assembled at Brushy Creek near Austin where Lamar harangued them. George Wilkens Kendall went along as historian. General McLeod commanded the soldiers, supply-wagons, beef-cattle and the single brass cannon that they had as they marched bravely forth.

The story begins gloriously . . . the herds of buffalo . . . the wild mustangs . . . the White Steed of the Prairie . . . the beauties of the Brazos riverland . . . the steep banks:

If Napoleon had faced the Bosque in crossing the Alps with its steep banks, he would surely have turned back.

But not the gallant McLeod who led his men across the Bosque and then over the Brazos at Granbury. Kendall, describing the Comanche Peak, records:

The Comanche Peak is high above the other hills, giving grandeur and sublimity to a scene which would have otherwise been far from monotonous.

The farther the expedition went the more trouble it encountered. Badly led and guided, it succumbed to fatigue, hunger, sickness, shortness of supplies, water-failure and general over-confidence. They sent word that they were coming to deliver Santa Fé and the Mexican soldiers had plenty of time to be there to meet them on the plains of the Brazos

[249]

Forks. There was not even a decent battle, the Texans talking themselves into surrender "on terms." They went to Mexico in chains and if it had not been for the American minister's intervention, General Waddy Thompson, they would have all been shot.

The Brazos always claimed Albert Sydney Johnston as one of its great men. He chose it. Claiming a survey in Palo Pinto County for its loveliness of scenery, another in Stephens County on the Clear Fork and building a plantation home in the lower Brazos country, he definitely preferred it. He had been a fellow-West Pointer with Jeff Davis and Robert E. Lee, graduating in 1826, fought in the Black Hawk War with Lincoln and came to Texas in 1834 when he quit the army.

Unobtrusively he joined the Texas Army as a private. Houston found him out and made him a Brigadier. Lamar later appointed him Secretary of War. He was a Colonel of First Texas Riflemen in the Mexican War, but 1849 found him paymaster of the line of Brazos forts — Graham, Worth, Belknap, Phantom Hill and others. Indians and outlaws alike respected him and his escort that carried the pay-roll.

When the 2nd Cavalry was formed in 1855 he rode to Texas in command of a regiment to keep the frontier peace. Later, he was to win his General's star for leading an overland expedition to quell a Mormon uprising in Utah. On his return from the west he was named Commander of the Texas Republic Army, but old General Felix Huston, who was supplanted by Johnston, challenged him to a duel over it. Although wounded in the encounter, Johnston recovered and assumed command. Huston, mollified and his honor satisfied, served under Johnston as if nothing had happened.

But when Sam Houston took over as President and reduced the size of the Army, Johnston took it as a slap at him and sent the President a challenge to meet him on the Field-of-Honor.

"Tell him I've had a number of challenges in my life-time," old Sam sniffed. "He'll have to stand in line and wait his turn."

With Davis, Lee and others, Johnston cast his lot with the Confederacy and brilliant was his record. He outpointed Grant that first day at Shiloh, but was killed on the morning of the second day — April 6, 1862 — and Lincoln often said: "What might have happened if Johnston had not fallen at Shiloh!"

The Brazos could claim Robert E. Lee for he served many a watch along the River of The Arms of God. A Lieutenant Colonel of the 2nd Cavalry, he commanded the 1st and 5th Squadrons at Camp Cooper on the Brazos in 1856. In letters he referred many times to his experiences on the plains of west Texas, along the River. When Johnston went on the Mormon assignment, Lee assumed command of the regiment and later of the Department at San Antonio on February 20, 1860. But by Christmas of that year he was back at Fort Mason and the other forts along the Brazos. While in command he put a stop to the practice of "branding" AWOL's and other minor offenders.

As the New Year dawned he was hurrying back to Washington to find out what Secession was about and by April had resigned his commission . . . his sword was Virginia's.

Fair women and brave men . . . a throng of them have marched up the Brazos valley through the years. Smithwick reflected on them once:

Men talk hopefully of the future, children revel in the novelty of the present, but the Woman, ah, there is where the situation bears the heaviest!

He had heard them speak sadly of the old life back home and the friends they had left behind. Contrary to the popular conception, many times there was not even the solace of hard work to divert them. There were no spinning-wheels and looms at first, no house to keep except a one-room cabin, the food was so scarce that they had little to do to prepare it, there was no company for miles to wait upon . . . only the fighting of the children and the dogs to break the monotony.

No garden to till, no books to read, no schools, no churches. Smithwick says further on:

It was July on the Brazos and the heat was intense. The only water obtainable was from the sluggish river, which crept along between low banks, thickly set with tall trees from the branches of which depended long streamers of Spanish moss swarming with mosquitoes, pregnant with malaria. Alligators, gaunt and grim, certainly the most hideous creatures God ever made, lay in wait for any unwary creature that might come down to drink.

This was the wilderness of the lower Brazos in the days when the pioneer men and women came to hew out homes and fortunes. Their accomplishment was in proportion to persistency. In the fitting words of Van Dyke:

> *O question not but honor every name,*
> *Travis and Crockett, Bowie, Bonham, Ward,*
> *Fannin and King, all who drew the sword*
> *And dared to die for Texas liberty.*
> *Yes, write them all upon the roll of fame,*
> *But no less love and equal honor give*
> *To those who paid the longer sacrifice —*
> *Austin and Houston, Burnet, Rusk, Lamar*
> *And all the stalwart men who dared to live*
> *Long years of service to the lonely star.*

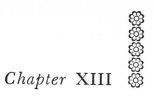

Chapter XIII

FOR THE GOLD THEY NEVER EARNED

"THE TOUGHEST FRONTIER in the world!"

That was the reputation that the Brazos had in the decade from 1810-1820. Men went heeled and lived by their wits and the quickness of the draw. If an adventurer got by the Comanches and the Kiowas, the Spaniards shot him on suspicion. Down at the very mouth of the Brazos, an ex-pirate of the high seas, Jean Lafitte, preyed on Gulf shipping and robbed slavers in the Middle Passage. The border-ruffians outdid the Indians in deeds of deviltry.

This Brazos-land has had turbulent times and the present peace has been bought with blood and tears. Explored and exploited in its early days by men of greed and avarice, crime was the simple expedient of their ends. Slavery, robbery, theft, and murder were quick aids to a return to the Old World.

The Spaniard that the valley saw was, for the most part, a ruthless invader; ambitious to improve personal fortunes, to impose his religion upon everyone, to discover cities of gold, to betray the friendship of the Indians, and to get what he desired by any means possible.

Successively the paths of the River have suffered from the demoralizing trade of the treasure-hunter, the smuggler, the pirate, the slave-trader, the outlaw, the bandit, the stage-robber, the bootlegger, the hi-jacker, the hot oil runner, the cattle-rustler, the bank-bandit, the black-marketeer, and all manner of folk who have risked their lives and traded honor for the gold they would not honestly earn.

Gamblers all. From the Spanish Queen who pawned her crown jewels to stake a Genoese sailor on his maiden voyage ... to Cortez who burned his ships to keep his men from running away until they had milked Mexico dry of all the gold they could take from the betrayed Montezuma . . . to Coronado who kicked the pitiful hogans of the Indians to pieces because they were not made of gold . . . it is a story of exploitation, along with all of its color.

When the Spaniard found that the Brazos valley contained naught but farmlands and forests, plains and peaks, he turned his back upon it and from 1500 to 1800 — three hundred years — he did nothing to develop it or to improve it for human habitation. It had no wealth in terms of his values and he contented himself with keeping others from exploring it lest they profit thereby.

The French were fully as preoccupied with avarice. La Salle sought silver mines on the Brazos and when they could not be found, his party began internal strife that resulted in the dashing adventurer's death. In 1816 Luis Aury, another Frenchman, declared himself Governor of all of the territory from the Brazos' mouth on up to present Richmond and over to Nacogdoches. He demanded that the Indians bring him gold and silver, while he preyed on Spanish shipping in the Gulf of Mexico.

When the tribesmen of the red men did not bring him treasure he held their families hostages and sold them into slavery in the markets of Europe, and wherever else he could. It is not a pretty picture, but his "province" was short-lived, for his buccaneering followers fell out among themselves and fought over the spoils until their band was dispersed.

In their wake and recruiting some of their people, Jean Lafitte set up at his Campeachy, down near the Brazos entrance on the Gulf. For a time he ruled from his pirate-roost, and Mexico City recognized his right. Andrew Jackson had enlisted him at New Orleans against the British in the War of 1812 where the free-booter paid off an old score. President Madison had pardoned him for his high crimes. For four years he was to carry on his buccaneering in the Gulf . . . until his ambitious pirates sank a vessel with an American flag in the Sabine and a cruiser of the new government in Washington called an end to his piracy.

He had a colorful time at Aury's old headquarters while he lasted. Personable rascal that he was, he was well-educated, spoke several languages, held letters of marque-and-reprisal from the Venezuelan Government, and never bothered anyone but the Spaniards against whom he had a grievance. He enjoyed the right of a Port-of-Entry for Galveston, his headquarters, from the Viceroy in Mexico City. When one of his lieutenants sank the Yankee ship, he hanged him. But when driven out of Galveston Island, he went to the Caribbean and was killed within the year by a Spanish cannon-ball.

In addition to piracy as a crime that was not regarded with too much opprobrium, smuggling was a pastime of sorts. Noah Smithwick, for all of his respectability in the early Republic, mentions that he and Joe McCoy, Jack Cryor and John F. Webber engaged in smuggling tobacco into Mexico and smuggling back trade-goods that people along the Brazos would pay good money for.

Life in the colony became stale and not so profitable as I could wish, so I sold my shop at Columbia, or Bell's landing and invested the proceeds in tobacco and set out for Mexico on a smuggling trip.

That he had to bribe the Mayor and other officials did not seem to bother his conscience. It appeared that in that day if you wanted something badly enough, you got up an expedition and went after it by might — if your might was powerful enough — and got it.

President Mirabeau B. Lamar listened to a plan to steal all

of New Mexico from the Mexicans without even asking the natives if they wished to be "liberated." He outfitted an expedition — the Santa Fé in 1841 — at the Republic's expense to take the whole area. That it failed was not due to any virtue but to farcical planning.

Even in 1843 when Sam Houston was President of the Republic, Snively's Expedition marched to New Mexico for the express purpose of preying on innocent wagon-trains for the booty to be gained. When they were discovered on The Santa Fé Trail, Uncle Sam's troopers served notice on them to get back into Texas, where they could hi-jack all they pleased, but if caught outside of the Republic's boundaries they would be fired on.

Bands of robbers would establish themselves — Border-Ruffians — in the wild fastnesses of the forests and raid the settlements. Magee was a Lieutenant in the U. S. Regulars, until he went out and broke up such a band of robbers on the Sabine. Then he decided that he would do some robbing of his own. "Filibustering" was the polite term for it. So he resigned his Army commissions and ran up a land-pirate's flag, aligning himself with some Mexican adventurers, and "taking" town and fort until tuberculosis and the Mexican soldiers snuffed out his career of freebooting and conquest in his first real skirmish.

Bernardo Gutierrez, a follower of Hidalgo, the patriot-priest of Mexico, had egged Magee and Kemper on to "take" Nacogdoches and La Bahia, but the venture was short-lived after Magee died.

The constant attempts of Filibusterers, using the aegis of Freedom and Liberty for their attempts at exploitation and conquest, kept the land of the Brazos in an uproar until the coming of Austin's people to the River. Then some semblance of order and law asserted itself and a standard was reared to which lawful folk could claim allegiance.

But from the earliest days, with the flood of emigration to

the Brazos, there came a steady stream of lawless people, many of them under indictment back in the old States — headed for Texas — changing their names — starting life over — or joining up with lawless bands and living by their wits and guns. Deserters from the Civil War armies on both sides, escaped criminals, remittance-men from abroad, they flocked to Texas and holed-up with their own kind in the hills, here and there, swooping down upon settlements, trail-herds, stage-coaches and wagon-trains to rob and pillage. The Brazos was not spared its share. As the settlements became more thickly populated with self-respecting people, they began to oust these robber-gangs and stamp out their lawlessness. The Rangers and the peace officers, the sheriffs' posses and the Vigilantes, along with the Fear-of-God and Old "Judge Lynch," that the settlers imposed by Colt and Winchester, cleaned up the Brazos valley and made it a fit place to live.

Back in 1875 the cattle-thieves got so bad that the cattle-men and nesters took the law in their own hands. "The Regulators," as these indignation-groups were called, fought it out with the hired gunmen who were imported to fight them. The poisoning of the farmers' sheep, the stealing of their stock, and the firing of their barns and corn-cribs ceased.

In 1877 the law-breakers refused to let District Judge W. A. Blackburn hold Court until several Rangers came to stand behind his bench. That was when the Frontier Ranger Battalion was sent in to comb the shinnery and the chaparral and smoke out the bandits. They brought in thirty of these desperadoes who were wanted in eighteen Texas midland counties. Judge Blackburn convened a Grand Jury that indicted twenty-nine of the thirty, but there were only nine people in that county eligible for jury duty, so the cases had to be transferred to another county.

The Brazos-land suffered during the days of Reconstruction from the end of the Civil War until 1874. Carpetbaggers made life a burden to the white people of the Valley.

Disenfranchised, property confiscated, the Riverland deprived of Constitutional rights, they could only endure and fight back with blunted weapons.

The day of the cattle-drives saw outlawry revived as the bandits preyed on the herds and the chuck-wagons. They remembered how they had benefited by robbing the California gold-rush wagons and again they came down out of the hills and buttes to make life miserable for the traveler. The Ranger, however, proved to be the nemesis of these outlaws of the short-grass country and, in the warfare between them, the Ranger prevailed.

The middle of the nineteenth century saw a new form of grafting-outlaw. *Comancheros* were unprincipled Mexicans, egged on by Don Juan Bautista de Anza, who had an alliance with the Comanche Indians to rob the white settlers of the Brazos valley as well as the overland wagon-trains bound for California.

Posing as *ciboleros,* or buffalo-hunters, they hid their weapons out in the canyons with trinkets and contraband goods that the Indians wanted. They became the Fagins of the open spaces. They urged the Comanches to bring them jewels, money, and other valuables that they could get from robbing the wagons. They would give the Indians guns, ammunition and whiskey. They kept within safe distance of the settlements but usually came in through New Mexico. They based in Santa Fé and eluded the soldiers by changing their hiding-places frequently.

They got so they would arrange for whole herds to be taken by the Comanches down in the Cross Timbers and delivered to these *comancheros'* drivers up on the Plains. The herds would be driven through to Kansas and sold there and the bootlegged arms delivered to the Indians. It was estimated that during the Civil War, when the men were away at the battle-front, over 300,000 head of stolen cattle and 100,000 horses were driven into the upper River region and disposed of by this illicit system. It was only when the Civil War ended and the forts began to be garrisoned with United States troops that this trade was stopped.

When Colonel Mackenzie strung José Tafolla up to his own wagon-tongue and left him there as a farmer would a dead hawk, spread out on the wire-fence, the Indians realized what would happen to any more trading of that kind and the people who indulged it.

One of the very earliest "bad men" of the upper Brazos region, a legend of that country, was Sostenes l'Archeveque — "Jean the Frenchman's" grandson — who cut a wide swath among the outlaws and Indians, but he double-crossed the Indians one day and they liquidated him. He ranged in Billy the Kid's territory . . . Santa Fé, The Plains, the Brazos Forks, Tascosa and the Panhandle of Texas.

The Kid — born William Bonnet — ranged all over that area and while not primarily a Brazos product was well-known to the towns and cattle-camps of the Forks country. He was often at Lubbock and came down farther to do his deviltry until Pat Garrett caught up with him and stopped his career.

Old newspapers and record-books of the Brazos valley are filled with the deeds of derring-do of their own bad actors — Jim Miller, Clay Allison, Kid Curry, Bill Longley, Ben Thompson, King Fisher, Tom Starr and the Marlow Brothers of Young County. They have each a long sheet of crime in their records and were the targets of Rangers and peace officers until they were exterminated by persistent efforts.

They tell a story around Walker's Crossing on the Bosque . . . of how on an evening in spring they were having a big gala dance at the Walker's to which the neighbors from miles around had gathered. Four personable young strangers came walking in.

"I'm Jesse James," one of them said. "This is Frank and . . ."

He introduced the others. They had a string of cattle out on the Brazos Forks in the west, the exact location of which they were not telling and had been holed up for the winter. When leaving the dance, James asked Mr. Walker for a change of horses . . . and got them.

Waco was a hilarious old town in those days and the hangout of many a desperate character. There were so many shooting-scrapes, gun-toting bad men, and suspicious characters strutting about the Square atop the bluff over the Brazos that Waco was known as "Six-Shooter Junction."

They tell the story of how ex-Sheriff Bill Harris and Doctor J. D. Lovelace shot it out. They met at Waco's old Turf Saloon and had about settled their differences when Harris' son heard that his dad was in a scrap and showed up with a loaded shot-gun. Lovelace began firing and when the smoke cleared away, the former Sheriff and his son were both dead and the Doctor had such a good self-defense plea that they did not even summon the Grand Jury to indict him.

There was Will Lambdin, who got into a running gun-fight with two assailants, and before he killed them he picked off two innocent by-standers besides. He was later a Brigadier-General in the Regular Army and served in the Philippines.

"Six-Shooter Junction!" the Katy brakeman would yell into the day-coach. "Thutty minutes for lunch and see a killin'."

John Wesley Hardin used Waco as the background for some of his early crimes. He was reared over in Limestone County and rose to the dubious heights of being known as "The World's Champion Desperado" with forty-three notches in his gun. He started out fighting with some Negro soldiers of the Carpetbagger regime who tried to arrest him. He killed them both and then went outlaw, ranging up and down the Chisolm, the Brazos, and over the Southwest generally.

Once at Towash Dam in Hill County on the Brazos banks he shot his way out of arrest in true Western-movie fashion, leaving three dead behind him. Another time he killed both of his Yankee soldier-guards who were carrying him to jail. Hardin had worked for James Barr on his Brazos ranch and made a drive or two up the Chisolm. He knew his way around and could hide easily. When Texas got too hot for him he took off for Florida, but there was a Ranger on his trail who met and arrested him in a Florida day-coach and brought him back to Texas so quickly he did not have time to demand extradition papers. He did a term in the state penitentiary and was shot in an El Paso saloon gun battle some years later.

It was not uncommon to see Jesse James on the streets of Waco in his heyday and not a hand laid on him. Sheriff Sul Ross arrested Belle Starr in Waco one day on a Dallas-issued warrant.

It was Sul Ross who cleaned up a nest of bandits on the Tomas de LaVega Grant in McLennan County. They were holed-up in a thick wooded spot in the middle 1870's. They were called "Modocs" and descended to terrorize the entire mid-Brazos region.

Then, there was Sam Bass who is a central Texas tradition of a "bad man." He sleeps today in a little cemetery in Round Rock and above his grave is the epitaph on stone: "A brave man reposes in death here. Why could he not be true?"

His main hang-out to hide was in Denton County, but when he yearned for a place to spend his time and his money on amusement he came to Waco. It has always been claimed that he spent his last $20 gold-piece left from his Union Pacific $60,000 holdup in Nebraska in 1877 at the old Ranch Saloon in Waco on the east side of the Square.

It so happened that he was planning to rob one of Waco's three banks when his pal, Jim Murphy, talked him out of it and into robbing the one at Round Rock near Austin.

Murphy had secretly sold Sam down the river to the Rangers and the trap was laid to catch him at Round Rock. Bass, Jackson, Barnes and Murphy rode through Waco on horseback and down to Round Rock where Ranger Major John B. Jones, tipped off by Murphy's post-card, was waiting.

On July 21 when Sam strode into the bank-store at Round Rock, two Deputy Sheriffs followed him in.

"You got a six-shooter in that bulge, Sam?" Lige Grimes flipped his badge in sight.

"Two of 'em!" said Sam, whipping his guns out and killing Grimes. He only winged the other Deputy.

The Rangers closed in and Ranger George Harold dropped Seba Barnes while Ranger Ward wounded Bass. But the wily bandit got to his horse and escaped. Ranger Sergeant Neville took up the trail and located the wounded bandit out in the brush, deserted by his two buddies at his own express orders. Sam died the next day and, according to Verse No. 162 of the mournful ditty that they sing to guitar music about him, his Judas — Jim Murphy — less than a year later "went out and hanged himself," so great was his remorse — and his fear that Frank Jackson would come back and get him.

Around Waco the Lindsay Brothers were bad cattle-thieves and one of them was strung up in a gulch not far from present-day Cameron Park in Waco, along the Brazos course, by the Vigilantes, who shot the other brother. They call it Lindsay Hollow to this day. King Fisher, whom Zane Grey put into his western novels, was a Waco "bad man" at one time and Tehuacana Bill Posey was another desperado of Six-Shooter Junction that the Vigilantes waited on . . . all seeking for the gold they did not earn.

Of gold . . . they still search with their locator-machines for gold on the Waco trail about six miles above the Falls of the Brazos for a large shipment that they claim the Mexicans buried when attacked by the Indians. There are many fabulous tales of the gambling-halls of Waco, Calvert, Hearne and other River-towns of the Brazos in those latter days of the past century. In Reconstruction times, the Yankee State Constabulary forces under Governor Davis' regime were supposed to be headquartered at Waco to keep the peace . . . but it was principally to collect graft. They were in league with every bandit gang.

A popular story of 1872, while this gang of high-binders were supposed to be enforcing the law, is told concerning Hoffman, one of the Carpetbagger leaders of State politics. He was being shaved in a barber's chair in Waco fronting on the famous Square. A man he had wronged came into the shop, removed the towel from the faces of several men until he came to Hoffman and then shot him dead before he could get to his feet. The man escaped on a fast horse over the bridge and not a soul stirred to pursue him. Nor could anyone be found to identify him.

Another of the easy-gold ventures along the Brazos was the famed Waco red-light district that went full blast until World War I and the army camp closed it down.

When Waco shaped up and made a town in the 1880's there was a question as to what should happen to the ladies of easy virtue, practising the world's oldest profession. Waco became the only town in Texas and second only to Omaha in the United States to license houses of prostitution under official regulation.

The lines were tightly drawn and the habitues of "The District" were supposed to stay strictly within it . . . but that did not keep the townspeople from slipping down to see them. A prominent killing brought many names into the newspaper, *The Waco Day.*

Hattie Tyree, it seemed, with her sister, Lily Murphy, were doing very well until Eva Clinton came along and took Lily's boy-friend. That Saturday midnight, when the parlors were filled with music, laughter, drink and leading citizens, there incognito — or so they hoped — Lily and Eva staged a knock-down-drag-out-fight right among the customers.

Eva was quick and mean with a knife and Lily died on Monday from the stabbing she got. Eva's hearing on a writ of habeas corpus application brought many prominent names to the embarrassing light of day. Five of Waco's leading lawyers represented Eva. One of the star witnesses, a man of great prominence in the town, got the newspaper to say:

The Day is reliably informed that ———— was in the parlor at Hattie Tyree's to look after a friend who had gotten deeply in his cups with a large sum of money on his person. It is a misfortune . . . but evidently not his fault.

Incidentally, Eva was acquitted on the grounds of self-defense. Even this widely-heralded exposé of vice did not shake the city fathers in their determination to keep the reservation licensed. For twenty-seven years, Mollie Adams in her high two-story house on Jefferson Avenue, ruled as "Queen of the Red Light District" in Six-Shooter Junction. It took a War to close it up. Now it is a Negro shanty-town.

Calvert and Old Sterling farther down the Brazos toward the Gulf and east of the Falls were gay old towns when Fort Worth was an Army post and Dallas a half-dozen log huts. Calvert boasted 4,000 people in those days and even the Carpetbaggers stayed out. The Negroes warned them: "When dem bad mens in Calvert stomps dey foot, dey guns jumps in dey hands!"

The town had eighteen saloons at one time and hauled in the whiskey from Kentucky by ox-trains. Gambling and saloons were wide open and the furnishings in the houses of the town rivalled New York. It was the hub of activities in the 1870's. Belle Starr operated a livery stable and Sam Bass was a frequent visitor.

Not all of the people were notorious who lived there, however, for Belvedere Brooks, founder of the Bell Telephone system, was a telegraph operator in the old days and the prominent Texas families — Mistrot, Sanger, Padgitt, Adoue and Littlefield — stemmed from there.

But, one day in 1873 they took a sick man off the train . . .

He had the Yellow Fever and from that day the cemetery grew and the town dwindled. Those who did not die ran away. When the railroad missed it, then its doom was sealed. But when it was going its greatest guns, it was one of the two towns where a road-show stopped — Galveston and Calvert. Though far from the sea, it furnished the Navy three Admirals of World War II — Spencer Lewis, Ernest M. Pace and Commodore Robertson.

Among Brazos folk who came to death by violence, William Cowler Brann, "Brann the Iconoclast," was one.

Illinois-born in 1855, he wandered about a great deal until he finally settled in Austin in 1891 to start his *Brann's Iconoclast*. He wielded a pen that dripped vitriol and his goal was to uncover hypocrisy and break idols. He fought the Baptist leaders' hierarchy bitterly and unloosed his guns on the authorities of Baylor University. No head was too proud nor station too high to awe his attack. He pilloried Governor Charles E. Culberson, later a distinguished United States Senator from Texas, castigated *The Dallas News* and did not hesitate to name any name or say anything he cared to about anyone.

His *Iconoclast* printed in Waco reached a circulation of 90,000 and every issue was sold as it hit the streets. He was a satirist of first rank and had a beautiful command of the written word. In one of his articles, printed in a two-volume collection, he wrote:

In the name of all the gods, which is the fouler crime, the greater "social evil": for a woman to deliberately barter her person for gold and lands, for gew-gaws, social position and a preferred pew in a fashionable church — even though the sale

[265]

be in accordance with law, have the benediction of a stupid priest and the sanction of a corrupt and canting world — or in defiance of custom and forgetful of cold precept, to cast the priceless pearl of a woman's honor upon the altar of illicit love?

He would refer to some adversary's mother as likely "off some place behind the barn scratching her ear with her left hind foot" and he did not care about whom he said it. Horse-whipped by Judge John B. Scarborough for some of his attacks on the Judge's womenfolk who taught at Baylor, he was nearly lynched by Baylor students in order to secure a retraction on another accusation that he made. He was the direct cause of the famed Gerald-Harris feud in 1897 which resulted in the killing of J. W. Harris and his brother, W. A. Harris, by Judge G. B. Gerald over a letter criticizing Brann.

In one election Brann attacked Tom E. Davis, son of a famous Waco pioneer lawyer, and on April 1, 1898, the two of them shot it out on the street in Waco and they both died of the wounds they received. It was the ending of a turbulent career which made Brann rich, but he never lived to enjoy the gold that he earned in this easy manner with his scurrilous pen.

When the Ranger boom hit and oil set the Brazos-land wild in the neighborhood of the Cross Timbers, there was a mad scramble for quick-money. The whirr of the gambling-wheels, music of the dance-halls, barking of the six-gun... the old West came to life in 1919 in the Brazos oil-belt region.

Bob Quantrell, gambler and killer, was known as "The King of Ranger." The law-abiding people prevailed upon Byron Parrish to come up out of the sheep and goat country around Mason with his big hat and fancy boots, his silver-mounted pistols and his diamond-studded holsters and be Chief of Police of the new oil town.

He hired as his assistant, Gene Reynolds, a young World War I Lieutenant of Infantry, 22, who was not afraid of either end of a six-gun; and they started in to clean up the town. It came to a quick show-down between Quantrell and Parrish and the new Chief pistol-whipped the gambler with his own gun and ran him out of town between suns. But . . . it went to Parrish's head and he was hard to live with in his success. He started dictating to the City Fathers.

Thereupon, they hired young Reynolds to stand up to Parrish and get rid of the ex-Chief. He did and ran his ex-boss out of town, fancy pistols and all.

The oil boom excitement all along the Brazos let down the bars for a time to lawlessness and crime. Vice throve in the busy, get-rich-quick days when everyone was grabbing for leases and no one wanted to take time to play "cops" to the many "robbers" who were there to share in the excitement. The bootleggers of whiskey and oil throve while the fancy women and crooked gamblers moved in overnight into hastily-thrown up shacks. It lasted for a season and then the Rangers moved in and cleaned it up.

Even after the oil industry settled down to normal production, there were certain silk-stocking grafters who wished to exploit the supply, regulate the price and rob the rich preserves for their own gain. With the whole picture decidedly hay-wire, in April 1831, when the East Texas Field was roaring in 160,000 barrels of crude oil a day and the price was down to 21c a barrel, the Texas Railroad Commission adopted a curbing plan of proration.

There was rebellion in the ranks of the greedy. "Infringement of our rights," they shouted, and it took the state militia and martial law to enforce the edict of the Commission until the Legislature could meet and set up laws to curb the waste. For twenty days not a drill-stem moved and not a barrel of oil came to the surface.

Then, when they had it flowing again under restrictions, according to the new law, the men devoted to easy-money began seeking to devise ways to beat the proration. Dummy derricks, by-passing, open check-valves, bribed inspectors, corruption in high places, violence and intimidation of officials, hidden lines, bootlegging by night of gasoline, evasion of taxes, destruction of records, diverting oil from one well to another and faked wells were some of the devices. Only when the Federal Government threatened to step in did enforcement become a reality and then it was more honored in the breach than in the observance.

Some charges were filed, indictments returned and a few trials had. A smudge of "hot-oil" appeared on several proud and ancient escutcheons in high places among Texas' foremost families, but very few ate cowpeas and pot-licker in prison for their violations of the law. The chapter on Hot Oil, however, ranks with the stage-coach robberies and the Sam Bass days . . . the difference being that the men of the black mask took a pay-roll or a few watches and the Hot Oil bandits made hundreds of thousands. Its day is not entirely past in the valley of the Brazos. . . .

The old River has its modern bandits . . . and one who stands out pre-eminent was Clyde Barrow. He was once a student at Waco High School. During that time he was arrested and convicted of auto theft, which was his first proven felony. Thereupon, he started his career of crime that was to take him to the top as "Public Enemy No. 1." He would come and go over the country but return to the banks of the middle Brazos, for there he reckoned was home.

In 1932 in the old limestone court-house at Waco he heard the first sentence that sent him to the penitentiary. But they gave him "a second chance" — to commit crime — and he came from "The Walls" at Huntsville to stick up a Hillsboro merchant, John Bucher. When the poor man demurred Clyde burned him down. After that it was open-warfare between Clyde Barrow and the public. Bonnie Parker out of the West Dallas slums joined him as his "gun-moll."

These two gangsters, with guns blazing from Iowa to the

Gulf, riding in stolen cars, blasting peace-officers when they attempted to arrest them, spread their reign of terror far and wide. On one occasion Clyde and Bonnie staged a delivery down at the Eastham State Prison Farm to release one of Clyde's pals who was working in the cotton-patch under guard. They released five in all and when a guard flickered an eyelid, he . . . never did again. But they neglected or overlooked freeing Bonnie's lawfully-wedded husband who was doing time down at Eastham.

Over in Austin, Lee Simmons of the Prison Board and the Governor of Texas went into a huddle. When they came out they had decided that Captain Frank Hamer, formerly of the Texas Rangers, was the man to get the rioting pair. Came an Easter Sunday when most Texas folk were in the kirk. A farmer near Grapevine, between Dallas and Fort Worth, saw a car in his lane. A few minutes later two shots rang out and two State Highway Patrolmen were dead in pools of their own blood when the farmer got there. But there was a whiskey-bottle . . . and it had Clyde's finger-prints on it.

Hamer took up the hot trail. He was just behind Clyde and Bonnie when a Commerce, Oklahoma, constable got a bullet for his services in helping Clyde's black sedan out of a chug-hole. It was time for them to hole-up, Hamer decided . . . too hot . . . where would it be safe?

Arcadia, Louisiana, was where the relatives of one of the men they had sprung from Eastham lived. Why not try there? The trap was set.

Nine o'clock in the morning and a black car came down the road at a lively clip. Hamer stepped out of a ditch and held up his hand. Clyde yanked at the rifle in his lap and the men in the ambush let them have it. There were over fifty bullets in Clyde and the cigar-smoking Bonnie. Neither ever got a gun in action, although they had them in their laps.

"We got the job done," Hamer reported to Austin headquarters and hung up the phone.

Chapter XIV

DOGWOOD BLOSSOMS AND POLITICS

IN THE SPRING OF THE YEAR in the east Texas valley of the Brazos, a lovely tree flings out white banners in the greenwood. Among the pines and oaks a snowy whiteness shines through.

The dogwood is in bloom.

Along the River of The Arms of God there is a legend that the Spaniards started . . . on the day of the Crucifixion at the place called in the Hebrew tongue "The Place of the Skull," the tears of the women who tarried near the Cross watered a tiny tree on which white blossoms grew. From that day each took on the stigmata of the blood by having a tinge of brownish-red on each petal of the cross-like flower. Every year in the spring at the time of Good Friday the same flower blooms. Some of the devout believe that the True Cross was made of dogwood.

"No smart politician will announce for public office until the dogwood blooms in the spring!" This is an adage in the Brazos valley and has been for many a year.

They have always taken their politics seriously in the Brazos-land. In many of its centrally-located towns and cities the parties and politicians have held their conventions and parleys. Oratory of the hustings has been heard on the course of the River, often and loud.

It is a one-party constituency. Unless you are a Democrat in the environs of the Brazos you are viewed with some suspicion or distinction, depending upon the leanings of the

viewer. Now and then a Brazonian will "stay out of the primaries," or "go fishing on election day" because he can not
stomach the man or issue that the Democrats support. It is
far more likely, however, that the voice that speaks out will
claim: "I've never scratched a Democratic ticket but I've
voted her straight every single time!"

Only once since the Civil War has Texas voted for a Republican President — Herbert Hoover over Al Smith in 1928
— and then there was a religious issue combined with the
political. The nomination by the Democratic Party in the
July and August primaries is tantamount to election in the
November General Election. But there are new-comers, free-
thinkers, more and more independence; and at each election,
the hope springs eternal in Republican breasts that they
may raise an issue, a prejudice or offer a candidate who
will swing the top-heavy majority aside and make at least a
close election between the two parties. It will be news when
the Brazos goes Republican again.

But back to the dogwood blooms. . . .

Come spring and the green buds burgeon out in the valley
of the River. A small town editor walks down to the post
office and picks up his mail, stops at the drug-store for his
morning cup of coffee with a few old cronies. He ambles on
down to the newspaper office on a side street just off the
Square. He takes a deep breath of the Brazos ozone and
wanders over to his ancient, dusty typewriter. Inserting a
roll of copy-paper in the machine he bites off a wad of Thick
Tinsley and begins.

There is talk that State Senator Lafe Emery will take out after
Congressman J. Whoopen Holler in the July primary. That
means that State Legislator Sam Houston Busby will be a candidate for Senator and Sam's seat is being eyed by County Attorney Ed Lamar, who would like a ticket to Austin. Things are
picking up in politics and by the time the tar begins to run in
the dog-days we will see the fur flying. The Old Settlers' Reunion

at Brazos Park on July 4th will find a large crop of candidates shaking hands, kissing babies and willing to make the sacrifice of holding public office.

It may be out of the whole-cloth and entirely in the editor's own imagination, but it will act as encouragement and if one or two others add their nods to his, local politicians will begin "seriously considering answering the demands of the people that I offer for public office."

From the days of old Washington-on-the-Brazos and San Felipe, the pot of politics has stewed, simmered and boiled with conventions and conferences, party pow-wows and huddles. Waco, Richmond, Lubbock and Marlin have been popular rendezvous points for the politicos.

Of the politics of the Brazos Indians we know little. They usually settled theirs by the strength and might of the warrior who could meet and beat all opposition. The Caddos had a political Confederation of sorts and the Comanches had their law-making bodies who debated policy and program in the canyons of the Brazos Forks. The Red Man was an orator and oratory is the bond-sister of politics.

With the Spaniard there was little of politics in his decisions in the affairs of the Brazos-land. The Viceroy in Mexico City got his orders from his King and gave them to his Governor. The soldiers saw that they were carried out. It was not until the free Indian blood began to show in the Mexican strain that ideas of Liberty began to be born south of the Rio Grande. This expressed itself for a time until Santa Anna converted his republic into a dictatorship and then his Anglo-Saxon *colonistas* up on the Brazos began to ask ... *why should we not help to make the laws that govern us? On what meat hath this imperious Caesar fed that he tells us what we can not do?*

Against the domination of *El Presidente* from Mexico City and the *alcalde* and the *ayuntamiento* locally, the settler along the River began to call his fellows into Consultations and conferences, to pass resolutions and protests. "Liberty under the Law" came to be the watch-word of the folk in the Brazos-land and they set about doing something about it.

Despite all that Stephen F. Austin could do to caution rational thought, within three years after his grants had been approved down on the Zocalo in the Mexican capital, Hayden Edwards was drumming for Freedom on the Brazos and declaring "The Republic of Fredonia." True, he did not last long, for his effort was early aborted, but he did express it. When slavery was forbidden in Texas in 1829, when further Anglo-American immigration was banned in 1830, when custom-houses were set up and a high tariff placed on goods, the fires were lighted along the settled banks.

By 1832 Austin had his hands full holding back his hotspurs. In July he hurried back to San Felipe from the meeting of the Legislature at Saltillo to meet Colonel Mexia with four hundred troops of Santa Anna in five vessels that entered the mouth of the Brazos and discharged at Brazoria on July 17. There was a big *fiesta* on the 25th and Captain F. W. Johnson paraded his "Santa Anna Volunteers," who had led the attack on the Spanish Royalist garrison at Anahuac. There was much speechmaking and Austin said:

I have not words to express my grateful feelings and unfeigned thanks for the kind welcome with which you have honored my return to the colony. . . . My leading motto has been and is 'Fidelity to the Constitution of our adopted country.' . . . The people have asserted their rights under the banner of that distinguished patriot and leader, General Antonio Lopez de Santa Anna. . . . You have resorted to arms . . . but have not for one moment lost sight of your duty as Mexican citizens, but have defended the true dignity of the national flag. . . .

There was a salute of twelve guns, the troops paraded and Lieutenant Colonel Ugartechea, who commanded the fort at Velasco, replied with a speech commending Austin. *Viva la federación y la constitución Mejicana!*

[273]

At the big banquet that night the Mexican commander was most cordial:

May the Supreme Being preserve the life of. Colonel Austin to the citizens of Texas twenty years and longer, so that they may have the benefit of his exertions to separate Texas from Coahuila and form it into a state of the great Mexican Confederation as the only means of securing prosperity and the true interests of the Mexican Republic!

These sentiments were approved by the *jefes* down in Mexico for they had been hearing disquieting rumors of assemblies, of grumbling at the way land titles were being dispensed to rich and powerful Mexicans for speculating in Brazos real estate, of the use of English to the exclusion of Spanish, of the spread of Protestantism and of the organization of local militia. Then, one day Austin came with the petitions of his colonists on these very subjects. . . .

They kept him cooling his heels until he wrote a letter home expressing himself strongly. When they read his mail, they put him in jail and kept him there for fifteen months before they let him out. By then he was thoroughly disillusioned, broken in health and spirit. When he got back to the Brazos, he said:

"War is Texas' only recourse!"

Then was when politics took over and the San Felipe Provisional Convention convened on November 3, 1835, sending a delegation to Washington, D. C., to ask for help and laying plans for a revolution.

For a time bullets and not ballots spoke in the land of the River and when it was over there was a republic to be set up, officers to be elected and laws to be made. Politics' banners were flying on the Brazos.

What should be done with Santa Anna? Who should command the new Texas army — Mirabeau Lamar or Felix Huston? Who is to be President?

In September after San Jacinto in April, old Sam Houston settled that by winning handily over Stephen Austin and Henry Smith. The new government met at Columbia and the sickly, ailing Austin was named Secretary of State. But by December 27th he was dead and in his grave at Peach Point Plantation. Thus passed from the scene the man who had carried out his father's and his own vision and borned Texas out of the wilderness of the Brazos valley.

By 1837 they had a Land Office set up and appeals went out for immigration from Europe and the United States. In nine years the population trebled. And a political feud was in the making. Two such dynamic opposites as Lamar and Houston could not exist in peace side by side.

Lamar wanted to exterminate the Indians, Houston liked them. Lamar wanted to attach New Mexico, Houston thought it might not be bad to take Old Mexico instead. He advised getting stronger before jumping anyone. Woll's invasion from south of the Rio Grande and the reprisal Mier Expedition against Mexico kept the sore open and bleeding. The Texas Navy acted more like pirates in Mexican waters than sailormen of the new Republic.

The laws were hard . . . in 1839 the Congress said by statute that if anyone stole a horse, mare, ass, mule, gelding, foal or filly, he would get the death penalty and lynching-by-law became the vogue. Two rustlers were hanged in the Brazos valley while two thousand spectators looked on and the account in the paper says:

They were sentenced to death rather than to submit them to the hardships of another month or two in jail in this bad Texas winter weather.

Sam Houston took the oath as President for the second time in 1841, and in 1844 Anson Jones beat out Ed Burleson. But Texas was about through "playing nation." Financially broke, militarily weak, unable to maintain an army and navy, currency worthless, England and France both

[275]

had begun flirting with the new Republic to accept a protectorate. Mexico was afraid of this and the United States grew apprehensive.

Most Texans wanted annexation to the United States. To the latter it was not too attractive. Would Texas come in as a slave state? What of her public lands? Who got them? What about her debts? Who would patrol her Mexican borders and fight her Indian wars?

These issues were carried into the political campaign in the States in 1844 when the Whigs and the Democrats fought it out at the polls. On December 29, 1845, after much discussion back and forth, Texas hauled down her flag of the lone star and became the twenty-eighth state of the American union.

The politics in the Brazos-land were thick and hot in those days as the various advocates tried to carry their several points. The location of the state capital had been a white-hot controversy. Lamar had moved it to Austin on the Colorado and how Sam Houston loathed the location so far from the coast! Too, he had a secret ambition that it be located down on Buffalo Bayou . . . perhaps, at the city named for him. At any rate he offered to bet that they would yet give Austin back to the buffalo and Indian and that he would live to see it. In January 1840 he tried to move it to the Falls of the Brazos but the bill failed of passage in the Congress.

It was at Austin that the first Governor, J. Pinkney Henderson, took over the new state government. For the next six years there were many political fights and repercussions until Secession surmounted them all. While they were trying to move things about . . . three lower Brazos Congressmen legged for moving the Supreme Court from Washington-on-the-Brazos to Galveston. After the Joneses — J. B. Jones of Galveston, W. E. Jones of Brazoria, Simon L. Jones of San Patricio — had made their stormy speeches for, the opposition boomed out:

Now, Mr. Speaker, where is Galveston? Sir, it is a little sandy spot set away out on the Gulf of Mexico where the pelican lays her eggs and the sea-gull screams, once the stamping-ground of Lafitte and his pirates and now inhabited by the worst set of damned rascals that my two blue eyes have ever gazed upon!

Until 1850 men and not issues were the themes of Texas and Brazos politics, but in 1856 The Know-Nothing Party carried Texas and declared against all immigration — "America for Americans!" — and they boosted Houston for Governor. He quit the Senate of the United States to run and was elected.

Things were in a turmoil with Secession looming. In February of 1860 they got a group together not far from the Brazos banks and "The Knights of the Golden Circle" was formed. They had an idea of forming a union of the slave States of the South, Mexico, the islands of the Caribbean, and some of the Central American republics.

George Bickley, their chief leader, claimed that he was working with Benito Juarez in Mexico and had the Cherokee Grays from Rusk County mobilized down at Brownsville to "invade" Mexico. Governor Houston ordered them to disband, for he had ideas of his own about this secession business. The Knights of the Iron Hand folded up without any further activities.

Back in the United States Senate, Houston had the chagrin of having the Texas Legislature declare his seat vacant. Texas was for Secession and its counties had so voted. Houston was against it, refused to take the oath of allegiance to the Confederacy and retired to Huntsville to die when Texas left the union.

But he was a Texan and when Galveston was captured by Yankee gun-boats and General J. Bankhead Magruder came down from Richmond to accomplish the delivery of the Island and drive off the enemy, old Sam sent him a congratulatory message:

[277]

Sir, you have breathed a new life into everything, have introduced a new era into Texas by driving a ruthless enemy from our soil. It gives me great pleasure to mingle my congratulations with the many you have received.

Politics took a holiday while the men of the Brazos-land fought with Hood and Terry in Virginia and Kentucky, but when they came marching home they found a mess of political brew confronting them that was to plague the pleasant land for the better part of the next ten years.

Yankee Carpetbaggers moved in to handle the military government and to exploit the Negroes. Lincoln was dead by the bullet of a crazed assassin and the decent people of the North were too busy with the rehabilitation of their own fortunes to care. Let the South pay . . .

They were bitter years for the folk of the Brazos-land, as the white man stood aside at polls, disenfranchised and saw the Negro cast the only vote that was counted. Property rights were snatched from these people who had won them the hard way or inherited them from their pioneer fathers.

Then, in 1873, a Brazos son was named as the Governor of Texas against the renegade Edward J. Davis, the Republican incumbent. Richard Coke of Waco was Governor and when Davis appealed to President U. S. Grant to help him hold his seat, he was refused. Once again the rule of the Brazos citizen was restored and he began the long climb back to normal times.

The new Constitution of Texas was written in 1876 and the finances of the State were put on a sound basis. A great agricultural and mechanical college was set up on the Brazos banks. The Ku Klux Klan that had elected Coke over Davis began to exercise selfish tyranny and the Texas people cast it forth. It disappeared from politics not to show itself again until the late 1920's.

In 1878 the Populist Party roared to the fore as Governor L. S. Ross sought to curb the trusts and monopolies that had grown up under Yankee rule. The new capital was building on the banks of the Colorado with Texas red granite walls that were purchased with many acres of west Texas land. The great of Texas came to dedicate it. Big Foot Wallace was the toastmaster, the heroes of Texas' wars were the honor guests as Terry's Rangers, Hood's Texas Brigade and Houston's Army of the San Jacinto mingled in the new capital and ate barbecue.

From down on the lower Brazos came a native son to hold the office of Governor. They had feared that the huge James Stephen Hogg would incline to be a demogague in politics, but he won the name of "Hogg the Patriot" and he set forth to curb the monopolies. It was he who fathered the Texas Railroad Commission that would curb the grabbers of privilege and encourage the normal development of transportation, industrial enterprises, and natural resources for the century ahead.

It took a bitter fight to elect Jim Hogg. George W. Clark of Waco, another Brazonian, waged him a contest that was close and hard-fought. There were others as time passed . . . once the Governor, Charlie Culberson called a meeting of the Legislature in 1895 and tossed in the matter of whether Jim Corbett and Bob Fitzsimmons should prize-fight in Dallas. Then, there was the greatest of political issues . . . prohibition.

For forty years and more that question — shall liquor be sold in the free land of the Brazos? — racked and tore public opinion and was asked of any man who aspired to hold public office. It was *the* politics of Texas for four troublous decades.

Colonel E. L. Doheny of Paris fathered local option, whereby many saloons were closed in dry territory. The Prohibition Party, The Woman's Christian Temperance Union, The Anti-Saloon League and the clergy were the war-element of the "Dry" or "Pro" advocates on down until 1919.

[279]

For the "Wets" or "Antis", the Texas Brewers Association, The Retail Liquor Dealers Association, The Citizens Forward Movement and a Negro organization, Rescue Association of the United States and Africa, of which Rev. J. L. "Sin-Killer" Griffin was the head, fought for the retention of liquor.

The hosts of the "Wets" heralded the names of Jake Wolters, O. B. Colquitt, R. V. Davidson, Nelson Phillips, Charles K. Bell, H. B. Terrell, John N. Garner and James E. Ferguson. Aligned against them were Morris Sheppard, Sterling P. Strong, William Poindexter, Cone Johnson, Thomas B. Love, Thomas H. Ball, Cullen F. Thomas, J. H. Gambrell, William E. Hawkins, W. F. Ramsey and Pat M. Neff. These were the names of the leaders of political thought in the valley of the Brazos as the early quarter of the century passed.

There were debates and elections, meetings and assemblies called on the Liquor Question. In 1911 a noted convocation at Waco was held to put over the Dry Amendment to the Constitution that the Legislature had submitted to the people's vote. It had started back in 1887 when Roger Q. Mills of Corsicana and Dr. B. H. Carroll of Waco met on July 6 at Padgitt's Park in Waco and first debated such an amendment to the Constitution. Governor L. S. Ross's administration had submitted the amendment and prohibition was defeated by 100,000 votes at the polls.

In that 1887 campaign the Brazos midlands were the storm-center for the fight on Prohibition. George Clark was for the Anti-prohibitionists as the chairman and Dr. Carroll, Dr. R. C. Burleson and Dr. J. B. Cranfill, sturdy Baptist roundsmen, headed up the Drys. After many debates and speech-makings, the final rally was attended by 7,000 people at Waco. The main speakers orated for one and one-half hours with one half-hour for rebuttal. There was no loud-speaker equipment then save the vocal cords of the orators, but free sandwiches and barrels of ice water were provided.

And so it went from the 1880's on down to 1917 when World War I decided the question as a "war-measure." Prohibition became the law of the land, followed by much more argument, infringement, attempts at enforcement, boot-legging and finally by repeal. Today it has ceased to be a political issue and rarely enters a local campaign in all the length of the valley. Old politicos marvel at its utter disappearance.

There were plenty of other political footballs to be kicked around in the Riverland throughout the years besides Prohibition. Jim Hogg waved the flag of Railroad Scandals in 1890 and declared war on "special interests" wherever he could discover them in Texas. The Grange leaders sprang to the aid of the farmers about the same time and in 1896 rallied their strength for the Populist Party, but inside of four years their sun had risen, shone and waned. Potent it was in the valley, however, while it lasted.

The farmers were looking for allies. They were uneasy and worried about economic conditions and the politics of their own situation. The railroads seemed to be getting all the governmental favors, the price of all farm-products was exceedingly low and an "Agrarian Crusade" appealed to the men of the Brazos soil.

Money was terribly scarce — tariff needed adjusting — Negro problem was worrisome. The old Greenback Party held out its promise but did not live long enough to fulfill it. By 1890 it was a thing of the past. Then in the decade of the '90's The Farmers Alliance and The People's Party, along with Populism, swept the Brazos valley. The people who farmed did not know which way to turn. Grange . . . Greenbacks . . . Alliance . . . Populists?

In 1896 the Democrats gobbled up all the best of the lures that each movement offered and the people voted their ticket again. The Grange had mustered 45,000 members of whom 6,000 were women and many lived in the environs

[281]

of the River . . . it had pounded for equal freight rates . . . grabbed at the Railroad Commission as a popular issue . . . gave its support to Hogg in a vain attempt at survival.

Caught in this whirlpool of agrarian reform, the farmer listened while "The Farmers Party" fought the farm-produce tax . . . "to set the smoke-house and the corn-crib free" . . . against usurious rates of interest . . . for deep water harbors. It fell of its own weight.

The Grange met at Bryan and the Greenbacks at Waco in the same year, each of them pounding on the table for the farmer . . . the remonetization of silver . . . repeal of the National Bank Law . . . tariff for revenue only . . . and deepening of Galveston harbor. The Brazos farmer was bewildered.

Finance had always bothered the folk on the banks of the River. They were so far from Wall Street and Washington that they did not know how to figure out their own monetary salvation. Back in November 1835, Gail Borden notified the Provisional Government that the treasury balance was $58.30 and R. R. Royal, President of the Council, donated $26.00. While he was President Mirabeau B. Lamar spent four million dollars, while Sam Houston pointed with pride to the fact that in his second term he only spent a half-million dollars in three years.

The Indians cost Lamar two and a half-million while they cost Sam one hundred thousand. By Annexation, Texas was twelve millions in debt. That was a tremendous sum, unless one reasons that in the decade of the 1940's it cost the State of Texas more to operate than in the previous 103 years as a Republic and as a State in the union.

At first, the Republic of Texas used Mississippi paper money without a financial system of its own. On April 1, 1835 the Coahuila-Texas Legislature had chartered a banking institution for the Department of the Brazos with a capital of $1,000,000 to be secured by mortgages on real estate.

Samuel W. Mims was authorized to set it going. It was equipped with directors, all the attributes of a bank and a loan rate of 8% when loans were not over six months and 10% for a longer time.

The revolution and setting up of the Republic was a severe tax on financial arrangements in the Brazos-land. There was little taxable property and few benefits that the tax-payer could get. From Annexation to the Civil War, the Republic and State finances were nebular and vague. The War plunged them into deeper gloom.

Plantations with their slaves and cotton were some of the few tangible assets the Brazonian could muster and the Civil War washed them out completely. Confederate securities did not even make good wall paper after a time. Northern and Eastern capital, with that from across the seas, vanished overnight. Cotton was at a stand-still and until the trails opened and the herds became realities on the cattle-drives, there was no hard money in the River's valley. It can be safely said that the Longhorn put the man of the Brazos on his feet.

Politics have always looked in the newspaper before venturing an opinion . . . People read the news, scan the editorials and then make up their minds. In many cases they follow the pabulum of the politician as it is reflected from his reported speech, or adopt the varied views of the editor. Sometimes they find out how the editor goes and vote the opposite way.

There were many newspapers that shaped public opinion in the early days. Back in 1813, José Alvarez de Toledo published *El Mejicano* at Nacogdoches and circulated it widely in the Brazos settlements. In 1819 Dr. James Long had his *Texas Republican* going strong, but when the Mexicans finally liquidated him and his dream of empire, a law was passed to require an oath of future colonists that "they would not disturb the peace by publishing or reading any seditious newspapers."

In 1829 Godwin Brown Cotton published a weekly *Gazette* on the Brazos and in 1833 *The Constitutional Advocate* was run off the hand-presses at San Felipe by D. W. Anthony. But that was a dismal year . . . the Brazos overflowed and when the waters subsided the cholera plague struck. Crop-loss and disease took their toll and folk of the River country lived on jerked beef that was hauled in until the 1834 crop was made. Many deaths were reported and the newspaper was among them.

In 1835 *The Telegraph and Texas Register* was the official press organization of the Provisional Government at San Felipe and so continued for the Republic and State for many years to come. So hard up, however, was the early Republic for a voice that the first copy of the Texas Constitution, adopted on March 17, 1836, had to await publication until H. S. Kimble, the secretary of the convention, could take it to Nashville and have it published in one of the papers there. Republished in the Cincinnati papers, it was not until August 2 that *The Telegraph* got set up to where it could print it. Then it appeared in Texas for the first time.

Where was the birthplace of Texas politics as they exist today? On the Brazos at Brazoria at the home of Benjamin Freeman in 1835. He had a meeting of some friends of Texas Freedom at his house and over old wine, that he was noted for in that section, they discussed their grievances against the Mexican dictates.

Somebody outlined them and they were written down . . . high duties . . . separate statehood . . . more representation in making the laws . . . the custom-house at Anahuac . . . the Deputy-Collector's tactics at Brazoria . . .

They were bold and when they were sent to Mexico caused furious resentment there. That little round-table discussion was to become the basis for a new government. Andrew Briscoe's bargeful of stuff was refused landing by the Mexican duty-official because he would not pay the high import duty and Barrett Travis seized the custom-house. When they arrested Travis the San Felipe Convention met and started resoluting:

We, the good people of Texas, solemnly declare, first, that they have taken up arms in defense of their rights and liberties which are threatened by . . . military despots.

At the blacksmith shop at Washington, four days before the Alamo fell they were saying to the world:

We, therefore the delegates, with plenary power, of the people of Texas . . . appealing to a candid world . . . declare that our political connection with the Mexican nation has forever ended . . . and that the people of Texas do now constitute a free, sovereign and independent republic . . . We fearlessly and confidently submit the issue to the decision of The Supreme Arbiter of the destinies of nations.

Wherever Sam Houston went he created politics. His story is one of the most varied and diversified of any man to enter American public life. Tried once by the House of Representatives for cane-whipping a Congressman, when he was in Washington advocating some reforms and relief for his Cherokee Indian friends, he served his adopted State of Tennessee as Governor and enjoyed a turbulent period of public life before ever coming to Texas.

Wherever he went he was drawn into controversy and elections. When he was running against David Burnet, with whom he had clashed in the days of "The Runaway Scrape" he charged:

You prate, sir, about the faults of other men, while the blot of foul, unmitigated treason rests upon you. You political brawler and canting hypocrite, whom the waters of Jordan could never cleanse from your political and moral leprosy!

He beat Burnet for President of the Republic. Always Sam played the rough, rugged soldier type to Mirabeau B. Lamar's effete, classical side. Lamar had been a politician back in Georgia and a strong advocate of Thomas Jefferson's principles. Beaten for Congress in Georgia, he tried his luck next in Texas and wound up as the first Vice-President that the Texas Republic had. Since Houston could not succeed himself under the Constitution it looked as if Lamar would easily step into the office.

But Houston did not propose to let him get by with it. He lined up the press, such as it was, against Lamar and stumped the Brazos valley against him. But luck seemed to be with the Georgian in this new land, for one of his opponents, Peter W. Grayson, drowned himself in the Gulf and James Collingsworth shot himself before election day, leaving the field uncontested for Lamar.

Houston went off and got drunk and Lamar went to the high office where he began courting England, France, Belgium and Holland to send ambassadors to the new Texas nation. He did several things — launched the University of Texas idea, planned a foreign conquest of Mexico and New Mexico, fought the Indians assiduously and bogged Texas down in debt unmercifully.

Although Samuel Bangs went to Galveston and founded a pro-Lamar paper, called *The Daily Galvestonian,* by next election the people had enough of the dreamer-poet and sent Sam Houston back for his second term. Things were in a mess . . . the "red-back" currency was worthless, Texas credit was a farce, Mexico was threatening re-invasion, the United States was strangely aloof . . .

Houston began by setting-up to England. What about a British protectorate? He let wind of it get to Tyler's Secretary of State in 1844 — John C. Calhoun — and evoked this utterance from the South Carolinian:

To the South the present issue is a question of absolute self-preservation; so much so that it were infinitely better for us to abandon the Union than to give up Texas to become a colony of Great Britain.

[286]

Texas became a political football in United States politics and in 1845 on the issue of Texas Annexation, James K. Polk and George M. Dallas were swept into office. Houston's ruse had won. He had no idea of playing with England, but it was smart trading and he had gotten into the Union, saved Texas' public lands for her own, retained her tidewater rights, secured slavery and reserved the privilege of dividing into five states if she ever was so minded. Sam was a good horse-trader, Washington found out; and then it was necessary for Texas to have two Senators . . .

"I nominate Sam Houston!" the redoubtable Sam stood up and said.

Lamar fired back a hot protest and Sam replied in kind, "But I put over annexation and I'm entitled to it as a matter of right."

"That's not true," Lamar's partisan *Galveston News* rejoined. "He makes a merit of his guilt and turning to the people he has dishonored, as if in mockery of all human virtue, he demands the patriot's reward for the traitor's crime!"

But Sam got the job and in Washington he made the decision that Texas would be Democratic instead of Whig. He got Uncle Sam to pay $10,000,000 into the defunct treasury at Austin, saw to it that immigration picked up, the banks opened and had United States gun-boats scaring Mexican vessels of war off the Gulf-coast of Texas.

Slavery, however, was another thing . . . the plantation-owners of Sam's lower Brazos had to have slaves to work their cotton-fields and sugar-cane patches. Sam was "agin it." He voted with the Abolitionists in Congress and when he ran against Hardin R. Runnells for Governor on the Independent Democratic ticket, while he was still a United States Senator, making anti-slavery the issue, Texas beat Sam Houston by 10,000 votes!

As the 1860's dawned, Texas politics had several jolts.

Senator Tom Rusk committed suicide over at Nacogdoches grieving over his wife's death. Lamar was off to Nicaragua to be the minister of President Buchanan to that country. Sam Houston was having the devil's own time with the issue of Secession. He opposed the Brazos-folk on this question.

Newspapers pumping vigorously for Secession and Slavery, turned their guns on the potent force that spoke against them. They began to say that the old warrior was over-rated, that he had not fought at San Jacinto until his men forced him to and that he had been too long in politics. Then, the Texas legislature withdrew his credentials and declared his U. S. Senate seat vacant, and the great man of the Brazos bottoms was done . . . another prophet was not without honor save in his own country and among his own people. In retirement at Huntsville, he heard the guns of Civil War boom and he saw Texas men march off to battle while he tarried behind in self-imposed coventry for his beliefs.

But his heart was still Texan for when the 42nd Massachusetts Infantry was forced to escape from Galveston in small boats to the Yankee vessels on New Year's Day in 1863, Sam's cheers for a Texas victory were among the proudest.

The Civil War did not come closer to Texas politics than an occasional nibble . . . Napoleon III sent out feelers from Versailles to see if he could not chisel Texas away from the Confederacy under a French protectorate, but it bore as little fruit as did his Maximilian venture into Mexico.

And then, one day, the quiet man in gray, who had learned a lot of soldiering on the upper Forks of the Brazos, surrendered his sword to Grant and with it the fortunes of the Confederate States. The news hit Texas on April 21 — the anniversary of San Jacinto — and old General Kirby-Smith who commanded the forces west of the Mississippi issued a *pronunciamento*:

"Stand by your colors, maintain your discipline, protract the struggle! You possess the means to long resist the enemy!"

General Magruder harangued the 2nd Texas Cavalry at Galveston in the same vein, "Don't allow this bad news to cause you to despair for a moment about the final success."

But the fires of the Southern Confederacy were drawn and on June 19, General Gordon Grainger landed 1,800 Federal troops at Galveston and President Andrew Johnson named A. J. Hamilton Governor of Texas.

The two Texas Senators — David G. Burnet and O. M. Roberts — were turned back at Washington and refused seats. General Phil Sheridan in 1867 came to New Orleans, removed Governor Throckmorton as the head of the Texas State and named Pease in his place. Texas was now in a military district, one of the five that Sheridan set up in the South. The Carpetbaggers took over the courts of Texas.

Finally in 1874, the Brazos Governor from Waco, Richard C. Coke took over the State. Of him, historian James T. DeShields writes: "he was one of the most heroic figures who ever appeared on the stage of Texas politics." He later represented Texas in the United States Senate.

Two other Brazos men from Waco filled that chair of Governor. One was Sul Ross, the dashing young soldier, who "rescued" Cynthia Ann Parker and who opened up the Brazos prairies and plains to settlement. He also started the paying of Confederate pensions. He began the war on monopolies in Texas, presided at the birth of the Prohibition issue and enlarged Texas A & M, later to be its president.

The third Waco man to ascend to the Governorship was Pat M. Neff, noted churchman, educator, fraternalist and lawyer. He waged a fierce battle with former Senator Joseph Weldon Bailey for the nomination and for four years he filled the position. He abolished the State Pardon Board and screened executive leniency where pardons were concerned.

Neff was a strong Prohibitionist, as was Governor Ross, who as a State Senator introduced the first bill in the Texas Legislature to prohibit the liquor traffic. James Stephen

[289]

Hogg was Attorney General during the Ross administration and the anti-trust laws were passed at that time, a year before the Sherman Act in the Federal Congress.

Waco was always a focal point in early Texas politics and some of the great political contests have been staged there because of its central location.

The Coke-Clark feud originated in Waco and was one of the great political stories. Back when he was fighting the Carpetbaggers, Richard Coke had his close friend and fellow-townsman, George Clark, at his side fighting for him. After a hard fight, in which the Ku Klux Klan was supposed to have had a strong influence in "reasoning" with the Negro voters and causing them to "go fishing" on election day, Coke was elected. He owed much to Clark.

But when Clark and Hogg were embattled in the fall of 1892 for the office of Governor of Texas, Coke lined up against Clark and backed Hogg who won by 50,000 votes. It was in this campaign that a Federal Judge granted an injunction against the operation of the Texas Railroad Commission and Coke shouted from the platform:

A whole cow-pen full of Federal judges cannot keep Texas from regulating the railroads inside her own sovereign borders!

The issue of States Rights is as green today as it was when the speaker spoke those words within sound of the Brazos.

They had a big debate in a Brazos county, down at Cameron, to which 25,000 people came to hear Hogg and Clark state their platforms. George (Little Giant) Clark yelled "Turn Texas Loose!", while the burly, oversize James Stephen Hogg placed all of his hopes in the Railroad Commission and the slogan: "Let regulation go along with development."

A great political issue of the Brazos-land was — Brazos Navigation. It was said that R. L. (Bob) Henry stayed in Congress for twenty years on that one issue. It was actually attempted once by a series of locks and dams to bring the waters under control and have boats ply from Waco to the Gulf. But the engineers discovered after much experimenting that the shifting sand in the banks and bed of the River confounded their efforts, especially near the old Coke-Horne Plantation, where Richard Coke had lived. The Brazos, it seemed, changed her channel frequently going south of Waco and the project was abandoned as hopeless.

On the lower Brazos they know and have always known hot politics. In the late 1800's "The Woodpecker Democrats" there declared for "honest government and honest taxing." Their opponents were known as "The Jaybird Democratic Association." They got the names from the old Negro ditty:

> *Jaybird flew to the Woodpecker's hole,*
> *And the Woodpecker said: Damn yo' soul!*
> *Walk about, Jaybird!*

Control of county politics has always been the fight with few issues other than men-in-office. Vote the rascals out and vote our side in! In 1889 the Reconstruction question was rife and if an agitator showed up at the Big Bend of the Brazos, a committee called upon him and "advised" him to move on. The Jaybirds set about ridding the section of all Carpetbagger remnants.

Military units were raised and Governor Ross was asked for Rangers. The Negroes armed themselves and both Jaybirds and Woodpeckers went armed. Ross went down with his Rangers — he had been one himself — and reasoned with the warring elements, but while he was arguing, there was a battle on the streets . . . Sheriff Garvey was killed . . . Kyle Terry was run out of town . . . Wasson Parker, a noted Carpetbagger hanger-on, swore he would never leave town . . . but did.

Henry Frost conferred with the Governor and asked him to intervene, but he never got to see his wish was carried out for he was killed in a street gun-fight fifteen minutes later. The Woodpeckers were told to get out . . . A Ranger was agreed on for Sheriff . . . and the Terry-Gibson fight made *The Police Gazette* for February 15, 1880. Carrie Nation's husband was there writing the story for Northern news-papers, but they horse-whipped him in Richmond and he and his hatchet-swinging wife went to Kansas.

The Jaybirds won out and still survive. Down on the lower River the Jaybird is something other than a scolding bird of bright blue plumage.

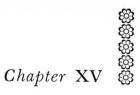

Chapter XV

BRAZOS ARTS AND ARTISTS

 ART HAS LINGERED ABOVE
the Brazos through the years.

Architecture, sculpture, painting, music, drama, folklore and literature have each had their artists, their devotees and supporters who have followed the Brazos' folkways. They have not always been world-acclaimed.

The prehistoric Brazonian was an artist . . . scratching his paintings and drawings on the limestone walls of his caves, expressing his impulse in the runics of his time. With paint and feathers, in the symmetry of bead-work, in the lines of an arrow-head or cleverly-turned piece of decorated pottery that we find in the kitchen-middens along the Paluxy and the Leon today, he expressed his vision.

The Spaniard was a writer. In his letters and his *relaciónes* of what he saw and did in the Brazos-land, our literature has been enriched. He was a fictionist and a lover of folk-lore. He wrote many legends and his enchanting imagery of the Gran Quivera and The Seven Lost Cities of Cibolo shows that he wished to believe his fairy-tales. In other fields of Art, he shaped buildings, painted and carved, decorated and embellished his missions and presidios until artists of our later day stand in wonderment before the surviving portions.

The Anglo-Saxons and the emigrants who came pouring in when the Spanish rule was broken on the Brazos added to the artistic accomplishment of the valley. The Germans and Danes, Swedes and Norwegians, the Czechs and Poles and all of the new people came singing their songs, dancing their folk-dances in costume and the architecture of their old lands was translated by them into the architecture of the new.

The cabinet-maker, the blacksmith, the wood-carver, the painter and the decorator hewed down trees and built a home, then a fort, then a church, then a school . . . then, he set about following his art and his craft until he had beautified his environment.

There was little room for books and paintings in the early covered wagons or on the frail ships that brought the *empresarios* to the Brazos-land. Pots and quilts and bull-tongued plows took up all the space, but the people pined after the other things. Stephen F. Austin was writing in 1830 to his brother-in-law in Missouri:

Bring all your books. Bring all the books you can. Bring me a copy of the laws of Missouri and the Constitution. Don't forget this!

Prescott, the historian, said that the surest test of the civilization of a people was reflected in their architecture, "which presents so noble a field for the display of the grand and the beautiful . . . intimately connected with the essential comforts of life."

We note the arrangements of smoke-blackened rocks in the caves of the prehistoric aborigines which can give us some conception of their ideas of symmetry. Each artifact tells its own story.

The Indian of the early known Brazos period of this four hundred years left us little to speculate upon. He was a nomad and a dweller in tents. He left no permanent structure in the land. But the Spaniard did. In his crumbling ruins we can trace his Moorish and Old Spain motifs. He was inherently an artist who loved the graceful line and worked upon the arch and angle. The slightest thing that he made for the adoration of his Deity or his Saints was possessed of all his artistic talent. Of his houses and homes we have little record preserved. He was a dweller in fort and convent and there his originality was expended.

Not so with the Anglo-Americans. They brought their architecture with them and since they had come to stay they began building for permanence. Here was an old colonial house after the way they built them in New England and Virginia . . . a baronial mansion after the manner of those on the Ashley and the Savannah, the Mississippi and the Suwanee . . . here a Byzantine steeple reminiscent of Central Europe . . . *fachwerk* design on the outside of a dwelling . . . rock and stone houses that one sees all over Northern Europe.

At first they were crude, one-room structures made of logs and River-stone, chinked with mud: Lean-to, hogan, dugout on the far plains where the wood was scarce, more substantial, two-room and loft cabins with the inevitable dog-run when there was labor and lumber to justify it. That was the architecture of the early Brazos.

Necessity dictated the first plans as the Brazos settler tried to get his shelter built before the snows came upon him and his little family. Quickly hewing and shaping, adzing and notching, he put a strong cabin together and hefted the stones from the field and stream to build the chimney. There came a day when that first cabin would be the barn.

Only in the churches and chapels was there early extravagance of effort and material. The Franciscan father, who was trained to be a builder by his brotherhood, gloried in the Renaissance rococo. He must have the belfries and the twin-towers, rose windows and niches, cloisters and colonnades, walls and turrets. Much of his art he developed in Mexico in his ecclesiastical architecture colleges and then came to prove it on the Brazos.

One finds old cabins and buildings up and down the

bank of the River today as he travels its course. There is a story to each. Not a glamorous or exciting story, but one of toil and sacrifice, bound up in pathos and suffering, courage and persistency. Each family reverences the cabin where its history first began.

There was no paint until whitewash, berry-stain or creosote could be secured. So the wind, rain and boiling-sun of the Brazos valley cured or cracked the wood and set the mortar. The windows had no panes, the loop-holes for the rifles were stuffed with cloth when not in use and the cat had a small opening in the corner of the door for ingress and egress.

If there was not enough timber for a cabin, the settler dug into the earth until he had a four-foot excavation, built up a bank or wall of sod, about three feet above the ground, set a ridge-pole and then with a roof of hides, used dirt and brush until he had a "dug-out" that would stand against the wind and weather.

It was 1850 before they started using milled lumber. Pine, cypress, magnolia and cedar were plentiful and the slaves became adept at brick-making for use in the chimney and in the sugar-mill ovens. When the planters of the lower valley became more discriminative and demanded stair-ways, balustrades, newels and fancy ceilings, artisans had to be imported.

The first house at Waco was made without a single bit of metal, entirely of mud, wood and rawhide and was owned by Shapley P. Ross. It was a good double log-house with chimneys of mud and cedar-limbs and the doors were of wooden frames with dressed hides attached. There was a puncheon floor of split logs.

Forts were built much after the same pattern as one can see as he visits the ruins of them today. Barracks, bakery, headquarters buildings, stables with an arsenal or powder-house off a safe distance from the others. Native stone and mortar manufactured from soils that were available and handy.

The Brazos developed no architecture of its own unless it be the type of cabin that the early settler built as best and as strong as he could. It served the purpose and was the work of his hand and every bit of it reflected his toil. "Architecture should bespeak the traditional language of a region." The cabin of the colonist does.

The Brazos' exponent of sculpture was Elizabeth Ney who lived and loved and lies buried today near Hempstead at old Liendo Plantation. She bought it in the latter years of her life. She was born at Munster in Westphalia in 1833 and came to Texas in 1870 with the praises of all Europe ringing in her ears as the result of her talent and artistry.

She did a statue of Sam Houston and one of Stephen F. Austin that are in the national Hall of Fame in Washington, D. C. When asked why she made them so small — life-size — instead of in the usual heroic pattern, she replied with spirit:

"God Almighty made the men. I only made their statues."

The Franciscans brought their own sculptors from Mexico to make the images and statues for their missions.

§

It was Simonides, according to Plutarch, who called "painting silent poetry and poetry speaking-painting," and through the years the Brazos artists have been devotees of both arts.

If you will pause and observe them, climbing down into the most inaccessible places and using your imagination at times, you will see where some prehistoric man . . . or woman . . . drew pictures, carved petroglyphs or scratched queer runes and letters on the cave-walls in order to set down some bit of history, acclaim some god or indicate a direction for another to follow. How we study these scanty few messages from another age to see if they have a meaning for us!

The Indians painted their shields and wigwams with suns and symbols in fancy colors; the Pueblos could work into their pottery fantastic designs and when the Spanish *padres* came and showed them the white man's art, they soon learned to express themselves in that form. They took berries and clay pigments from the soil or the bushes and their tints excelled and outdid the ones that the Spaniards knew. Ram, a Spanish writer, has this to say:

They have vermilion in abundance and use it to decorate their tanned leather. They have excellent dyes that they use for their clothing. The blue is particularly fine. Their green comes from a cuprous metal. They know of a wood (perhaps, black walnut) so good that the deerskins they color with it have the appearance of black velvet. They get red and yellow ochres and white clay from earth pits. These with charcoals they apply as kalsomines. They have vegetable dyes such as vivid yellow of the Osage orange.

The Anglo-Saxon painters have been many. William Huddle came to paint three pictures which hang in Texas' State Capitol building today: *Surrender of Santa Anna, Dawn at the Alamo* and *The Battle of San Jacinto.*

One of the earliest of the Brazonian painters was Eugenie Lavender who won acclaim in the salons of Paris in 1851. She took recourse in the native paints of the River land when her French supply was exhausted. A misfortune befell her when her husband was made captive by the Indians for a long time. She is noted for her *St. Patrick.*

In 1876 a lad by the name of Frank Reaugh came to the Brazos-land in a covered wagon, became a cow-hand with a penchant for drawing pictures. So imbedded in his mind and heart was the way of cattle that when he went off to St. Louis, Paris and Holland he remembered the Longhorns and put them on canvas.

The Columbian Exposition in Chicago in 1893 exhibited his *February in Texas* and *Springtime.* In 1894 he showed

The Roundup that had 5,000 Longhorns in it. He painted much and taught landscape-sketching at Baylor University. He died in 1945 and his culminating work was a series of pastels *Twenty-four Hours with the Herd.*

There are many cowboy songs, Negro spirituals, river-chanteys, Mexican *canciónes* and tender ballads of the outlaw and noted characters that have found expression and become a part of the Brazos folklore. Mary Austin Holley, who added to Brazos art-life, said in her *Letters of An Early American Traveler* concerning her muse:

I shall send you to be published a Brazos boat-song, which I have composed and set to music and sung to the delight of the Texas people, especially Colonel Austin.

Albert Pike was not only explorer and writer but versifier as well. He came to the Brazos-land in the 1830's and wrote thereafter *Prose Sketched and Poems written in the Western Country,* among which was, *A Dirge: written over a companion killed by the Comanches and buried on the Prairie.* He used the name of the Brazos in much of his poetry and prose.

The most abundant rhymster and perhaps the most distinguished that the Brazos boasted was Mirabeau B. Lamar. He was ever ready to subordinate his state or military duties to entertain the muse. His *Verse Memorials* (1857) were typical of his range. Themes patriotic, religious and narrative gave him subject and his often long versification ran the full gamut of the scale.

Charlie Russell penned many a Brazos lay and Mollie E. Moore Davis in *War Times at La Rose Blanche* gives us a picture of old Columbia in the days from 1857 to 1872. Charlie Sirango in 1886 with his upper Brazos breeziness gave posterity the memorable *A Texas Cowboy* that Will Rogers said was *The Cowboy's Bible.*

John A. Lomax and his son, both of whom resided in old

[299]

McLennan on the Brazos, took guitar, note-book, recording-machine and went into the cow-camp, the penitentiary, the cotton-patch, the honky-tonk and the River-dock to hear and set down what folk-songs the Brazos people sang. *Cowboy Songs and Other Frontier Ballads* were entwined with the saga of the Brazos-land, while *Songs of the Cattle Trail and Cow Camp* were reminiscent of the herds that splashed across the River in the early days. Negro folk songs abound in their collection and much has been added and preserved by the skill and artistry of Lomax *pere et fils* in their peregrinations up and down the out-of-way places.

There was a Brazos artist whom they developed for posterity. Huddie Ledbetter, or "Leadbelly" as he was better known, ran the course of the Brazos-land from the prison farms of the lower valley to the cotton-fields of the upper Forks. A huge giant of a Negro, he had a form, a voice and a personality as well as a memory for songs and a rhythm in his soul that will live far beyond his day . . . he passed in December 1949 in New York where he was making broadcasts and recordings of his famous folk-songs of the River and the canebrakes that he knew.

Once Governor Pat M. Neff pardoned him for his appeal in song sung to his guitar in a manner that touched the Governor's heart. Lomax collected *Negro Folk Songs as Sung by Leadbelly* and the pages are filled with his ballads and blues, chants and work songs, railroad and cowboy ditties.

There is one man who has given much to poetry in the River land.

> . . . *every common bush afire with God;*
> *And only he who sees takes off his shoes.*

This man *sees* and the distance between foggy, staid old Wimpole Street in London and the high bluffs of the Brazos at Waco is effaced and Dr. A. J. Armstrong has brought the Brownings twain to Baylor and the valley.

He came from his work in the British Museum in 1912 and decided that a shrine to Elizabeth and Robert Browning should be established in Waco . . . it has. Illustrious people have come to pay their tribute . . . Edwin Markham, Katherine Cornell, John Masefield and others.

Here he has gathered several thousand titles, original manuscripts and editions, the original bronze cast of the two poet's hands clasped that Harriet Hosmer did, letters from Robert and Elizabeth, a first edition of *Pauline* valued at $18,250, and a ring that Robert wore when first he went to Wimpole Street.

They have reared a building on the Baylor campus at the Doctor's persistence where almost a million dollars has been invested, practically all of it of his raising. Each stained glass window depicts a Browning poem, bronze doors have the self-same pattern as those in the Florence baptistry in Italy where Elizabeth won back her health, a Michelangelo ceiling and a foyer of meditation are in this new Georgian marble temple.

In addition to the host of valuable Browning relics, the kindly, white-haired, firm-lipped Doctor has implanted in the minds and hearts of Baylor young men and women for nearly forty years a deep appreciation of the poetry of this famed pair.

The land of the River has never lacked for "concord of sweet sound." Indians sang and chanted and whooped in unison. The Spaniards and Mexicans brought their strings and wood-winds and taught the aborigines of the Valley the soft music of old Santander and Andalusia. Said Father Juan Augustin Morfi, a Franciscan, of the Indians in 1778:

They play the instruments well and we may teach them the harp and the guitar for the Indian has an ear attuned to music.

There was the spirit of music in the battle at San Jacinto for they marched to the strains of Frederick Limski's flute and the beat of a drum — "Come to the Bower I have shaded for you" — Texas came singing! It has been followed by the folk-music of the Czechs, the Swedes, the *lieds* of the Germans in their *saengerfests*, the lusty songs of the Bohemian *sokols*. These have been preserved in the religious and social life of the Valley, along with the native cow-country dances — *Put your little foot* and *Ten Pretty Girls*. The present day sees the revival of the old tunes and dances when the Brazos folk are surfeited with new songs:

> *Swing your partners round and round,*
> *Pocket full of rocks to hold me down,*
>
> *Ducks in the river going to the ford,*
> *Coffee in the little rag, sugar in the gourd.*
>
> *Ladies to the center, how do you do?*
> *Right hands across and how are you?*
>
> *Two little ladies, do si do,*
> *Two little gents, you ought to know,*
>
> *Chicken in the bread-tray kickin' up the dough,*
> *Granny, will your dog bite . . . no, by Joe!*

The cowboy crooned many a song to his herd that he made up as he went along . . . *Home on the Range* dates back to 1872, says Lomax, the noted curator of The Archives of American Folk-Song of the Library of Congress . . . no one knows who started imploring the world not "to bury me on the lone prairie."

Brazonian Oscar J. Fox contributed his *Hills of Home* . . . epics of Billy the Kid . . . Sam Bass . . . Jesse James . . . abound in the Brazos valley and the radio has given them a new revival. The Negro spiritual is still popular . . . *"Jesus rides a milk-white hoss"* . . . on a cotton-wagon, in a little wooden church out in the lone field, or in a brush-arbor . . . *"My Lawd is a battle-axe, a shelter in de time ob storm"* is still sung lustily along the River of The Arms of God.

In the old days concert-singers and operatic companies played the music-halls at Richmond, Calvert, Navasota, Waco, Fort Griffin and other places . . . Wagner, Beethoven and Liszt were familiar.

In one Brazos settlement in 1838, they are said to have built a theatre before they built a church. Many of the noted actors of other days came to regale the Brazos people with their interpretations. Joseph Jefferson played the Waco Music Hall in 1845, while Booth, Bernhart, Mansfield and Langtry were often seen up and down the River doing one-night-stands. They had a music-hall at Fort Griffin that had many of the good companies, but they had to burn feathers to kill the smell that the buffalo-hide dealers brought in with them from their wares. That was in 1876.

There were newspapers circulated in the settlements before Austin's time. *Gaceta de Tejas* was published about the time of the Gutierrez-Magee Expedition and between 1821 and 1845 *The Texas Gazette* was a standard journal at San Felipe. . . . *The Texas Republican* moved to Brazoria from Nacogdoches and kept going. . . . Gail Borden began his *Texas Register and Telegraph* in October 1835 down at San Felipe. . . . Santa Anna dumped a lot of his presses and equipment into the bayou, but Borden was back in business at Columbia by October 1836 as lively as ever.

Fort Griffin had its *Echo* and when the Fort folded it moved and became *The Abilene Echo* where it heralded the fact that:

A long-winded speech is unnecessary but for $2 cash we will give you the news of the town, country and a little state news 52 times a year.

The ink-supply was a problem and the early news-sheet depended on what they could get . . . once *The Fort Griffin Echo* came out in red, blue, green and violet to show its variety of ink. The Brazos-land had its famed writers of the news . . . George Wilkins Kendall followed the Santa Fé Expedition as its "war correspondent" and preserved much description of the Brazos and Comanche Peak.

The Waco Daily Examiner was started by Major Robert Lambdin in 1873 as *The Waco Era,* its predecessor, started in 1850, folded up. . . . W. H. Parsons published a rabid Secessionist sheet in Waco but went off to the Civil War to fight and was killed in battle.

We look for Brazos valley news of the cattle-drives, of the Reconstruction days and post-war politics in *The Weekly Register,* an out-and-out Republican sheet that was the only one supposedly allowed in Waco and central Texas until 1872 when the Carpetbaggers were kicked out.

Folklore and folk-ways have been rich and abundant from Quintana to Muleshoe, through the years from Indian days to the present. Varied and picturesque legends, myths, wild tales of explorers, experiences of the *padres,* Indian wars and depredations, exploits of Rangers and "bad men," tall stories the cow-boys tell, the pirate yarns, the imageries of the Negroes, form a fantastic collection of folk-tales.

Ghost-lights on the high Plains . . . "hanted" houses in the Brazos bottoms . . . superstitions of the cotton fields . . . Paul Bunyan's accounts of the oil belt . . . the ardent recitals of lost treasure upon which the Mexicans dote . . . they are all part of the Brazos story.

Read Davy Crockett's rambling writings. He lived for a time on the banks of this River and his wife is buried at Acton in old Hood County. He says on one occasion:

One day I war out in the forest with Kill-devil, and ther war a deep snow on the ground, and I see'd a fox a-crossin' my track and jumpin' up and down in the snow, but couldn't git ahead tho he tried mighty hard to get outa my way. So I telt Growler to be still and I walked along as if I hadn't see'd him, fer Davy Crockett war never a man to take advantage of fellow-critter in distress.

There are many of the same type and to such stories as
Sam Bass' eulogy there are as many verses, of which this may
or may not be the last one:

Sam met his fate at Round Rock, July the twenty-first,
They dropt the boy with rifle-balls and then they took his purse.
Poor Sam he is a dead lad, and six foot under clay,
And Jackson's in the mesquite, aiming to get away.

John C. Duval was an early Brazos writer who loved a
folk-tale and he hitched many a one onto Big Foot Wallace
as he wrote his engaging tale: *The Adventures of Big Foot
Wallace, Texas Ranger and Hunter.* If there was a good
story, Duval attributed it to his hero and it includes many of
the myths, legends and traditions of the Brazos valley.

There is an interesting bit of folk-lore that a lady of the
near-Brazos country, Mary Daggett Lake, a noted folk-lorist,
has gathered from the cotton-patches of the Riverland and
preserved in her book *The White Rose of Commerce.*

Much of the folk-lore of the Brazos has been preserved in
the valuable archives of the Texas Folk-Lore Society and
published in its year-books. They conduct vast research and
are fortunate to have these yearly compilations edited by
that versatile man of Texas letters — J. Frank Dobie. The
surface has only been scratched . . . Indians, pirates, *conquis-*
tadores, pioneer, cowboys, Rangers, Negro cotton-pickers, settlers, Frenchmen, and Mexicans.

Cabeza de Vaca in 1542 wrote and published in Zamora,
Spain, his *La Relación de Cabeza de Vaca.* Coronado saw to
it that there was a careful journal made of his upper Brazos
Fork journeyings, unsuccessful though they were; and Pedro
Casteñada left us an interesting account of that barren waste-
land in his day.

The "Gentleman of Elvas" who marched in the De Soto
Expedition in 1542 left many valuable notes for the archivist
to pursue anent the Brazos story and chronicle . . . those

[305]

Gentlemen-Sailors of Essex wrote down their impressions of the Brazos in that early day of the 16th Century . . . Henri Joutel's *Journal of La Salle's Last Voyage, 1684/7* adds his contribution to the Brazos tale . . . while the best "history" of the time, when history had hardly begun, was Fray Juan Agustin Morfi's *History of Texas, 1673-1779*.

Posterity owes much to the meticulous literary genius of Stephen F. Austin for *Austin's Papers*.

The first novel with a Texas back-ground was *L'Heroine du Texas*, published in Paris in 1819 and had Lafitte and his pirates in the tale. The writer was anonymous. Austin in 1829 published the first real Texas volume, *Laws, Orders and Contracts on Colonization*.

His cousin, Mary Austin Holley, wrote her first Texas history in 1833 after a short visit to the Brazos settlements, but despite its limited research it gives us a very fair picture of the times along the River. Her style is pleasing and readable.

Of the two great combatants — Houston wrote scarcely a thing and Lamar never stopped writing. There is a six-volume assembly of "The Papers of Mirabeau Buonaparte Lamar." Noah Smithwick, from whom this narrative often quotes, is a most interesting *litterateur* of the Brazos as well as a most remarkable one. He lived as a young man in the days of the Texas Revolution and was the *confidente* of the Brazos great. When he was 89 he dictated his memoirs, *The Evolution of a State,* to his daughter, Nanna Smithwick Donaldson. He died October 21, 1899, at the age of nearly 92 and the memoirs were published in 1900. It is a feat of astounding memory.

Two great contributions to the early literature of the Brazos are this book of Smithwick's memories and experiences, and that of Davy Crockett, whose *Exploits and Adventures in Texas* is standard literature along the Brazos. William Kennedy gave his history in 1841 and Henderson Yoakum in

1855 told of the events along the Brazos in the early days . . . that was the history of Texas in the main.

They liked Mrs. Holley's *History of Texas* so well in 1836 that *The Intelligencer* of Lexington, Kentucky in its May 20, 1836 issue said:

The public may not generally be aware that a complete and authentic history of Texas down to the present time, with a description of its geography, topography, etc., by Mrs. Mary Austin Holley of this city is now in the press and will be published within a few days.

Her book was widely read in Kentucky, Texas, Washington and Europe . . . Henry Clay bought many copies and gave them to his friends and wrote the author that it was authority in the United States Congress.

The Brazos West came in for mention in Captain Frederick Marryat's *Travels and Adventures of Monsieur Violet in California, Sonora, and Western Texas,* published in Leipzig in 1843. Many German writers came and visited their people along the Brazos and went home and wrote the story for contemplative emigrants to read. Dr. Ferdinand Roemar — The Father of Texas Geology — published at Poppelsdorf and at Bonn in 1849 his book of travels in Texas.

He set forth in minute detail the physical appearance of the country and *The Cretaceous Formations of Texas and Their Organic Inclusions.* His accounts of German settlements and Indian depredations were as meticulously correct as his geological findings and add much to the archives of the Brazos.

John C. Duval wrote many books during his period of 1819-1897 that added to the literary luster of the Brazos-land . . . Andy Adams with his *The Log of the Cowboy* . . . Charles A. Sirango and his *A Texas Cowboy* put the men of the boots and saddles into the Brazos literature for the first time . . . J. W. Wilbarger in 1889 left a monumental collection of his

Indian Depredations in Texas which he gathered from eye-witnesses or from the children of those who perished at the hands of the redskins.

George W. Saunders did for the trail-drivers what Wilbarger did for the Indian-fighters and victims in the two-volume book *Trail Drivers of Texas*. The value of it lies in the fact that Saunders saw to it that the old fellows each set down in his own language his own story of the trail and put his picture in the book to go along with it.

Clarence R. Wharton, indigenous to the Fort Bend Brazos country, wrote much of the valuable story of that section and preserved its story for posterity. Dorothy Scarborough in her books keeps her mid-Brazos homeland alive with her *Land of Cotton,* her *On the Trail of Negro Folk-Songs* and her novels. Edwin Lanham of Weatherford, originally, preserves the story of that section of the Brazos-land that is Parker County and the trial of the Indian Chieftains wherein his distinguished kinsman served as prosecutor.

J. Frank Dobie has written the story of the lost mines, the cattle and the wild coyotes, besides contributing much to the literary life of the Brazos country in all of his many books. ... George Sessions Perry, although a Rockdale native, dealt in 1939 with the fishing people of the Brazos in his *Walls Rise Up* . . . while John L. McCarty touched on the upper Brazos region in his *Maverick Town, the Story of Old Tascosa.* . . . Boyce House wrote the story of the Brazos oil boom in the Ranger and Stephens County field.

John W. Thomasson, the Marine officer, wrote of the Brazos . . . while Laura Krey's *And Tell of Time* has the River for its locale. . . . William C. Holden of Texas Tech's History Department has given us a writing of the Forks Country in *Alkali Trails* . . . as Judge Coombes did in *Prairie Dog Lawyer.*

Now and then a Brazos writer preserves the works of others and renders a valuable service. Eugene C. Barker's *Austin's*

Papers and H. E. Bolton's *Spanish Expeditions in the South-west, 1592-1706* are examples. Samuel Wood Geiser gives us his *Ghost-Towns of Texas, 1840-1880*. Frederick Law Olmsted in his 1857 *Journey Through Texas* reveals much of the land as he saw it then. Elizabeth Custer, the gifted widow of The Hero of Little Big Horn, wrote a book *Tenting on the Plains,* an interesting account of Army life in the early forts and camps.

PART FOUR

Cruising Down The River

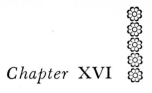

Chapter XVI

FROM MESA TO MESQUITE
"Unto the place from whence the river comes." Eccl. 1:7

FREDERIC REMINGTON, WHO
caught the spirit of a scene and put it on canvas in terms
of the western way, painted among his immortal pictures of
the high, dry plains of western Texas "Coronado leading his
army." He depicts the ambitious *Gran Capitan* trudging
along the weary wastes while the Spanish *conquistadores* in
casque, helmet and breast-plate, armed with their long lances
and heavy swords follow along in his train.

Out of New Mexico as we know it today they came, plod-
ding along in the dry dust, searching the far-off horizons for
the glint of golden cities, wondering when they would find
trees and water and people again. The thirty-year-old Captain Francisco Vásquez de Coronado had put a million dollars of his wife's money into this venture and had turned his
back on the province of which he was Governor in Mexico —
Nueva Galicia.

Three hundred soldiers and many camp-followers marched
with him on this vainglorious trip, led by a deceiving Turk
who kept promising that they would find golden streets and
houses roofed with jewels on which the sun shone with
radiant brilliance.

They wandered the land of the upper Brazos Forks, wa-
tered their horses in the shallows and drank from the springs.
If only they had paused near where the thriving town of
Muleshoe is today in Bailey County and sought out some of

the tiny lakes and streams west of the townsite, they would have come upon the place that the map-makers tell us is the far source of the Brazos' fork.

It is in Texas, the beginning of this Double Mountain Fork, far up in the northwest corner of Bailey on a plateau that the Spaniards called the *mesa,* or table-land. Sometimes on top of and then again under the surface the timid little stream slants across the highway and the Santa Fé Railroad's right-of-way and moves eastward and south to Soda and Spring Lakes in Lamb County. There it gathers strength and courage and becomes a determined stream across Lamb and into Hale County, far up there in the land of The Staked Plain.

Why "Staked Plain" you ask? This is the story they will tell you up there: when the *padres* came in 1734, a long while after Coronado, travelling from the old settlements in Santa Fé seeking the mines of San Saba in western Texas, they marked their trail with stakes driven into mounds of buffalo skeleton-heads.

Out of this high country the River runs straight south from Hale until it comes into Lubbock County by Lubbock town, when it starts southwestwardly again, nipping the corner of Crosby and liberally watering the wastes of Garza. Down there on the edge of the Caprock it picks up another Fork from the south of Garza, while the Salt Fork rises in the high canyon country to parallel the other two forks and flow on evenly into Kent. There the Salt and the Double Mountain bisect Kent and flow on through the treeless plains.

This is the first lap of our journey from the place where the River rises on down to where she meets the sea at old Quintana on the Gulf of Mexico. It will be about eight hundred miles.

At first glance one would say that this was a dry and arid country where no trees thrive, where the River often dries to a trickle or is a narrow ribbon off in the distance gleaming in the sun. But it is not a barren land. Treeless, yes, but there is vegetation. Bunches of bear grass and clumps of buffalo grass, patches of broom-weed and stands of cactus, and there is water beneath these growing plants . . . "and everything shall live whither the river cometh."

A vista of splendid distances, untenanted for the greater part, a long stretch between towns, even between wind-mills. It is a place to meditate upon as you drive through. A writer named Wickeland did in 1800:

I am sure that the time is not very far distant when these plains, over which the Comanche and the Apache speed their course amid the loneliness of rude nature, will resound with the strange sounds of cattle-bells, cracking whips and the whistle of loco-motives.

Were he here this day he would see a straight line of paved highway from Muleshoe to Post, as if drawn with a straight-edged ruler. A railroad track parallels the road. He would see huge gins, vast warehouses, mills, cattle-pens, and the cotton in the fields in mid-November — baled, piled and unpicked — would amaze him.

It has taken a century and a half for this land to be settled and developed, first into a cattle-land to raise huge Herefords that move by the thousands each year to market; then to make a cotton-land without precedent in America in enor-mity of production; an oil-land where the fever of discovery is as acute today as was the crave for gold when the men of Coronado marched this way. These are the marvels of the High Plains today — the dreams of wealth in men's minds.

The Brazos is not imposing up in this country. Plenty of river-bed, a token flow of the current, occasional sheets of shallow-water, great sprawling sand-bars, but the River itself is never deep. Yet it is a threat, the natives here tell you, for in the spring it will come tearing down these beds, over-run these banks and be a russet tide and torrent as it races over the flat, even land.

One dare not estimate distances in this plains-country. How far is it, do you reckon, to that butte off yonder or to that flat plateau on the horizon? Miles and miles lie between with a limited carpet of vegetation . . . no evidences of civilization except the paved highway. Joaquin Miller said:

> *Room! Room to turn round in,*
> *To breathe and be free,*
> *To grow to be giant,*
> *To sail as at sea,*
> *With the speed of the wind*
> *On a steed with his mane*
> *To the wind without pathway*
> *Or route or a rein.*

Now we wander down the stream and see the thrifty, wind-blown little towns, clean-as-a-whistle, slumless, new and growing fast, where people of purpose who believe in their future live. They used to say in the old days that this land of the Brazos Forks was a "land of ranches, rascals, rattlesnakes and remittance-men." But not any more.

Gins, silos, wind-mills, grain-elevators, maize-mills, radio-stations, combines, trucks, tractors, trains, airplanes, lighted football fields, drive-in theatres — these are the minions of industry that one finds in the towns of the high plains these days.

But out on the *mesa* you are back in the primitive sweep of the land that compares in vastness to the sea. The tiny prairie-dog scuttles for his hole, whipping his furry tail behind him; the long-eared jack-rabbit almost out-runs himself as he bounds in great leaps between the clumps of range-grass. The sky presses down on all sides of you like a giant cup of inverted blue.

It is high and the air is rare up at Muleshoe and Progress — 4,000 feet above the sea.

This is ranching-country and the old Muleshoe Ranch covers a wide, sprawling area . . . they call that ridge over there "The Sand Hills," and they run east and west . . . they tell you that they are of the same sand that dunes down on the coast are made.

You see many cattle through here. There is hardly a windmill with its long feed-troughs and blocks of sulphur and salt nearby but that a few square-bodied Herefords are not congregated. They lie about and rest or nibble a patch of grass. On the distant sward, miles away, is the main stand of the russet herd . . . all grazing together, facing in the same direction, broad rumps to the breeze.

But this is a cotton-country from Muleshoe to Post. Giant piles of it stand in the fields where the Mexicans have picked it and dumped it from their sacks. There have not been enough wagons and tractors to haul it to the gin and, if there were, the gins are clogged down — running night and day — and could not accommodate it.

Around the farmer's house will be a great dune of the white fibre, the field-hands will be picking furiously and whole acres are still white unto the harvest. At the railroad station hundreds of bales lie in fields awaiting transportation.

This is really cotton-land in mid-November.

What is the secret of it? All of this abundant growth and not any more trees than we see? Irrigation is the answer. The water is just under the surface and they bring it up from the shallow depth. They make five crops of alfalfa, they tell us, here in Bailey County in a single year.

And now this is Lamb County. Sudan is a highway town with huge grain-elevators for storage. They raise much wheat, and down at the rail-yards several thousand Herefords complain at being penned up. They are being fed-out for market. Dropping over to the Brazos North Fork we find the big cotton-wood trees, tall giants that keep close to the water-courses for sustenance.

The Mashed-O Ranch set out a lot of trees in the 120,000 acres of its jurisdiction. They run over 8,000 head of Herefords. We see little lakes where wild geese pause in abundance in migrating time . . . lots of quail — Mexican blue and bob-white — and when they let you hunt antelope, there are some in this vicinity. They were here once by the millions, old-timers will claim.

They believe in such things as auction-sales in this country. Cattle, furniture, farm-implements, household-goods, horses. Folks drive from miles to participate and professional callers are able to make a good living. Rodeos, horse-races and square-dances are the social events, but in the fall they take their high-school football seriously.

Ever see a tumble-weed? Or heard them sung about?

We pass a field where they are growing. They are indigenous to this country and there are literally millions of them. When they are ripe for picking the wind attends to it. Jarred loose, the big round weeds — too large for a man to reach around the circumference — start rolling over the flat land. When they come to an obstruction, a barbed-wire fence, usually, in through this country, they pile up. At first glance you would bet it was a brush fence, so solid and thick are they along its line.

But the plainsman smiles at your guess. The wind built that fence in a single day and it is a fire-hazard, what's more. It could burn down the cedar posts and ruin a lot of good wire, so the ranch youngster has the tedious chore of tossing them over the fence or else burning them in piles.

On a high windy day in this section it is almost uncanny to see these great balls travelling across country impelled by the gale, an entire field moving at once. At times they pile so high that they climb the brush-fence that they themselves have made.

Here in Lamb County, near the Brazos Fork, was the first cow-camp in the Panhandle of Texas, not far from Amherst.

They have a tablet there on a shaft that is called "Sod House Spring Monument."

Littlefield is a Plains town just about where the River, the road and the rails run out of Lamb going south, sea-ward. Cotton built this town and cattle helped. From the time when irrigation came into vogue the land began to give promise. The nesters had fought a hard fight of defense against the cattle-men, but when a smart, shrewd nester discovered something that the buffalo had been trying to teach man for generations, he won a victory.

Nature taught the great beasts to wallow in the fine dust and sand of the prairie until they had reached the near-surface water. It accumulated in the wallows and then the great shaggy beasts would come back and drink it. Finally, man caught on.

Now, there is modern farming here. There are few rocks and ravines; it is level land with no stumps. Cotton, maize, wheat and alfalfa thrive. Mexicans from south of The Border, on an immigration arrangement effective only during the season, come to pick and harvest the cotton. They take a tremendous wage out of this county . . . ah, *Conquistadores,* your *compadres* have found gold at last in the valley of the River where you watered your horses and passed on!

This was the "dug-out" country in the early days. The people lived *in* the earth for an hundred years.

Lubbock . . . the chief city of importance on the high Plains in this leg of our journey and one of the most important places on the Brazos course. Back in 1891 they were fighting over the name and location of it. Finally, they called it after Colonel Tom S. Lubbock who went with Terry to Virginia to get commissions to organize Terry's Texas Rangers and enlist them in the Confederate cause.

They tell a story at Lubbock, when you mention the great quantity of cotton you have seen, about how it got started. Seems as if a man brought some cotton-seed in the early days of this century to use for stock-feed and decided to plant some of them instead. Now they have taken the country.

Ranches are plentiful around Lubbock. The Spade or Yellow House Ranch covers 80,000 acres with Herefords as the chief asset. There is a Yellow House Canyon up here and some maps list the Brazos Fork as the "Yellow House Fork." They have a State Park, named after General Mackenzie, the old Indian-fighter who did a great job ridding this country of savage Comanches who preyed on the settlers.

You can drive for miles and never see the vestige of a tree as you make your way down the Brazos Forks . . . a windmill, yes . . . Pedro de Casteñada, the chronicler of Coronado's Expedition, wrote about this country through which we travel:

The country is like a bowl, so that when a man sits down, the horizon surrounds him all around at the distance of a musket-shot.

His musket must have shot a far piece! This is what he wrote of the Indians in this country when *El Gran Capitan* passed this way:

They go about with the buffalo, eat the meat raw, drink the blood of the cows and then tan the skins for clothes.

Lubbock was a typical frontier town of the 1890s with trail-drivers, buffalo-hunters, cattle-ranches, cowboys, wild horse hunters and men who changed their names when they crossed the Sabine or the Red. Now . . . it is a fine college town, high on the Plains, with a huge campus and many imposing buildings, hundreds of instructors and thousands of students. From the high pole this National Holiday morning the garrison flag flies to show that they have a cadet corps training.

Lubbock has Cotton Carnivals, glories in mills and museums where the artifacts of the Plains have been gathered and is the center of wealth for this vast area about. They have the first store-building preserved. It was owned by Singer and in the days when it throve was a popular meeting-place at the military cross-roads of the Panhandle and the Plains.

If you wanted to arrange a rendezvous in the old days it was — "Meet me at Singer's Store at Lubbock" — "I'll see you at the Falls of the Brazos at Marlin" — "Let's make it down at Old Fort Bend at Richmond." It depended whether it was to the upper, middle or lower Brazos that you were heading.

Down through the corner of Crosby County we come and here is what is known as "The Caprock." It is an escarpment or an abrupt uplift of the earth's surface of from 400 to 1,000 feet. It is high and flat and the buttes and plateaux stretch to the horizon on all sides. It is magnificent to be able to see so far . . . as the land starts its sloping toward the plains and the sea . . . on top of the world.

The Caprock ends and down yonder is the Brazos' prairie-land. Draws and gulches, arroyos and canyons sweeping away to the rim of the earth where the sky comes down. The drop is from 4,500 down to 2,500 feet. You can spot the towns off on the flat-land, dotting the ribbons of white roadway that race across the treeless country . . . and there is the snake-like Fork etching a crooked line across the yonder-land.

One of the Double Mountain Fork tributaries starts on the Caprock of Lynn County, while the Salt Fork has its source in Crosby, east of the main stem of the River. There used to be great ranches through here in the days before the Great Drought. The Two Buckle Ranch was on the south Fork that rises in Lynn, but . . . she's gone with the tumble-weeds of yesteryear.

We are going on into Garza County where all three of the Forks are found and the Salt Fork becomes quite prominent. The Indians made their journeys here in the old days for salt.

[321]

The Tahoka Lake over in Lynn is definitely established in the minds of these people as the camp of Coronado's men. They mine sodium sulphate out of it today when it runs dry . . . they show you ruts that they claim are those of the old stage-coaches and the California-bound ox-wagons of an hundred years ago.

They have found many an Indian relic and those that go back to prehistoric times. Many people lived here in ages gone. They invite you back for the big fiesta when the harvest is gathered; they make very merry then.

Coronado was not the only dreamer who came to Garza County. C. W. Post, the breakfast food man, founded this little Plains town of "Post" back in 1907 and planned to make a model farm-city in this wide country . . . but he died before he could set his dream into reality. Today it is a little windswept city at the foot of the Caprock where the cattlemen come into town from the Slaughters' "U-Lazy-S" and other nearby ranches. The famous "Currycomb Ranch" was near here and the Boy Scouts preserve the old headquarters as a club-house. Quanah Parker and his Comanches used this vicinity as their main stamping-ground at one time.

Ever see a "catalo"? It is a cross between a buffalo bull and a domestic cow. There are not many, but they are not so uncommon that they become zoo or museum pieces. There are persisting fossils and bones seen through here of the prehistoric sea-animals.

As you come down out of the high country you catch a glimpse of the Double Mountain over in Kent County. It is really a triple-mountain for there is one flat-top and a double jagged peak that is visible for miles around as the highest point above the plain. We are along the Salt and the Double Mountain Forks now and the mesquite is beginning to put in appearance.

Over there is where the O-Bar-O used to have its headquarters . . . cattle meant much to the people of these plains, but it took a lot of care, driving them to water, getting them to market and feeding them in the winter. Railroads, irrigation, windmills and fences have had their effect.

After the Civil War the Galveston newspaper said editorially that this Plains country would never be opened up because the fencing of a section would cost more than $1,000, which was more than the land was worth. But it reckoned without a man named Joseph Farwell Glidden, a Yankee out of New Hampshire, who invented barbed-wire to keep the dogs out of his wife's flower-beds back East. It was the answer to the fence problem of the Brazos valley.

Here on the Salt Fork they break the white salt with a plow and load it onto trucks. Nobody would ever *buy* salt in this country . . . here is where the Indian trail led and where the troopers from the forts came pursuing them . . . and over this route came the Swedes to Clairemont to settle this land and stay with it to this day . . . there still is heard the sound of the *nyckelharpa* and the singing of the *folkviser* in this land.

There are no bigger names in all the cattle country of Texas than the ones you hear here on the Brazos Forks — Swenson, Connell and Jaybird. The history of these ranches goes back into the past.

Stand on Double Mountain and look the world over!

The air is like wine and your breath comes in puffs after the slightest effort. That's Blanco Canyon off over there to the right and the White River runs through it. The White feeds into the Brazos' Salt Fork.

Those jagged peaks of the Plains escarpment you see there rise as high as 400 feet. How peculiarly night comes in this high Plains country. There is a brief twilight, the pink of cloud-banks there in the east suddenly goes gray and before you can look back, the curtain of dark has come, and the sun has gone . . . the low-hanging stars come out all at once. When night starts coming to the Plains, "it doesn't fool

[323]

around," as one native son commented when we remarked on it.

The counties through which we pass on this lap of our trip are a part of *The Great High Plains,* as they are geographically known, at the base of the Rockies from Canada to Mexico.

We are travelling "the short-grass country" — the land of the antelope and buffalo, big hats and tall boots, coyotes and jack-rabbits, rattle-snakes and prairie-dogs, wheat and cotton, blizzards and sandstorms.

They claim that over three million buffalo were killed in this country in the 1870's and that they were never missed from the herds. The people who whipped this country and made it yield for them with only a dirt hogan-house to live in deserve a lot of credit.

Hardship was written on every flinty rock for the early folk. Talk to the old-timers . . . find out how they burned buffalo-dung for fuel, gathered up the whitened bones of the buffalo and hauled them to the market for fertilizer, dug oil wells in self-defense, planted cotton when everybody said they were foolish.

What a wild, distorted, rocky-strewn land it is from Post down to the Double Mountain Fork near Justiceburg. White, bare buttes with a single green cedar high on the side of a steep hill . . . a stock-tank in a natural depression that is purple in color for some unknown reason . . . tumbleweeds gathered at a wire fence . . . no timber in sight for miles and a plateau that runs for five miles at least without a gouged-out break in its straight-lined top . . . and the Fork of the Brazos must go underground here, for it has run out of water . . . but here is where it *would* be if only there were a spring rain or two.

There is a rich, red loam underlaid with gypsum one to four feet thick along here and before the white man came and found water under the surface, the Comanche was the only human being who could live on it. Coming from the bleaker Wyoming hills, or down from Colorado's waste-land for salt, or following where the herds of buffalo led him for food, the Indian came to the western Brazos plains and stayed.

In 1599, the explorer Juan de Oñate sent his man Zaldivar into this country to catch some buffalo and bring them back for experimental purposes. He was the first of a great band of despoilers — the buffalo-hunter. How abysmally dismal this land must have seemed to him when he started across the *mesa*, utterly devoid of water, food, vegetation or a marked trail. Much is owed to those who had the fortitude to mark the way and then build a road through it, over which civilization travelled to the sources of the Brazos.

In 1720 the Frenchman, Captain Jean l'Archeveque, came up into this country with orders to make trouble between the Spaniards and the Indians that would redound to the value of the French, but he ventured too far. The Indians killed him and his party for their guns and horses. Zebulon Pike came through here — in chains — bound for Chihuahua in 1806. He had relied too much on the word of the Spanish authorities who knew the country of the Texas plains far better than he.

And over this wide sea of land the Conestagas of 1849 moved to the gold-fields of California. The climate through here was milder and the winters less severe than in the crossings farther north.

While we have found no abundant waters in the upper Forks, no wooded banks and shaded pools, we have noted the occasional peaks that rise, bare and stark from the level plain. The Comanches had one in the early days that they called "Iron Mountain" and it was their belief that it was a sort of Mount Olympus for their Sun-god. The metal was malleable and brittle, with little rust or oxide on its surface. It was pure iron in a malleable state.

[325]

Loneliness — isolation — solitude!

Those are the emotions of one who travels these plains on the high Forks today. Awesome silence grips you. There are no signs of human or animal habitation and the sky is devoid of a single winged bird. You could be an old *conquistador* of the 1500's yourself were it not for the roadway of concrete.

Pause and study the tumbled, jagged rocks in wild disarray . . . cards of red stone that a giant shuffled a hundred thousand years ago and when they scattered never bothered to pick them up . . . the sun shines blazingly hot up here and the wind whips the dry sand into your face and into the pores of your skin . . . the hot air rises to make stiff winds when the higher colder air sweeps in to take its place. They breed stout-souled folk up here with grit in their craws.

It can get very cold on the Caprock in wintertime. A brittle cold with a dryness to it that cuts deeply. Every little pool of water is glazed with ice. The elements try themselves in this country and to stand up to them — summertime or winter — takes stamina. Even the flowers bloom close to the ground and the tumbleweeds give with the wind.

They had stores in dug-outs in those days. W. C. Dockum ran a supply-store in one in 1877 and had the only postoffice at Dockum's Creek west of Fort Griffin. Kidwell Brothers ran the KID Ranch up here in Lubbock County. Andy and Frank Long had the OS Ranch in eastern Garza and the "2-Circle" was down in Scurry, lapping over into Fisher. A Scotsman by the name of Weir owned the 2-Circle.

On the Salt Fork they lead you to the ruins of the old ranch-house of The 22 Ranch and a dug-out that they used covered with a dried beef-hide. There is no telling how old it is. They had two Dutch-ovens — one for meat and one for bread — and they used wolf-hides for blankets. A frying-pan and a coffee-pot were their household goods. Coffee and flour were all they imported. Mined their own salt, used buffalo skulls for chairs and a lamp was made out of a tin-can of tallow with cotton rags plaited for wicks. When they needed hogs for lard and meat they went down to the main Brazos shinnery and staged a hunt.

When the night comes on in the Plains you find it hard to describe the stillness that falls with it. It does something to you ... the still intimacy of the stars that seem to shine with a supernal brightness ... the frost appears to form while you watch it ... there is an elation of compelling isolation ... the vastness of the outdoors' emptiness ... the grandeur of a calm sameness ... the grasping of the scope of these distances ... the wild eerie aloofness of the wilderness of it. The sight of a windmill in the far-off haze of the flickering twilight startles you into thinking things animate exist around it.

It is as if you and Nature and God and this vast Unknown are all waiting — expecting something to happen — balanced on a mood of silence — holding a reverence for something that you can not define, but of which you are tensely aware. You await the answer but know that it will not come ... save in the moaning wind or the rumble of something afar off that you like to think is thunder and not doom ... An ageless solitude while Nature holds her breath.

Did old George Causey, you ask yourself, the buffalo-hunter out of Lubbock, after whom they named this high sandy ridge, have the same feeling when he took off out into this country to kill buffalo for a living? He says that he saw herds of the big bisons that took six and seven weeks to pass a given grazing-ground.

Has this midnight sky been as close and as velvety to the herdsmen of the years gone by, to the wraiths of yesterday's hunters and cowboys who camped here once, to the soldiers of the *Capitan* out of old Spain who also saw a rocking, racing moon hurrying through the fleecy clouds back in his day?

There is poetry in this night and it struck Coronado too, for he inscribed this thought:

I seek a land whose ruler is lulled to sleep
Each day by the tinkling of innumerable bells
Of pure gold, which hang in the boughs
Of a giant apple tree.

You get to wondering in the darkness what Espejo, Sosa, Humana and Oñate thought of this land as they toiled over its plains and drank in this loneliness. One must be a sort of romanticist to be an explorer . . . perhaps, even gold-seekers have the star-light of romance in their eyes . . .

But here we are at the lower levels of the Caprock, following the Forks as they take the trail of a crazy snake through the more populated counties. The mesquite is becoming more abundant, hunted creatures can hide in here, birds can build their nests. It is a different land we are to gaze upon tomorrow as we journey down the Brazos.

But a hail and farewell to the men and women who came here to the high Caprock in the old days, who raised their cattle and now their cotton and valiantly their oil from the depths of the earth. Men who could venture more, stay longer and dare to linger in a land instead of scanning its horizons for golden cities and jeweled roofs . . . doubloons and pieces-of-gold to be spent in the wine-shops of Barcelona.

The wagon-trains are moving westward.
A magic word has come and they set out, the
seekers of a distant Canaan,
Tall determined men with a dream of harvest
in their eyes;
And a passion clean and sleepless as the
Holy Ghost,
And ample-bosomed women with their babes
in their arms.
The pioneers are coming.
Push back the mountains!
Give them room!

—W. E. BARD

Chapter XVII

FROM THE FORKS TO THE FORTS

THEY ARE FAR, FAR AWAY from the Brazos, those little English towns that Hilaire Belloc had in mind:

> *A lovely river, all alone,*
> *She lingers in the hills and holds*
> *A hundred little towns of stone,*
> *Forgotten in the western wolds.*

But the grassy hills of the rolling prairies, the land between the Cross Timbers and the Caprock Escarpment have some of the same beauty and much of a charm peculiarly its own. These are the beginnings of the little farmlands of the Brazos, the planted fields and the frequent homesteaders.

Aspermont, Roby, Rotan, Old Glory, Sylvester, Hamlin, Anson, Tuxedo, Rule, Haskell, Benjamin, Rhineland and Stamford. These are some of the "little towns" in the counties of Scurry, Fisher, Jones, Haskell, Knox and Stonewall that make up the second lap of a journey down the course of the River of The Arms of God.

What a wild country it is in Scurry as we come down to meet the rising of the Clear Fork in the eastern part of that county not far from Snyder, the county-seat. There is a spur of the Double Mountain Fork that rises in the hills and the high country of Scurry, too.

Red, jagged rocks, exposed to the relentless winds in a mad confusion, as if giant children had been playing at

[329]

blocks with them, had kicked them apart at the end of a tired day and gone home without putting their toys away. Buttes and gulches with hard, harsh lines, uninhabited ... "treeless, flowerless, untended, unkissed by God's kindly rain" ... a little cedar high up on the side of a butte clinging there precariously, a single dab of green against a sepia curtain of bald hillside. An occasional bush left alone and deserted by its fellows or condemned to an exile in this abandoned quarry.

Sandstorms are frequent here and the elements turn loose with abandon. Good roads winding across the terrain up and down the hills are the only water-mark of civilization to be seen.

We are all of a sudden in one of the sandstorms ...

It begins with the sight of tumble-weeds moving briskly across a bare spot and you note them picking up speed. They are on their journey wherever the wind listeth. Then comes a whirl of fine sandy-dust against your car windows and you make haste to close them.

For the next half-hour you are a ship in a gale, bucking this stiff sand-wind. It whirls clouds of dust against the bare sides of the buttes with fury, it whips the Fork of the Brazos into little wavelets with a white cap here and there, it bends down the mesquite trees to the ground ... the whip-lash of this visible wind ... the brownish swirl that lambasts the tortured hillsides and speeds the tumbling weeds in varied directions.

You actually *see* a wind!

The car tosses from side to side and you know that you are eating up gas as you buck this sand-gale. It whirls and eddies in the dust of the shoulders of the road and the red gulches are brown and red alternately as they receive the force of this wind. Over there that little bit of stock-tank water is purplish for some unknown reason as the sand whips it into agitated choppiness.

We pass the Yellow House Fork of the Brazos — as some call it — and it is as dry as a bone-yard today, but there are two wind-mills on the river-bank and they are whirling like mad in this sandstorm. They are laughing, as it were, at the futility of the wind that is only causing them to pump that much more water.

A sandstorm is an emotional whim of Nature here in this vast, desolate-looking country. It does no apparent good. It is a tantrum of the desert, a whipping that Nature gives in retaliation for the ennui of this silent, weird land. That a river should *dare* to exist here.

So, we see how Nature vents her fury against things. Now, for a glimpse of how Man is telling Nature what *she* shall do on the banks of the Brazos in Scurry County ...

We spoke in a former chapter about "Oil the King"; upon how men in the valley have drilled and explored for oil with varying degrees of success. Here is where the bit found oil — abundant oil. It is a glittering story of this present day.

The Canyon Reef ...

The smart brains of the oil industry had overlooked Scurry County until about 1948. There was a 6,500 foot deep limestone reef here that the *conquistadores* of Coronado, the Indians, the cattlemen, the cavalrymen, the surveyors, the railroad-builders, the nesters and the people who pioneered The Plains had walked over for years without dreaming of what it held.

There was a time when the Humble Oil people let all of their leases in Scurry lapse since all of the test-wells had been discouraging. Then the Standard of California in late 1948 brought in a well that caused the oil-thinking world to hold its breath.

Local folk had always believed that "there was oil in them thar hills" and among them was a young woman — Edith McKanna, an ex-GI — who ran her leases up to close an hundred thousand acres. She has many producers now to show for her faith and her foresight since the Truce of Rheims in 1945 released her from her uniform.

C. T. McLaughlin happened to have the center of the Canyon Reef just below his Diamond M Ranch of five thousand acres and he has no idea how much he is worth. He thought ranching was his avocation for the last fifteen years but he is in the big middle of the oil business now. A meat-butcher is reputed to be worth a quarter-of-a-million. A cotton farmer of last year is getting $3,500 a month in royalties today. Another oil-family — a rancher and his five sons who had some land — went out and worked on rigs for wages until they all six knew what drilling an oil well was all about. Then they started putting a well down on their own property. They have a family income of $5,000 a month now.

Jackson Ellis and his folks are really in "the high cotton" as they say along the Brazos now.

How did it happen? "Oil is where you find it!" This little cattle and cotton town of Snyder went from three to fifteen thousand people in nine months and that period of gestation was exciting! The oil-crazed prospectors moved in and took over all the buildings, the food and the facilities at the asking price. Trailer-camps grew like mushrooms, schools had to be enlarged and oil well supply yards extended out of town clear onto the prairies. Where would they ever get the water, the sanitation, the accommodations? People do not ask about such things when they are intent on winning. Snyder will double again before they take the next census. It is difficult to get a room to sleep in there now!

Movie-stars with fabulous incomes, wild-catters without a dime, big companies with plenty of money and independents who were willing to get their feet wet ... all began drilling like mad up on the Brazos Fork and it is estimated that about six per cent of all the oil rigs on the North American continent today are there in Garza County. Some say it may even eclipse East Texas and old Juan Ximenes Survey.

Joe York, his wife and four youngsters with a well on their 286-acre farm will be getting $15,000 a month soon. That well was brought in on his land in November 1949 and it proved up another big lot of acreage.

Let's swing up into Stonewall where the Salt Fork and the Double Mountain Fork snake their way over a large part of this country. We stand on one of the high peaks and look the wide, even stretches of land over — 2,250 feet above the sea-level of the Brazos' mouth here.

The towns are very few and wide apart on the highway ribbon and the railroad. Peacock, Swenson, Aspermont and Old Glory. There is an ancient red court-house of antique architecture — old for this new country if it dates back to the 1890's — and some genuine cowboys lolling against the drug-store wall.

We see more of King Cotton in those fields.

Miles of stalks with much of the whiteness still on them — hundreds of Mexican *braceros* picking in the fields — huge piles at the rows-ends — dunes of white cotton around the farm-house and outbuildings — wagons standing at the gins piled high with picked cotton waiting to be ginned and small chance of it being reached soon as the work-load is so heavy — bales in great numbers in the fields, strung out there because there is no room for storage in warehouses. That is the cotton situation here in mid-November we see as we drive along and marvel at its quantity.

There is plenty of mesquite. The crooked boles and the leafy branches that are ever green betoken shelter and cover as we drop down into Fisher County where the Clear Fork of the Brazos follows the highway through Roby, the county-seat. Then it runs eastward, picking up many a tiny tributary stream en route.

Monument Peak over by Sylvester is about 2,000 feet above the sea and these are the chief mountains of the Brazos-land. There is much more man-raised vegetation than we have seen up until now and evidences of cultivation. You get the feeling that here is a place that you could find shelter from the enemy, the elements and the prying eyes of the curious . . . could "hole-up" if you had to. The Brazos is still with us as we follow the Clear Fork through the county of Jones bound for the ruins of old Fort Phantom Hill and the lake that bears its name on the eastern border.

North of Jones the Double Mountain Fork skims the western edge of Haskell and joins up with the Salt Fork to flow on into Knox County in its southwest corner. Then it heads east over the south half of the square area on its way to the Possum Kingdom Lakes as a single stream.

It has been a queer sort of River up until now. Treeless banks were in the Plains country, but now they are becoming wooded with willows. There are fewer sand-bars showing through the shallow tide. There is more moisture here, vegetation and rows of trees that follow where the stream-bed leads. Towns are more plentiful, ribbands of roadways run white against the brown of the prairie, railroads gleam in the sun-light as their twin rails give the V-sign going away from you. One is not so inordinately lonely here as he was high up on the Caprock.

This was a great Indian section once. Here they hunted the buffalo herds, forayed down into the lower Brazos valley to do their pillaging and came back here to live. Their wigwams and council-fires were here and here they found salt, food and water along with the shelter that they craved. The buttes were their telegraph-lines where their smoke-signals went up into the Brazos sky. It was a natural home for them.

Buffalo grass and broom-weed. Jack-rabbits zig-zagging off in great bounds at the first hint of danger . . . or just to be on the safe side. A land of lush greens and deep browns, with a dark purplish haze off on the horizon. Good grazing lands with an occasional farm nestling down between and a substantial farm-house.

At the entrance to this lap of the journey into Scurry County, we were struck with the wildness of the approach . . . but not now. Where Scurry, Fisher and Stonewall were fierce in their starkness of scene, Jones, Haskell and Knox seem of a sudden homelike and civilized. They have a sustaining beauty of another sort . . . "the parched places in the wilderness, in a salt land and not inhabited . . . the heath in the desert."

There's cactus blooming — orange with a faint crimson tip to the blossoms — but very thorny spikes to the plants just the same. In season you will see a yellow huisache and in the spring a red-bud. You may depend on the mesquite to stay green. Nature will splash her brush around here in the spring with thistle and Indian-blanket, verbena and daisy until there will be a riot of color. But now it is November and if a country can be lovely in its hunting-habit of brown-and-dark green this is.

Above, the buzzards are circling. It is not a good sign but for the farmers and ranchers it is a significant one. A calf has been lost out in the shinnery and the rancher can charge that one off. The buzzards are his guides.

Now we are seeing birds in through here when we come to the trees. Back when we drove into Scurry one was lucky to see a kildee at a water-hole, a vulture or an eagle in a great while, but now there are larks on the fence-wires, mocking-birds in the mesquite, scissor-tails on the telegraph-poles and other birds if you search them out.

There are deer in this country, but not many. Game used to abound until the white man and Indian drove it out. The wild fowl migrate through here and sojourn on the open stock-tanks and lakes in the fall. Now that we come to cover and water we find the small creatures venturing here to live.

They tell you thrilling stories about this country when the soldiers and the Indians matched wits and battles in these draws and canyons. The men wearing the cross-sabers came

[335]

out from the forts and rode these hills and buttes looking for the raiding redskins. It was not as easy going as it is nowadays . . . frontier Indian-fighting was rugged.

They tell you of how Orient flared up for a time. It was a get-rich-quick promotion for a salted silver-mine. A boom-town sprang up and folk came in abundance to lose their shirts . . . but you'll find old-timers through here who will spin a tale of Spanish mines of gold and silver in the early days around Rath City and Orient. Some of them have the maps to prove it!

The last silver to be shipped out of this country went in about 1892. Two mining companies operated out of Stone-wall County. They hauled the ore to Abilene and shipped it to the smelter at El Paso. It cost $20 a ton to haul it out and it brought $18 at the smelter. The next year the miners planted cotton.

These little towns hidden away in "the western wold" are each interesting in its own right and each has a pic-turesque history about it. But it is the wide country in be-tween that intrigues the most . . . a cottonwood grove by the Brazos Fork . . . poplar leaves glinting silvery in the sun as the wind riffles them . . . salt cedars up on the gray, slate-like landscape . . . high, tall pecans where the River is a deeper current and has an all-year round flow . . . weeping willows dipping down into the stream by this bridge . . . a great Hereford herd scattered out over that sloping swale . . . a gulch carved into the terrain by some long-forgotten stream . . . a tank gleaming silver against the brown sward . . . an occasional corn or cotton-patch in the most unex-pected places . . . a windmill or an oil derrick punctuating the sky-line, no telling how many miles away.

There is sage-brush here and some nettles and soap-weed to give a touch of color. You wonder how anything can grow and thrive on some of this land, but these plants reach down to water and come up to green the surface. They will not grow very high. There is just enough vegetation to keep the country from blowing away when the sand-storms come.

It is an old country through which we are passing. At Hermleigh in Scurry, south of Snyder, not far from the Brazos Fork's inception in Sandstone Canyon, there are Indian picture-writings that go back perhaps thousands of years and then we find others that are more recent. Buffalo-hunters of the 1870's scratched their names here, cowboys of the early part of this century followed, and then tourists of later days. They used to post their cattle-brands here on the walls of this canyon as a sort of bulletin-board.

Don't think that Snyder was always an oil or cattle or cotton town. It was a wild buckaroo in the old days, they brag. "Robbers' Roost," they called it when the law and the rustlers slugged it out. At the site of the old West Side Saloon they can tell you about a man who got named Sheriff because he stopped a gun-fight, single-handed, armed only with a pool cue.

Which one of these canyons that we pass by did the Indians use for winter-quarters? You get to wondering about *people* as you pass through this bad-lands with its barren solitude . . . "the mother-country of the strong."

Haskell is a picturesque place to stop and see. Born in 1882 with a combination grocery-general-store-saloon that was named "The Road to Ruin," they held church in it on Sunday. The Forty-Niners passed through in great numbers on their way west, you are told time and again as you chat with the folks whose people settled this country a hundred years ago.

When the Kickapoos, Kiowas and Comanches who used to frequent this country were pushed farther west the buffalo-hunters moved in on their heels. The names of the towns you encounter suggest history — Paint Creek, California Creek, Lipan Point and Double Mountain. Each has a bit of history bound up in it that is important to it.

Indians, Swedes, Germans lived here once, but the Indians moved on. The Swedes came here to Jones County in 1877. The SMS Ranch has its headquarters not far from Stamford near the Jones-Haskell line and there are many Swedish customs, feasts, festivals and church gatherings among the people. It is a distinctly Norse flavor that you find.

The July 4th Cowboy Reunion at Stamford is a great time for the gathering of the cow-folk, as is the Cowboy's Christmas Ball at Anson. People come from far and near in costume to these occasions to keep alive the tradition of the horse-wrangler and the men of the herds. There is no dude ranch, drugstore-cowboy cast to these celebrations, either. They are genuine.

Wild Horse Prairie . . . as we drive along down the Forks of the Brazos we find that we are traversing the wild mustang country of a century ago. You can imagine the droves of these free, magnificent animals running the *mesa,* standing on the high buttes and looking like a cavalry troop against the sunset . . . manes a-flying, heads up and tails waving in the flight . . . all gone now.

This was the country in which they feuded and fought. Nester and cattleman went gunning for each other. The country wasn't big enough for both, they allowed, and they shot it out in these scrubby oak and mesquite thickets with Winchesters and Colts. They even hired paid-gunmen to come and help them carry their point. The movies have found the stories and the scenes of this country, right in through here where we are journeying, a rich field.

The tales of stolen water-rights, cattle-rustling, sheriff-and-outlaws, stage-robberies and bank hold-ups are of this very section. The readers and movie-fans never seem to get enough of the bravery and fortitude of these people of the Old West. This was *it* in the old days!

Again and again we find the trail of the archaeologist. Amazing stories with the artifacts to prove it. Caves and river-beds, gravel-pits and canyons produce queer bones and fossils.

This was where the wood or "box-houses" began, for they had wood in Jones, Haskell and Knox Counties that could be cut and hauled. The forts were not far away and the Indians were afraid to venture too close in their raiding. The dwellings were crude and the corrals were hard-built by driving cedar-stakes into the flinty soil. But the men who had the stamina to frontier this country wanted a place to pen their stock about the ranch-house.

In 1878 they called Snyder "Hide-Town" because they were bringing the buffalo-pelts in for shipping. Reynolds City was a hang-out for hunters, too. They founded it over in Stonewall County in 1876, but in two years the market moved and the town folded . . . Four general stores, a dozen saloons, a Chinese laundry, a hotel and a livery stable . . . and a grave-yard. A big one, too.

It was a lonely country in the 1870's and as late as 1883 you could go clear from Albany to Lubbock and see but one house. Haskell was not a town until 1884. The drought of 1881 dried the country up. The Clear, Salt and Double Mountain Forks stopped flowing entirely as did their tributaries, lakes and creeks. Water was hauled and sold by the barrel. Immigration halted and when they dug wells no water came forth. It was reported that even potato-bugs emigrated out of the country, it was so dry. Congress made appropriations and the Red Cross aided. Cattlemen drove their animals to where water could be located. Foreign capital went broke during these years and it was not until the spring rains of 1887 came that the real drought was broken.

The progress and prosperity of this country through which the Forks of the Brazos pass is interpreted in terms of Water. Until Man's ingenuity improvised windmills, immigration projects, water-control, conservation, lakes and dams, it was a bleak place to settle and try to exist. You can estimate the location and extent of water by the vegetation as you travel.

Around a creek, a lake or where the Brazos Fork has a good flow, there will be a pecan, walnut, elm or hackberry grove with other hardy trees of large bole-growth. Here a settler would likely build his cabin in the earlier days and later on his house. He would build on a slope commanding a view of the flats so that the Indians could not slip up on him under natural cover.

The wise ones built on a rise if there was one so that a breeze could blow through the center or "dog-run" of the cabin. The corrals and stock-lots were about two hundred yards from the main house with the chicken-shelters closer in. The fence was of hand-hewn post oak rails. If heavier timbers were needed for the beams and sills, they were cut in the heavy timber country and hauled in. Rawhide and such wire as could be obtained was used for making fences or a stake-and-rider rigged up after the ways they learned in the old States. A few oak trees for shade was a god-send. Shade was at a premium.

They say that a buffalo-camp in this section in the 1870's was a putrid-smelling place that could be located for miles away. Ever smell a green hide drying? Well, acres of them would be set out in the sun to dry — to be turned every two or three days — and then stacked, baled and loaded on wagons for Fort Griffin and the factor's scales.

Too, there were scaffolds of cottonwood on which were stretched tongues, humps and back-strips of the buffalo. The air above was thick with buzzards.

It has not been the vast, wide land of the Plains that we have been traveling, but the reclaimed border-land — The Land of The Desert-Rose — where for a time the Indian chose to call "home." Then, the buffalo-hunter delighted in it, the cowboy rode it in untrammeled abandon, the farmer bent its will to his plow and hoe and the oil men now wrest from it its long hoarded treasure.

The greatest charm that it has, perhaps, is to the fanciful who can see in it the true picture of the Old West ... with the sheriff and his posse chasing a group of bandits across the *mesa* and through the shinnery, mile upon mile ... as real as a neighborhood movie.

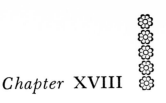

Chapter XVIII

FROM THE PLAINS TO THE PEAK

IN THIS LAP DOWN THE Brazos we see her gather her Forks together, blend and meld them into a single stream in her Possum Kingdom Lake area and move majestically for the remainder of her course towards the sea.

> *Ne'er saw I, never felt, a calm so deep!*
> *The river glideth at her own sweet will.*

Even as Wordsworth's favorite stream, so does the Brazos water these frontier counties of Baylor, Throckmorton, Shackelford and Young with their ruins of the old forts, their open and near-open ranges . . . and then, through the woodlands of Stephens, Palo Pinto, Parker and Hood, we see her wind through picturesque country. Redolent with memories of the olden days when the Indians made of these forests "The Dark and Bloody Ground," rich in cattle, thriving in cotton and ambitious in oil, we see a diversified valley.

Instead of a dry stream-bed in which a tiny brown or red trickle of acrid alkali flows hesitatingly along, or a broad, sprawling, shallow sheet of shimmering stream, punctuated by broad sand-bars, where the Forks zig-zag across the prairie-land, here, at last, is a recognizable River. Not a series of Forks — narrow ribbons blown across the Plains in a breeze — but a dignified stream cleaving its way through a land and through banks of exceptional beauty.

There is glamor of scene and story to this series of counties. Indians, troopers, settlers, travelers paused along here to make history and others have recorded it with far more exactness than they did the story of the Plains and Prairie Counties through which we have just passed.

There are old newspapers to read in the basements of small town libraries or in the back of editorial offices ... chats with old-timers around stores or at Old Settlers' Reunions ... or a story to pick up around an Old Fiddlers' Contest or at a County Fair ... or perhaps gather a gem over a cup of tea in a front-room with some little old lady, her hair tightly drawn back from her forehead and whose eyes sparkle with reminiscence as she recalls how the Comanches burned the Sheltons out just a whoop-and-a-holler from where her father's cabin was. You can see the blaze against the midnight sky as she describes it to you ... for she watched it through a chink-hole in her cabin as a little girl, while her father and mother stood to their guns with a fearful silence pervading the log hut.

The Brazos Salt Fork comes down across Baylor and heads for Seymour, the county-seat. Then it snakes off through the southeast corner, spurning the large lake in the north part of the county — Lake Kemp — that gives the Wichita River its contribution.

The vegetation is thicker and trees are the rule now instead of the exception. This is what is known as the Cross Timbers and the Plains and Rolling Prairies are behind us. Cotton is fairly abundant but not as plentiful as on the Plains. There are oil wells, too, but shallow ones for the most part and you can see many a field of pumpers and drawing-lines gathering the few barrels that each well contributes to the "allowable." The mesquite is fenced, and some of it is burned over, when they have not "assassinated" these tough trees by the injection of poison into the boles. Cutting or grubbing the tough roots is no easy task.

This little western town of Seymour was settled by the Oregon emigrants in 1878 just about the time that the nes-

[343]

ters and the cowmen tangled in their famous warfare. The new-comers met it full in the face. The cowboys thought that these folk from the Northwest were a part of the in-road — and perhaps they were — so, the cattlemen came riding into town, burned the houses, drove cattle across the planted fields until the Oregon people high-tailed out.

In Baylor County today you hear a lot of Bohemian spoken. The Czechs are well entrenched. They grouped together in this new land, read the newspapers in the old country language, had their festivals in costume on feast-days and sang the songs of the homeland.

There was no disloyalty to the new country, no desire to go back over the ocean to stay. They were happy and contented, for the land yielded them abundance.

The Salt Fork clips the edge of Throckmorton County in its journey east and south. There is a wide expanse of land between it and its sister-fork, the Clear, that zig-zags in through the high Antelope Hills in the southwestern part of the county. We have dropped down from the high 4,000 feet elevation that we had up at Muleshoe back at the Brazos source ... these are only little hills here in Throckmorton compared with those of the Plains.

The Comanches loved Throckmorton. It had cover and shelter, buttes for their signal-fires and game for their hunting. They fought the troopers in blue for it and the buffalo-hunters throve here in the latter days of the last century.

This huge county is rural and ranchy, with fenced fields and low protecting hills, wooded, and with little farms and ranch-houses nestling in the sheltered spots. There are none of the little village-clusters of houses that one finds in these people's old part of Europe. The farmer or the rancher has his house close to the land and his nearest village may be ten, twenty miles away. Off he goes in his car, attends to his business, hurries home to his rural-electrification, butane-gas fuel, long-distance telephone, home power-plant, septic-tank, radio and television. If he works he has his power-driven tractor and a maze of farm machinery for every job.

Camp Cooper was once an Army installation in Throckmorton. A Comanche reservation was *attempted* here, but they did not fence it in! The Caddos abode here in about 1851, while the 5th U. S. Infantry kept a watchful eye on them from Camp Cooper. In January 1856, Lt. Colonel Robert E. Lee's diary shows that he was at Camp Cooper doing duty with the 2nd Cavalry. George Thomas, W. J. Hardee and John B. Hood — all of them Civil War Generals — served on the plains of old Throckmorton County and the Indian frontier.

But Camp Cooper bowed out to Fort Griffin when the army decided to make it the big post hereabouts and they made Throckmorton a county in 1858 by act of the Legislature. Civilization was advancing its frontier . . . the Butterfield Stage Line ran this way . . . the California Overland Trail split the county in twain.

In Shackelford the Clear Fork clips off a slice of the northwest corner and then runs out into Throckmorton only to come back in again and wriggle out through the northeast corner. It misses Albany, the county-seat, by a liberal margin, but the hills and lakes of the northern half furnish uneven terrain and moisture to make the Fork a formidable stream the year around.

We stop as the Clear Fork enters the county and visit at the ruins of Fort Phantom Hill . . . a strong-point once against the Indian depredations. A busy place in 1851 when Major J. J. Abercrombie of the old 5th Infantry with five companies came here from Fort Belknap to garrison it. By the time they built Fort Phantom Hill, the other line of forts — Worth on the Trinity, Graham on the Brazos, Gates on the Leon — were short of the Indian country. In 1853, Belknap in Young, Cooper and Phantom Hill here in Shackelford, and Chadbourne in Coke were needed.

[345]

That old square rock ruin of a building, standing in the sun, was once a part of the old fort. It also served as a station of the Butterfield Stage-line....

The Rangers had been here patrolling since 1846 when five companies were thrown in at the pleas of the settlers. They operated out of Ben Bryant's Place on Little River and Torrey's Trading-House on the Brazos. Three years later the U. S. Government began building a line of forts to protect the wagon-trains and the stage-lines to California.

"Not for the settlers' sake," Washington said, "let the Rangers protect them or let them fight back at the Indians." The settlers had no lobbyists in Washington such as the stage-line folk had. When the capital of the North and East began running its coaches through here and the mail contracts waxed fat, the "yaller-legs" and their bugles came to the Forks.

Fort Griffin . . . One tramps through the mesquite thicket on the top of the high flat hill where the site of the old fort lies. The story of the fort has been told elsewhere. The mesquite must be new although the twisted trunks are old enough to have been here many a year. The ruins of the different buildings intrigue. It is quiet on the hill and we stand at the flag-pole and look the country over for miles around . . . still and quiet . . . the ghosts of the old Indian-fighters have gone back into the shadows . . . Miles, Shafter, Mackenzie, Sturgis . . . Charley Griffin, Lieutenant General of the 6th Cavalry and Commander of the frontier, after whom they named this fort . . . *they* lived here once.

At the edge of the hill we look down at the scene where the Brazos flows through the willows and thick trees . . . that was a thriving settlement once. It is a deserted spot today with only a few small houses, a school . . . where once saloons, dance-halls, stores, warehouses, general stores and Indian tepees strung out for a distance down the stream.

Fort Griffin was through by 1881.

We follow the Clear Fork of the Brazos through the northwest corner of Stephens. Hills and swales and little creeks abound. The huge Possum Kingdom Lake system laps over into the county.

King Oil claims the county of Stephens as one of his strongholds along the Brazos. A lot of drilling was done here in the Ranger boom days — Breckenridge, Caddo, Ivan, Necessity, Frankell and Breckwalker — these are oil-field towns where leases on land brought fabulous prices and where many locations were made. You are hardly ever out of sight of a derrick in Stephens.

There is history in this county. They called it Buchanan County at first, but politics were changing fast. When Alexander H. Stephens got to be Vice President of the Southern Confederacy, they named it after him. Breckenridge, the county-seat, was named for the Vice-President of the United States.

We pause at Picketville and Owl Head to see where they forted-up against the Indians ... Fort Davis on the Clear Fork had such an unmanned fortification.

There is an Indian story here. The Browning boys lived here on the Clear Fork. In June 1860 a large party of Indians came on a raid. The boys were grazing horses and the Indians killed one of them, but the other one, wounded, got away. When he got to General John R. Baylor, the old Indian-fighter gathered a posse and took off after the redskins. After a five-day pursuit he caught up with the Indians at Paint Creek and joined battle on sight. Thirteen Indians "bit the dust" and the others high-balled out of the county. The triumphant posse took the scalps of the "Unlucky 13" into Weatherford and exhibited them in the public square as they would varmint-hides. A big barbecue was held in honor of the occasion.

We learn from sources here of a pow-wow between the whites and the Indians in Stephens County in 1854, to which as many as 25,000 representatives of the tribes came.

It is hard to find positive confirmation and it may be that it was the council down at Comanche Peak in Hood to which they are referring. It is claimed that the emissaries of the Government and the Indians arrived in March and stayed until May, camping along the Brazos, holding war-dances, horse-racing, sun-worshipping, shooting-matches, gambling-bouts and carousing. Only the chiefs were at the meeting proper.

The Government wanted to settle the Indians on the Brazos near Fort Belknap in Young, where they could be watched. Old Yellow Wolf, however, would not agree to any-thing except drawing a line from the Red to the Rio Grande that would pass through San Antonio. He wanted the whites to stay east of it and the Indians west of it.

"No!" said the United States Government representatives. So, Yellow Wolf and his Comanches picked up their traps and pulled out. The other tribes signed.

But when the other Indians checked up, Yellow Wolf's crowd had stolen all the Lipan horses when they left. There was some borrowing on the picket-line and the Lipans took off to catch the thieves in Coke County where they suc-ceeded in killing Yellow Wolf and many of his warriors.

The Rangers had a story on Yellow Wolf that he "was kilt for his beliefs."

"Who ever heard of that old skunk being religious?" the credulous would ask.

"He had the belief that all the hosses in the county was his'n!"

With Yellow Wolf dead, the Comanches came onto the reservation which they used as a close base for their depre-dations into the River counties. "The Reservation War" resulted. But when the troopers settled the matter once and for all by herding the wild Comanches up on the Wichita in what was called the Chickasaw Nations, the foreign emi-grants poured into Stephens County. Many of the old names from across the waters show up today on garage signs and in small towns, but the accents and customs of "The Old Country" are not apparent.

In Young County, we see the wedding of the Forks. The Salt swings down through the southwest quarter into the Possum Kingdom Lake. The Clear comes at long last to a union with it and the lakes in the south of Young. From here on the River is a single stream.

Although not densely populated this has always been a cross-roads county where many folk have traveled, paused and tarried. Indians, traders, soldiers, buffalo-hunters, stage-coach drivers, Rangers, cotton-farmers, oil-well people. It is a busy place and always has been.

The markers alongside the road call to mind the time when the old Butterfield Stage whirled along this very road . . . Graham to Newcastle to Olney . . . scrub oak and sandy land that they call "shinnery" . . . mesquite in abundance on the low, flat hills . . . wild and unsettled in spots . . . fit for grazing and for scenery only, but picturesque and as western as a ten-gallon hat and a pair of chaps.

The old California Trail came through in the days of '49; and in June 1851 they ran the flag up to the top of the pole at Fort Belknap. It is an interesting restoration. Many of the buildings of native stone are in good state of preservation, with the crude square architecture of the early forts predominant. Here the 5th, 6th and 10th Infantry did duty, while the 1st Cavalry and the 2nd Dragoons rode the range after Indians. A lively town sprang up outside the fort and it is matter of history that R. S. Neighbors, the Texas Republic Superintendent of Indian Affairs, was shot down in the streets. The Confederates manned the ramparts in the Civil War and the Rangers headquartered here for a long time.

There is a bakery, a powder-house — square and steep-roofed — with an old road leading into town where the soldiers sought excitement and where the news of the frontier was swapped over red-eye whiskey and keg-beer in the several saloons. The people came here to buy salt for there was a sort of refinery. Charlie Barnard moved his trading-post here from down at Fort Spunky at the Falls. It looked as if the government was to make a permanent camp of Belknap, but not even Uncle Sam could hold back the frontier. When it moved, the fort folded up.

In October 1858, General D. E. Twiggs, who later got into trouble for surrendering the forts to the Confederates, reported to the War Department a victory of the Fort Belknap soldiers over the Comanches that he called "a victory more decisive and complete than any recorded in the history of Indian warfare."

Four companies of Cavalry and one of Infantry (they called all of them "companies" in those days in the official files, it seems) had marched from Fort Belknap against the Comanches on a thirty-seven-hour forced-march. They came to a village of one hundred and twenty lodges that contained about five hundred Indians. In thirty minutes the fight was over — 56 Indians killed, lodges burned, 300 horses captured and the survivors in full flight. Five troopers were killed and several wounded.

There is another Indian story...an old Methodist preacher — old Dad Tackett — back in 1859 lived down on Boggy Creek. One morning he found an arrow sticking in the neck of one of his cows. He followed the bloody trail in the snow to Tackett Mountain where he and his boys rounded up the rest of their cattle and started for home. Suddenly, up jumped a band of hostile Indians. Jim, George, Lycurgus and their old dad let the redskins have it, killing one on the first volley. Thinking that the whites were unarmed and would have to re-load, the Indians charged, but were surprised when the boys each had pistols and dropped four more on the charge. They beat a hasty retreat and there was no more molesting of the old preacher and his boys at Tackett Mountain.

Here in 1869 the Indians massacred thirteen Government teamsters on an Army supply-train over by Flat Top Mountain and the soldiers came against them and made them pay dearly ... down on Rock Creek near the Clear Fork of the Brazos where there had been a Fort Belknap once, but was out of commission when this happened, a war-party of about fifty Indians attacked a cattle round-up. Jason McLean of Keechi Creek and I. E. Graves of Weatherford were there at the time and passed the story down in their families ...

It seems that a Negro ex-slave was in charge of operations for the Indians while the Chief of the tribe stood on a nearby butte and directed the strategy. He was careful not to expose himself because the whites had long since learned that to kill the Chief was to take the fight out of the Indians. The Texans fought with six-shooters while the Indians had long-range rifles. It wound up by the whites losing about eight of their number before the Indians drew off having taken a much larger percent loss of their force. This was down in the Keechi Valley of Young.

That's Cox Mountain over there. In 1864 Cox and some of his men were out "hunting" cattle when some Indians chased them, driving them toward an ambush where some sixty of their warriors were hidden. In the fight, Cox was killed and two of the whites escaped to carry word back to the Fort that Captain Peveler of the militia was killed, too. But he was only wounded. Feigning death he lay doggo until he got a good shot at the Chief and when he killed him with a well-planted shot, the Indians quit. Peveler rode eight miles to safety with an arrow in his neck and sixteen other wounds. They named the mountain there after Cox.

Fort Murray was about eight miles from Belknap — just a forting-up place — and once when there were several hundred Comanches raiding through here they captured the wife and children of old Brit Johnson, a Negro ex-slave, who was at the time working on Moses Johnson's ranch on Elm Creek.

When Brit got home and found out about it, he quit his job and took off for the Comanche country to get his family back. The story of how this intrepid Negro went from place to place, village to village, hunting-party to hunting-party, is a most interesting one. Finally, he found them and the Chief restored the family to Brit for his pluck and "adopted" him into the tribe.

With no other choice facing him, Brit went along until the summer of 1865 when he managed to escape with his family, carrying a white captive woman along with them. But the Comanches never forgot this "desertion" and committed all of their warriors to watch out for Brit.

In January 1871, Brit was traveling the old military road east of Salt Creek with two other Negroes when he was attacked by a band of Comanches in full war-paint. He knew that it was a fight to the death, so he drew his bowie knife and slew his faithful horse, using the animal's body for a barricade. Firing from behind it, he spent the last round of his ammunition before they got him. In Young County, it is traditional that he accounted for one hundred seventy-three Indians with one hundred seventy-three empty shell cases about his dead body ... that may be a part of the tale, but it is a good one. The ex-slave was buried with full honors.

This is a fisherman's country. The Possum Kingdom lakes abound with fish for the skilful and there is a great deal of this country that is "birdy" for the quail-hunter. Doves abound. By some queer quirk of Nature there is a great quantity of petrified wood in through here and the people use it for common building purposes, regarding it with no special significance other than for its utilitarian value.

We leave the Brazos to visit in Jack County. Here at Jacksboro was Fort Richardson that rode guard down in "The

Dark and Bloody Ground" of the Brazos in the old days. The road coupled up Fort Richardson with Fort Belknap and Fort Griffin. The Butterfield ran through here.

Fort Richardson is well preserved and the buildings are used for military purposes today by the National Guard. The restorations are accurate. The officers quarters, the powder-house and the hospital are identifiable. In one of these buildings they were holding levee for General Sherman when he was informed of the Satanta Raid. In the old court-house square of Jacksboro, where the buildings are ancient for this country, is the site where the Indian chiefs were tried for the massacre of the wagoners.

We come down to the wooded glens and sweeping bends of old Palo Pinto, the near-mountains and the sloping hills. Here is a land where the Brazos and its plentiful creeks and tributaries make their way through the forests. The purple cast of the cedar-brakes on the Palo Pinto hills has a peculiar tone and shade of its own in the Brazos panorama. At Christmas time Jack Frost makes a wonderland of this cedar country with icicles glinting in the sunshine. Abundant Christmas-trees are crystals upon the slopes of the hills.

The Indians loved this country and it was perhaps their partiality for it that caused them to visit their wrath on the settlers who pushed them out of it. The cover, the game, the rich land, the plentiful water and the healing springs made it an ideal habitation for the nomadic people. Travel about they would, but they always came back to the Painted Pole land for their abiding-place.

How carefully they guarded the secret of the mineral waters! When forced out of Waco village, they came here and settled. They named the water "Crazy" in their tongue. It is still the trade-name of the crystals that are popularly used today. A settler named Lynch settled near the springs and found the water to be bitter. He feared to drink it until Lynch's wife, who had an ailing arm, used it for bathing and drinking. It aided her infirmity so that the fame of the mineral-springs spread.

They use native limestone and petrified wood for building in the towns and farms of Palo Pinto. It became a county in 1856, but Court did not meet here until 1858 when Judge N. W. Battle set the case of B. F. Harris for trial at the old Palo Pinto county-seat that is still in use. The charge was "Permitting liquor to be drunk on the premises where sold."

In 1880 the railroad reached here and the section grew rapidly. After that, it lost much of its reputation for being dangerous country. Wilbarger in his book on Indian depredations has this to say:

We do not hesitate to say (in 1889) that there is no territory upon the face of the earth of equal dimensions to that embraced within the boundaries of Palo Pinto, Parker, Young and Jack Counties whose inhabitants have suffered as much at the hands of bloodthirsty savages as have those who, at an early day, people the counties named.

Marcus L. Dalton dared to settle in here in 1855 and stood out against the Indians for a long time at the mouth of Rock Creek. But one day at Loving's Valley, six miles north of present Mineral Wells and twenty miles from his home on the Brazos, he and two men were returning from Weatherford where they had sold some cattle and made some other business transactions.

Indians attacked them from ambush, killed all three, scalped them and took their equipment and goods, but left $11,000 in an ironbound trunk and $11,000 that Dalton had in his shoes. They did not know the use of the money and did not care to be bothered with it.

The cover and shelter afforded in Palo Pinto attracted big game in the old days. Bear, wildcat, panther, deer, turkey were thick in here, but today only a scant remnant remains.

General Albert Sydney Johnston conducted the first survey of this area in 1830 and was so impressed that he selected a section of land for his own. His name appears on old deeds and plats. It has lovely vistas, commanding views from high palisades and tall rocky cliffs. . . .

Inspiration Point near Mineral Wells has a commanding view of the Brazos that is a favorite rendezvous for tourists to the famous resort who come to enjoy the waters.

Through the southwest corner of Parker County the River flows through the hills of Big Valley past where Nebo Mountain rises above the fertile plain. It is a country of diversified terrain and natural contrasts . . . here is a wide ranchland with rolling hills and a few bald buttes toward the horizon with barely enough brown grass for grazing . . . then one sees windmills, small farm-houses in the wooded copses along the streams, where cedar, pecan, hackberry, willow and cottonwood abound.

It resembles the weather of the Brazos valley . . . one old-timer testified that he came through Parker County with two oxen one winter day . . . it got so hot that one of them died of the heat and before he could get it skinned a Norther blew in and the other oxen froze to death.

Weatherford was a buffalo-hide center and collection-point in the early days of the real frontier. The soil is rich and yields peaches, melons, pecans and other fruit and nuts in abundance.

The line of settlement in this county moved slowly to the west and it was 1849 before it got to Walnut Creek and the Littlefield Bend of the Brazos. It was a daring venture, for the Indians were thick and Fort Richardson was not close enough to keep them from roving on moonlight nights.

One can find old Indian relics, arrowheads, stone-hatchets and other artifacts. G. A. Holland in his life-time was a collector of such historical evidences and maintained a museum on his place near Weatherford. He had a cabin with Indian bullets in it and the story that a settler was killed at the front door of it while the brave wife fought off the Indians from a chink-hole with the family guns. He was a noted rattle-snake collector, too, going out on a sunny afternoon with sack and forked stick and bringing in a bagful of rattlers caught sunning themselves on the limestone rocks. He rendered out snake-oil, sold the hides for decorative purposes and made necklaces out of the vertebrae as a hobby. He did much to preserve the folk-lore of Parker County and left a valuable collection of relics.

One day back in 1861, William Youngblood was out cutting cedar rails when nine Indians attacked him. They killed and scalped him, but it did them little good for just after leaving him they ran into a group of Rangers who wiped out every Indian . . . found the wet scalp of Youngblood, recognized it . . . hurried to find the body of the slain man and gave it Christian burial with its own scalp attached.

Old Isaac Parker, a member of the Legislature in 1855, gave this county his name, while State Senator Jefferson Weatherford gave his name to the county-seat. Judge Nat M. Burford held the first session of Court under a big post oak on the Fort Worth-Fort Belknap Road several miles north of present-day Weatherford. They had a newspaper by 1858, *The Frontier News.* Parker County gave Governor S. W. T. Lanham to Texas.

At last we come to Hood County. The waters of the Brazos wind through the middle of it, passing Granbury, the county-seat, where one remarks the ancient court-house in the plaza. Pausing by the banks of the Brazos where the steel bridge crosses we gaze upon the magnificence of Comanche Peak.

It is an awe-inspiring pile of masonry, high and visible for miles around. It is a long, flat mountain with a leveled top. Much history has been made on and about it. Little of it has been recorded.

Back in the 1830's on the earliest maps of this country, the surveys showed the peak. It acted as a marker and aiming-point for the surveyors and cartographers. The Santa Fé Expedition guided on it and crossed the Brazos near it.

The county was not created until 1866. Lipan in the northwest corner was named for the Indians who dwelt near here ... Thorp Springs, an early college town, was where the foundations of Texas Christian University, now at Fort Worth, were laid ... Cresson is a rancher's cross-roads town ... Acton has the cemetery where Davy Crockett's widow lies buried ... Tolar is where the Norse folk abound to indulge in hard-ground agriculture ... Mambrino is a farmer's hamlet nestling among the high oaks.

The Texas Republic Congress on January 14, 1843 passed a law setting up a military post near Comanche Peak and Torrey's Trading Station on Tehuacana Creek. This was done in 1844 and Fort Spunky came into being. An Indian agent was stationed here and it was used as a fort-settlement until Fort Belknap came along farther west in the 1840's.

They claim that Indian smoke-signals went up often from Comanche Peak and were visible for a great distance away. The Indians could do strange things with smoke ... make it go straight up despite a cross-wind that was blowing at the time, or make it spread out, or spiral flat at the top, or disappear in a sudden puff.

"If you see'd one of them signals," says Uncle Ed, wrapping his thin legs about each other and crossing his elbows on his knees, "you wuz boun' to see another un answerin' him from a hill way off yonder."
"Did they ever teach y'all how to handle smoke, Uncle Ed?" a goggle-eyed youngster at the Reunion asks.
"Nope," the old man spits emphatically. "The redskins war plenty particular not to learn no white man them tricks. But we got so we could figger them out after we'd see'd them purty often. They could say anything they wuz a mind to. I've see'd three or fo' signals in the air at one time."

Hood County is in the very heart of the Grand Prairie. The oaks and sturdy pecans abound. Mesquite in the flats and cedar on the bald knobs . . . hardy land with many a bare stretch . . . treeless for miles and then thick woods. High hills . . . Johnson's Peak, Top Mountain and Little Round Top . . . but none as high and imposing as old Comanche!

They have drilled and drilled in Hood for oil and sometimes they get "showings." The wild-catters still persists.

We pick up Indian lore as we go along. Flacco, Chief of the Lipans, was a brave and friendly ally of the whites, but Castro was a mean and unreliable old redskin who followed along after him. . . . They had a fight near Hanna's Mill on the Paluxy when fifteen settlers shot it out with twenty Indians and the whites won — with not a dead man on either side! Nathan Holt in 1859 was out looking for his cattle on the banks of the Brazos and the murdering Indians killed him and shot his horse full of arrows, just for meanness, sending the crazed animal galloping home to the cabin with the terrible news to Nate's little family. The Indians did really scalp a Negro here once, no matter what the tradition says, for back in 1863 when Jeremiah Green and five white men were out hunting cattle and were set upon by sixteen Indians every white man was killed. Jerry, the Negro slave, was found wandering about, his scalp lifted. He died a few days later. Seven Lipans came through here heading down east on Squaw Creek and gathered up about two hundred settlers' horses, but a posse of settlers came out of Thorp Settlement and pursued them. They came up on them in a ravine, where they had taken refuge, surrounded and killed every last one. Wilbarger says they scalped every dead Indian except a squaw who was discovered disguised in man's clothing. Two whites were wounded and one of them died later on. They named Squaw Creek after this occurrence.

Today it is pleasant and peaceful along the banks and you

can find many a good fishing-spot or swimming-hole in old Hood. The pastures are green and the shade of the trees inviting. No great industry, just a seasonal income for farmer and rancher.

Chapter XIX

FROM THE FOREST TO THE FALLS

"THROUGH THE HEARTLAND of Texas" . . . if that is the course of the Brazos then truly is this leg of the journey down the River through "The Heartland of the Heartland." The sylvan counties of Somervell, Johnson, Bosque, Hill, McLennan, Falls, Robertson and Milam are its very core and center.

When the Mexicans and their Spanish forebears looked upon this part of the valley, they gave to it their soft and beautiful name — *el bosque* — which, interpreted, is "The Forest." Cool shade, green fields, and lush pastures abound in the midlands of the Brazos.

Cotton and corn journey in complacent rows down slopes and hillocks to the water's edge in this region. There is not much uncultivated waste-land as there is farther up the course of the stream. One begins to see many more people through this region . . . a tenant-farmer sowing or reaping . . . a Negro field-hand picking or chopping. The trees and plants cluster about the houses and along the stream-beds. The herds that stand in the shade and chew a reflective cud are not as purely thoroughbred as they were up on the Plains.

The vistas are not so grand, the views much less sweeping than they were on the Grand Prairie. But it is more home-like here and less lonely.

This is the River's old and settled land. She tarries here and takes her time as she winds through tree-lined banks. The color is a deep yellowish-red from the clay and phosphates of the soil through which the Brazos flows. There is a peaceful purple to the twilight when a Bob-white whistles up his covey for roosting after sun-down and the pale wood-flowers shade off into darkness.

This is blackland, well-watered, that will yield its abundant fruit. There is none of the rocky, flinty surface that we saw in the uplands. Men and animals, birds and insects live without the effort that they exert on the plains and prairie-lands. The soil is deep enough for cotton and sugar-cane. There are no hills or buttes in this region but their opposites — creeks and flats — and little streams flowing over pebbles. People fish in the waters, boys swim in the "holes" and cows come to stand in the shallows to feel the ripples over their hooves on a hot day.

We start our journey in Somervell County, the tiniest along the River's course. It is a rural paradise where the Paluxy joins the Brazos. There are scenes and beauty-spots that make this a resort and vacation-land. Mineral springs and hotels, church-encampments and pleasure-parks, picnic-grounds and private camps attest to the popularity of the area.

A man came here, a story goes that we pick up on "The Square" of the county-seat, in the middle 1860's who called himself "John St. Helen." They firmly believe that he was John Wilkes Booth, the man who killed Lincoln. He lived out his life, died here and is buried in the little graveyard.

Small Somervell was carved out of her neighboring counties in 1875 and her people are farmers . . . in the stirring days of the Prohibition Era they made a wicked sort of concoction here in the hills that was known far and wide as "Glen Rose Moonshine." It is still a standard in the Brazos country for potency.

The Brazos washes Johnson County on its southwestern side. It began as a county in 1854, but Alvarado and Cleburne, two of its good towns, were both settled earlier and in 1856 Judge Nat M. Burford held the first session of Court. It is a farming and grazing country with deep-rooted grass, fruit orchards and staple crops supporting the land and people. Many little towns dot the area.

Find the historically-minded old timer (and he is scarce, too, for they are busy with the present in Johnson County) and he will show you where Philip Nolan and his men, who were supposed to be "wild mustang-hunting" met the Spanish soldiers out of Nacogdoches and where Nolan met his death. They buried him here on the lone prairie in 1801 and he never got back to report to Aaron Burr on his "filibustering."

There is quite a high hill — Lookout Point — in the state park here where you may stand and look along the Brazos for miles, glistening in the distance. The glint of the bare limestone hills is off yonder in the distance.

We can see the tall rise of Sugarloaf Mountain which is one thousand feet high and a mile long.

We visit Keene. Here the Seventh Day Adventists control the town and all therein. No meat, tea, coffee, tobacco or alcoholic drinks are allowed. Women eschew cosmetics and jewelry. There are no ball games, hot-music or fiction, nor are there cinemas or jails. But they are busy: a junior college, a planing-mill, a broom factory, and a printing-plant supplement the everyday activities of the people who have chosen to build Zion here.

Across the River is Bosque County . . .

Here we find the headwaters of the Bosque River, which flows parallel and on to the next county to join the Brazos there. It enriches a land that the Norse people have settled. The hills reach up to 1,300 feet. No great cities or towns but sturdy little villages, small towns and farm-houses with great barns in back of them. Plenty of thickets and cover for small game but a populated land and well-tilled.

Indians prowled here in the early days and "stole the

Bosque folks blind," as the saying goes. There were plenty of hills and woods for the redskins to hide in.

They will tell you how Ole Canuteson in 1854 had his house pillaged by Indians when he went to town in his wagons to bring more Norwegian settlers out to the Bosque. His family had to take to the woods for safety, But the Norsemen organized a posse and set out after the Indians, chasing them to the Paluxy, near Glen Rose's present site, and clearing the war-party out of the country. Thereafter, they were prepared for them when they came raiding.

In 1854 they made Bosque an official county and through here the noted Santa Fé Expedition passed on its way to New Mexico . . . the buffalos were as thick as bees in this vicinity once and old timers still remember that when you saw them in a valley the whole land looked black, so large were the herds.

They had a famous militia company down here under Captain Allison Nelson. It gave a good account of itself in the Indian-fighting.

The thrifty Norse folk learned how to dress hides from the friendly Tonkawas and went regularly to Waco to trade their finished products for wheat, powder and lead. They made fine Norway-style saddles and were noted for their craftsmanship. It was a community rule among these Norwegians that each shares with his neighbor.

They journeyed up from Bosque to Fort Belknap in the early days to trade pigs for tobacco and their cotton wagons went all the way to Houston to trade for salt and staples. When the herds came through they were ready to trade for the sickly and lame, nursing them back to health and augmenting their own herds.

The beauty of this region appealed to Major George B. Erath when he was surveying it and it was he who sold Ole Pierson, Canute Canuteson, Jens Jenson and A. Barton on bringing the first Norse families in. Then, one day Cleng

Peerson, who had come out of Norway and traveled the wide land over to find the replica of his homeland, felt that he had truly come upon it where the Bosque and the Brazos make a fertile valley. He prevailed upon his Norse friends in Kaufman and Henderson Counties to come and live here.

With their own Indians the Bosque folk were on good terms. The Tonks along Meridian Creek and Neils Creek were very friendly, but when the Plains Indians came, . . . that was another story. The Indians knew Meridian Peak as a rendezvous-point. There is a story that once in the early days a redskin war-party was raiding around the town of Meridian when they encountered Uncle Peter Johnson and his ten year old boy. They had a wagonload of supplies and were about where Iredell is now located. They killed the old man, rifled the wagon, and took the boy captive. They were bound for Comanche Peak to meet other parties of their people, but Patillo Fuller spied them and got away on his horse.

The Indians knew he would give the alarm and reveal where they went. So they sent one party down the Bosque and another down the Leon, dividing their stolen horses and loot between the two. Little Peter managed to escape but was very lightly clad and came near to freezing before some cattle-hunters found him.

The posse took out after the Indians who got away as fast as they could, killing the entire Wood and Conly families and two Monroe brothers lest they tell on them. One of the parties got to Neal Creek in Hamilton County and killed a man named Knight. Jim Babb happened upon two of the Indians drawing water at a spring the next day and killed them both, finding Knight's boots and hat on them. The main parties got away scot-free.

The first election in Bosque County was held in October 1854 and Judge R. E. B. Baylor held the first session of District Court on June 9, 1856. An amusing incident attended the opening of court . . .

"Open the Court, Mr. Sheriff," the Judge directed.

"Jedge," replied the Sheriff, "I ain't never opened no Court."

"Well, just go to the Courthouse door and shout as loud as you can 'The Honorable District Court of Bosque County is now in session'," said the Judge and then with a sigh he added: "God help us!"

Not realizing that the Judge was sighing over the ignorance of his Sheriff, that worthy went to the door and yelled: "The Honorable Deestrict Court of Bosque County is now in session. God help us!"

Across the snake-like course of the Brazos from Bosque is Hill County. There at Whitney they are planning a huge dam and lake that will insure moisture and the preservation of the Brazos springtime waters for the benefit of all this territory.

Here the Towash Indians camped once and had their settlement. There was a Towash Dam and a mill of native limestone blocks taken from out of the Brazos-bed. The mill was fortified and used for forting-up when the Indians came. In peaceful times they ground corn for the neighborhood between its stones.

Here old Fort Graham stood. Back in the days of '49 when they were mining for gold at Sutter's fort out in California many a covered wagon came past this fort. They had soldiers here in garrison and it flourished for four years but by 1853 the frontier had moved so far west that the soldiers had to move with it. Today it is a crumbling ruin.

The Caddos lived in the western part of Hill once and in 1839 Colonel Neil took a village that the Iona Indians occupied on the site of old Fort Graham. He was a valiant hunter of Indians and they say that he chased them all the way to Comanche Peak before he let up on them that time and came back by way of the Trinity looking for more.

It was a "gamey" country — bear, deer, antelope, mountain lions, lobos, wildcats, coyotes and badgers abounding at one time. They used heavy guns in those days . . . the Sharp's rifle or buffalo gun, 50 calibre, with a heavy ball that would kill up to 1,500 yards. Then, they had an old Springfield musket, the Henry rifle, the Spencer carbine, a muzzle-loading Kentucky type and a Spencer model of rifle.

The Indians made a brave stand to keep Hill county. It was not until 1835 that the surveyors from Waco made it as far as the Fort Graham site so obstinate were the red men. Then a long period elapsed and it was 1849 before W. H. Kirkpatrick and his family built a cabin, the first in the county as it was later constituted. A ferry was established at Fort Graham and a settlement grew up about the fort.

After the county was organized they built an elm-wood court-house, but it had a dirt floor and the jail was far more commodious, having a capacity for two hundred and costing $1,793. The Baptists set up for business in Hillsboro in 1849 under Rev. J. M. Stanford, while the Methodist movement began in the Peoria community. Hillsboro had two newspapers before the Civil War, *The Hillsboro Express* and *The Prairie Blade*.

Originally Navarro County was formed from a slice of Robertson and Hill was carved out of Navarro. Lexington Village was settled on Jack's Branch in 1851, but it was not until 1853 that the seat of the county was moved from Jack's Branch to Hillsboro. Woodbury and Hillsboro fought bitterly for the county-seat, but the latter won.

Fort Graham came into being because of the Indian depredations in Hill County. The Indians opposed every attempt to penetrate into their area. They were finally driven out and Hill became a sort of highway when the herds started moving North.

Today this is a thickly settled country, prosperous and complacent, about as rich a blackland cotton county as the Brazos boasts. No great pretentions to industry and no oil wells.

At last we come to the "Capital City of the Brazos," as

they like to regard it at Waco. It is the pivotal area of the River, the cross-roads of her traffic, and the most significant city along the stream, perhaps. Her people have kept well preserved the lore of the place and its deeds. There was published a centennial edition of *The Waco Tribune Herald* that was a tremendous historical document. To it this narrative is highly indebted for many facts of the Brazos midlands.

Although the Anglo-Americans came in numbers to the Brazos in the 1820's, it is singular to note that it was not until thirty years later that they actually established a city on the bluffs where the Indians had built their most important village.

There was an excellent ford of the Brazos at Waco, fine timber and good springs of fresh water.

Game came to drink and tarry in the Brazos shallows, the ground was rich and black, yielding wild fruit and berries as well as easily-produced domestic crops of corn and maize. The climate was mild and temperate, the rainfall good. The Indians found it a goodly land and took up abode there.

While San Felipe, Richmond, Washington, Calvert and Navasota could be settled, Waco had to be won. The Indians stoutly asserted their rights and offered to fight to retain it as their own. When Captain Thomas H. Barron and his Ranger Company came in 1837 from Nashville about eighty miles down the Brazos with a Vienna-born Sergeant named George B. Erath, they built a fort of sorts. They called it "Fort Fisher." But it was too far from base and Barron evacuated it in three weeks after he noted the way the Indians were grumbling and planning their strategy.

Erath never forgot the place. He was a surveyor, fought at San Jacinto and served in the Texas Congress. In 1839 he brought Neil McLennan to look at this site that he liked so much for a city. There was a trading-post across the Brazos in 1844, but the Indians died hard on yielding the south and west bank. In all of their treaties and "understandings" with the whites they put Waco Village in *their* territory and insisted that it be left to them.

The Mexican authorities down in Coahuila had issued promiscuous land grants to this territory along the Brazos where McLennan County is located. From the River out they let great blocks of it go to rich Mexicans in favor with the government. The settlers knew this and were afraid of the land title matters.

Chambers' grant covered most of the better part of the Waco Village site. He was a prominent man in the founding of the Republic, was potent in selling Washington on Texas' future, promoted the "Twin Sister Cannon" gift from Cincinnati and was a very influential man. He owned the land where Ed Burleson founded the town of Waterloo — that later became Austin, the State capital. He took title to most of Waco and McLennan County.

Until he sold it to a Galveston party the wise people laid off and would have nothing to do with it. The new owner secured the services of the dashing Jacob de Cordova, a native of Jamaica, map-maker, land specialist, surveyor and *entrepreneur* extraordinary. He was to lay out a town and start the settlement.

It is claimed by some that Erath first interested de Cordova and that together they prevailed upon Shapley P. Ross, Ranger and Indian fighter, to move his family in and become the "First Citizen" of the new town. He was to get the ferry rights, four town lots and the pick of the farms. He accepted the proposition, raised his banner and the settlers came pouring in.

On March 1, 1849, Erath, John McLennan and others began locating people in the present town-site of Waco and sold lots as fast as they were surveyed. It was a bare place with the rubble of the Indian village scattered about on every hand. Barron had situated his settlement back from the River because of the title difficulties. Captain Ross' ferry was the only one across the Brazos that high up from the mouth. Families proceeding to the east bank used it to cross. Town lots sold for $10 and $5 each according to their desirability. Dr. Alexander Montgomery Barnett and his family drove all the way from Kentucky by wagon, got ten acres of land in trade for a rag carpet and two bed quilts, and settled down to stay.

Ross was also the postmaster and it is related that he carried the letters around in his tall beaver hat, sweeping it off on meeting an addressee, and delivering the mail on the spot. He also ran the water-works which consisted of having his slave draw water from the spring and haul it at 5c per bucket to the cabins. Also he ran the first hotel and wagon-yard and had something to do with organizing the first stage-line that went from the Brazos banks down to Austin and San Antonio.

There are many picturesque views of the Brazos along its wooded banks in MeLennan County where the Bosque joins it after picking up several small streams and creeks. Stately groves of trees on the high Balcones Escarpment add much natural beauty to the River's banks. Amid them Waco's tall, lone sky-scraper and the twin towers of Baylor rise on the sky-line.

A. M. Strand had a trading-post of sorts in 1834 in this neighborhood and the Huacos gave their begrudged approval until he won their confidence. But when Boyd tried to build his house in 1835, taking advantage of the surveyors reaching to Fort Graham, the Indians made ashes of it in short order.

A detachment of the Santa Fé Expedition that Lamar sent out in 1841 passed through Waco and the chronicler wrote down in his diary:

All around the village were cornfields and pumpkins and melons. The wigwams were built in rows and had an air of neatness and regularity about them that I have never before seen in an Indian village. . . . They lived in some comfort and showed evidence of a more elevated humanity than exists among most Indian tribes.

There is authentic information that the wily de Cordova tried to take this Waco country by a *coup* before he decided to acquire it by more peaceful and perhaps more ethical methods. It is said that in 1839 he tried to stir up the Cherokees to wipe out the white settlers in McLennan County and promised Mexican military help. But President Lamar ordered several Ranger companies in and they waylaid the Mexican *guerillas* on June 1, 1839, decisively defeating them and adding their equipment to their own inadequate quartermaster stores. There were said to be about 5,000 Indians waiting for this Mexican contingent to arrive. The first they knew of the defeat of their allies was when the Rangers attacked and chased them to Fort Graham. DeCordova changed his tactics after that and began using more orthodox means.

The Indians who came from the old States now and then paid off old scores of hatred and revenge on the whites through this central region of the Brazos. Cherokees, Caddos, Ionas and Anadarkos preyed on the white settlers and a band of rascally white men, criminals and outlaws, gathered in the Bosque and Brazos woods to establish a reign of terror of their own until Captain Ross and his *vigilantes* wiped them out in 1846.

Although Waco is considered a Baptist stronghold, it was a bold and stalwart old circuit-rider of the Methodist faith, Joseph P. Sneed, who stood under the shade of a hackberry tree in 1849 and flung his Wesleyan gospel to the breeze for the first sermon of the Protestant faith thereabouts. He set down in his diary that "the howling of the wolves across the Brazos scared him worse than they did Elijah." He had a Methodist meeting-house going by the time the county was organized in 1850.

Judge R. E. B. Baylor held court here first in April 1851 and licensed Richard Coke to practice law. In 1856 *The Waco Statesman* began publication. The Waco Female College was operating in 1859 and the Baptists had Waco University going full blast in 1861, but it took until 1885 for Baylor to move up, consolidate, and begin its career on the Brazos that would blossom into the great university of the present day.

"The Queen of the Brazos" was the name the cowboys of the cattle-drives gave to Waco and they delighted in driving through because of the dance-halls, saloons and gambling-joints on Rat Row and the Square of the post-Civil War town. There was a big fiesta when the Suspension Bridge was opened in 1870. It boasted four huge towers, 475 feet long, three million Waco-made brick and great cables shipped out of New York and ox-teamed up from Galveston. It was the biggest at the time in the United States and the second longest in the world. Waco and the Brazos-land were indulging in Texas superlatives even in 1871 . . .

Captain J. H. Rainey in 1890 decided to attempt Brazos navigation up toward the source of the River but he was gone only a couple of days when he was back, reporting too many sand-bars barring his progress.

McLennan County is full of Indian lore much of which has already been included in this narrative. The Baylor museum contains the greatest collection of local relics and artifacts of the region. The Spanish style is preserved in an all Mexican Church — St. Francis-on-the-Brazos — a copy of the Mission San Jose at San Antonio. The Negroes allude with pride to Paul Quinn College in East Waco and the Masonic Grand Lodge of Texas meets in annual session in its new temple, wherein are the minutes of the San Felipe Lodge in 1828 over which Worshipful Master Stephen F. Austin presided . . . although it conflicts with the story of The Masonic Oak of Brazoria and the later establishment of the first duly constituted lodge.

One may travel a few miles from Waco up the Mexia road, go aside into the State Park and see reproduced the stockade on the very site where the Indians burned the original Fort Parker and carried Cynthia Ann away into captivity . . . and so to The Falls of the Brazos . . .

Falls County contains many interesting spots for the traveler to visit as he cruises down the River . . . "meet me at the Falls of the Brazos when the harvest moon is full." This was a well-identified rendezvous in the old days. The sight of the River dashing itself to pieces over limestone rocks with the silver lichens clinging to them in the days when the settler came to Bucksnort trading-post for supplies never failed to delight.

This was the land of the Tehuacanas for a long time, which they left with reluctance. To Chilton came the German settlers to build houses and churches after the kind they left behind in the little villages of Bavaria. One sees thrifty farms, big barns and houses built high on the hills, while in the quaint church-yards the old emigrant fathers take their long rest. Walk there and piece together the history of the land for yourself . . . Hans . . . Emil . . . Erich . . . and old German patronymics that bespeak the sturdy yeomanry that made of this section the thickly-settled area of homes that it is today. You see a tractor now, modern farm machinery and well-planned crops. No great display of wealth or abundance, but you feel that these people are living off the land and within their income. It is a region of old settlements.

The bones of some of the Indians in the burying-grounds show that they had arthritic conditions and the teeth of them show pyorrhea. One ponders whether they came here to use the healing waters of the springs.

Dr. James Long, who came in 1819 to start his filibustering, records that there was a trading-post at the Brazos Falls established by his brother, David Long and one Cap Johnson. In early 1830's Sterling R. Robertson established Sarahville d'Viesca. But we look in vain for someone to point out where it stood. It was moved and became Fort Milam and if you search far enough you will find a marker that the State has placed on that site. The Indians discouraged this attempt at settlement. We can find this record:

The town at the Falls of the Brazos in the Nashville Colony, heretofore known by the name of 'Viesca' should be changed to Milam. This whole territory bordering the Brazos south of Waco is known as 'The District of Viesca' and the principal settlement is at the Falls of the River. This is all in the Nashville Colony, one of the early *empresario* grants. Two hundred families were colonized here in 1830 and others came in later.

There is an Indian story with some pathos to it they tell at the Falls . . . in 1833 Chief Canoma and his friendly Caddos fraternized with the whites and was their friend. When a band of Tonkawas killed a white stranger named Reed and took his stock and wagon, Canoma and his braves pursued them and recovered his goods and Reed's scalp. Later, Canoma acted as intermediary between the white men and the other Indian tribes, negotiating for the return of children who had been captured. Once, he warned of an Indian raid that was planned against Bastrop and frustrated it.

On a trip to recover some stolen horses, he bore the credentials from the Falls white people when he fell in with a detachment commanded by Edward Burleson. That hot-headed, impulsive Colonel, who had given Sam Houston trouble during the retreat before San Jacinto, tore up the credentials, declared them to be false and killed Chief Canoma and his small son. The squaw escaped and brought the word back to the Falls. The word was sent to Burleson not to show himself around the Falls of the Brazos again and he carefully avoided it thereafter.

Tenoxtitlan existed in 1835 and it was quite a Spanish settlement in its day. It was at the Falls that David Crockett

[373]

made engagements to meet his Tennessee friends and the first place that he stopped in the Texas land. Also they organized a Ranger company here, said to be the first, and called it "The Range Men." Judge Perry, after whom the little town of Perry not far from the Brazos is named, was a Lieutenant in that company when it built Fort Milam.

In 1837 the Mexicans and Indians teamed up to attack the settlers at the Falls fort and killed many of them, among them Coryell, after whom the adjoining county was later named. The families that escaped fled to a nearby point, forted up, and founded the site of present Marlin. It became a stockade and was called Bucksnort for sixteen years.

The leading Indian atrocity hereabout took place in January 1839, on New Year's Day, when the Indians swooped down upon the Morgan family, nine miles north of Marlin and slaughtered all the adults of the family and many of the people visiting them. Three small children and Miss Stacey Marlin, who feigned death, escaped.

Chief Josef Marie (José Maria to the Spaniards) led the attack in person. James Marlin's family and Jackson Morgan's, together with Mrs. Jones were at George Morgan's place while the rest of the families were at John Marlin's seven miles lower down the Brazos. Every person at Morgan's Point was killed except little Isaac Marlin who hid and then ran seven miles to report what had taken place.

Ten days later the same Indians were back, attacking the house of John and Ben Marlin, but the whites were lying in wait for them and killed seven Indians in the first onslaught. Captain Bryant raised a posse and pursued the Indians to where they crossed the Brazos at Morgan's Point and trailed them to a post oak grove near a dry branch.

José Maria and his men opened fire, Bryant led a charge in which he fell, and Ethan Stroud took over command, driving the Indians into a ravine. David Campbell's shot hit the Chief as Albert Gholson's shot killed his horse, but José

Maria was not dead and the Indians got him clear away. He always boasted that he was whipped until the whites got to celebrating their victory. There are historical markers to be seen today at the home of George Morgan and also at the home of John Marlin.

But on Sunday morning, May 27, 1839, the Indians took a real defeat. Captain John Bird with thirty-one Rangers left Fort Milam at the Falls on a scouting expedition. They had gone about five miles when they came upon twenty-seven Comanche warriors skinning a buffalo and chased them to the main body about three miles away. The Indians retreated but Bird held off until he could be reinforced from the fort. Returning they were ambushed by forty Indians and driven into the ravine for shelter where there was a spring.

By smoke-signals the Indians summoned about three hundred others with old Chief Buffalo Hump, a wily old rascal, in command. Giving the Comanche war whoop they charged but could gain nothing by a frontal attack. They divided into two parties and attacked again. Captain Bird and six Rangers were killed. Then James Robinett, a young German among the Rangers, drew a bead on Buffalo Hump and knocked him from his saddle. The Indians withdrew with the body of their chief, noting one hundred killed to the Rangers' seven.

In the summer of 1861 a settler named Butoff left his clearing on Elm Creek in Falls County with four yoke of oxen and started for Johnson County with a hide-press. Six Indians waylaid him, slew him and pillaged his wagon. Another settler, William Glassinjim, was out "horse-hunting" and saw it all. Since he was too late to do Butoff any good, he decided to ride for help. The Indians pursued him and overtook him. He whirled and drew his pistols. Cursing the Indians madly, he dared them to attack.

"I'll kill two of you thievin', murderin' bastards," he shouted. "Come on, which two is it going to be?"

Realizing that he would do just that and none of them wishing to furnish the target for his pistols, they broke out laughing at his pluck and rode away.

Falls County was organized in 1850 and its county-seat named for John Marlin. The first court-house was a log hut. They had a ferry over the Brazos in 1855 when Churchill Jones ran it. The first bridges over the River were toll-bridges at Belton Crossing, built in 1870 and erected on pilings driven a few feet apart in the River's bed. The Brazos had plenty of water then:

In these days small steamboats transported a large part of the traffic up and down the Brazos River. As the size of the vessels increased, however, they were not able to utilize the shallow waters of the Brazos and traffic by water diminished.

The first stage-line up the Brazos came through Marlin traversing Falls County and going into Waco, but it took until 1888 for the S. A. & A.P. to run a rail-line through the Falls country and immigration was slow until it did.

In 1861 when Secession was a hot issue in Texas they took it seriously at Marlin. Sam Houston had been rocked in Waco when he tried to talk against it, but that same night in Marlin he got a worse reception. Up rose Lawyer Stewart in the audience on the courthouse steps in Marlin.

He accused Houston of being "an old man who would mislead the people" and a hot debate followed. It is recorded that Judge James D. Oltorf gave a barbecue at his home for General Sam that evening after the speech-making and Houston stayed at his home until midnight. Then he climbed into his buggy and drove on to Huntsville . . . what must his thoughts have been as he drove down the valley of the Brazos . . . here where he had made so much of her history . . .

Marlin is an old town, but it was not until 1891 when they were drilling for drinking-water that they struck a great pool of hot water that was due to pour forth a quarter-million gallons a day. They tell the story that there was not much made of the hot water until a tramp came along with a bad case of eczema. When he washed in the hot water he was relieved. They began investigating the curative properties of the water. Now it is a famous spa with bath-houses, sanitaria, and a home for crippled children where the ailing benefit from the waters.

The last two counties in this old country of the Brazos, Milam and Robertson, are divided by the waters of the River as they flow to the sea. Cameron and Franklin are the county-seats, respectively, and are thriving little towns of central Texas where cotton and farming of sorts are the mainstays. Calvert, once a wild and woolly place, elsewhere treated, is a reformed little city leading a most circumspect life.

Robertson, on the east bank of the Brazos, was the huge area out of which most of the adjacent counties were formed in the 1850's. To this region came sturdy settlers from Baden and Bavaria along with Czechs and Bohemians. The architecture is quaint and European with columns and façades of the continental style. Farming and grazing occupy the people and they live thriftily and comfortably from the land.

Milam, on the west bank, complements its neighbor with many little towns and farm-villages. Cameron was settled before Texas was free of Mexico and named for Captain Ewen Cameron, a noted Indian fighter of the early days. There are Indian stories galore in these counties . . .

On Pond Creek there was a family of McLennans who tried to set up. But the usually-friendly Wacos got on a rampage and raided the lonely cabin and murdered all of the family except John, 9, whom they took to their village in Palo Pinto County. He learned six Indian tongues and became quite an interpreter for his captors.

Bremond in Robertson was a wild place in the old days and one hears interesting tales . . . "few strangers arrived from the outside except those who were running from something and going nowhere" . . . fugitives from justice, fleeing the old States, formed a regular colony around Duck Creek in the 1860's. They would come into Bremond armed and in parties, defying the law.

The town had a hard name until the railroad came in 1869 to make it a permanent camp. Paul Bremond for whom it was named said: "The fellow who traded a hack and two ponies for this town was one mule-skinner that got skinned himself." The railroad brought a wave of new-comers and the main street was six miles long with many a saloon and gambling-hall running wide open. Today, Bremond is older, wiser and considerably tamer.

Hearne was just as wild. Back in 1873 there was an old saying that the towns on the railroad were: "Houston, Hempstead, Hearne and Hell." Gambling, desperados, lawlessness throve along this part of the River. But they sent a young Methodist preacher in, Horace Bishop, who started holding services over one of the saloons. He kept on until he had rallied the law-abiding in a campaign to clean up the town and build a school-house and a church.

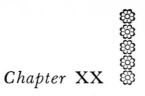

Chapter **XX**

FROM TALL PINES TO TIDE-WATER

"EVER THE WEARIEST RIVER winds somewhere safe to sea." And so does the Brazos on this lap of our journey "wind safe to sea." This is the part of the valley where strong men and women passed the River on its way seaward while they were moving westward against its tide, braving the wildernesses and daring its dangers.

Here began the march of the white man that was to forge its way upward to the source of the Brazos. Indelibly the marks of her Low Country, her Midlands and her Plains fastened themselves upon the characteristics of the people who dwelt in the River's sections. They were different civilizations as they were applied to the various regions, but the Brazos would unify them into her own peculiar composite to make them kin. They were indigenous to their own area, but even there they were pointed out as part of The Land of The River.

This part of the cruise (the old historic counties of Brazos, Burleson, Washington, Waller, Austin, Fort Bend and Brazoria) has been the highway over which Texas history has marched. These counties were the stage upon which the characters of Houston, Wharton, Bowie, Smithwick, Austin, La Salle, Erath, de Cordova, Caulfield, and Buffalo Hump, Chief of the Comanches played heroic roles.

The broad-water is here. Many trees and much undergrowth line the banks. Tangled forests and water-hyacinths, sweeping bends and imposing bridges, with far-flung vistas capture the traveler's eye. He does not have to apologize for the River here and say "Here it was . . . or will be when the rains come."

It has places that are redder than the Red River and muddier than the Mississippi. Elsewhere the green expanses of what might be a mountain lake mirror the moss-bearded trees on its surface. It can swirl and churn, eddy and rush; leaving on the barbed-wire bits of its driftwood and brush to show where it once reached. Marshes and fens, swamps and rice-fields, shallows and depths, are the attributes of the lower Brazos through which we pass.

Austin had two colonies. The lower at San Felipe was his favorite and was the one to which he gave his interest and devoted his life. The upper, around the old Nashville Colony site above the San Antonio-Nacogdoches Road was a venture, a speculation to which he loaned his name and use of his influence. His success there can be read in his writing:

I am of the opinion that the upper colony will totally ruin me . . . Cursed be the hour I ever thought of applying for that upper colony.

In February 1831 Austin and Sam Williams got permission from the Coahuila-Texas authorities to settle eight hundred families up in that region that straddled the Brazos immediately north of Brazos and Burleson Counties. The grants went to rich and politically influential Mexicans who never came to see what they had but took titles to over 1,250,000 acres in the name of about thirty-one speculators.

Austin and Williams did not attempt to develop this territory. In Tenoxtitlan, on the west bank of the Brazos about eight miles from Caldwell, in 1834 the land office was opened. It was in Burleson County and the site of a Mexican military post founded there in October 1830 by Lt. Colonel Francisco Ruiz.

The two promoters did not control the project much after

1834 and the peculiar nature of the grants marked it for early failure. The people would not move into this controlled region and immigration was slow north of Burleson County. Many lost faith in Austin and it is said to have cost him the first Presidency of the Republic and hastened his death.

Sterling C. Robertson was an earnest colonizer, who brought three hundred families into the Nashville Colony before the Mexican Exclusion Act of 1830. After much wrangling with Austin he acquired all of the rights of Austin and Williams in the Upper Colony. After 1834 Robertson was able to go ahead with his colonization and when San Jacinto was won, immigration proceeded with rapidity.

Brazos County, our first to encounter, is watered by the Navasota as it hurries to meet the main stream and furnishes the boundaries of Grimes and the eastern limits of Brazos. Here we find Texas A & M with its huge campus and its towering edifices of steel and stone. Here we find that combine and plow, transit and machine gun, are fitted into the hands of Texas' young men, fitting them for peace or war, "a fight or a frolic," cotton-bolls or battles.

We are in a cotton country here. Tall stalks stand high but not as many have bearing-bolls as we saw on the high Plains. But the farming is intensive and shows the effect of scientific guidance, carefully husbanded and conserved. Cotton fields are smaller than we have been used to, and are bordered by young oak trees with thick copses to mark the tortuous wanderings of the Brazos. Unlovely little cabins in the cotton are serviceable rather than ornate. The theme is utility rather than luxury, comfort instead of ostentation.

You can read the lineage in the names on the stores of the little towns. There are Czech, Bohemian, German and Italian people in this section, second-generation or third, but they still have a slight accent and lapse into the old tongue when they are together in store, parlor, or church.

The Negro is entrenched upon these small farm-lands and

has been for many years. Country-folk are these people, thinking in terms of share-crops, small incomes, hard work in the cottonpatch, hog-killing in winter, and wary of change.

You realize this country is getting old as you stop at the little wayside cemetery and read inscriptions on the tombs. You see some 1700 dates appear in a few instances; and wonder what became of the big houses where the planters and the land-owners dwelt.

"Boy," we ask of a sixty-five year old hitch-hiker whom we lift to the next little group of stores, "how long since your people came here to the Brazos?"

"Well, suh, m' Maw she's eighty-fo' an' she come yuh in slav'y time . . . she f'gits right smart of what she knowed."

We are intrigued with Brazos navigation. The old newspapers and yellowing pages of books attest to its authenticity. Just after the Civil War the records show that a small steamboat made some trips from Waco to the Gulf down the Brazos . . . the *Kate Ross,* named after Waco's first white child.

The railroads, they explain, knocked Brazos navigation in the head, for the rails ran straight up the valley, but here is a story of 1890 vintage of a brave try . . .

Professor J. H. Hurwood of Waco, sponsored by the Board of Trade of that city, with a party in row-boats started down the Brazos on July 15, 1890. He was back by August 12 and reported five hundred miles of travel in all with the sinuous twistings of the River. He claimed to have reached Richmond and reported many interesting items:

"Sixteen miles of shoals, several sets of rapids, monotonous landscape, but beautiful . . . only a little wild-life . . . the havoc of floods . . . inexpressible loneliness . . . an occasional Negro fisherman who evidenced no interest in the explorers . . . small villages and the fewness of them . . . the mosquitoes and the petrified wood."

The Professor came home by rail.

Between Grimes and Washington Counties the Brazos acts as a boundary-line. Grimes boasts the town of Navasota and Washington has famed Old Washington-on-the-Brazos, Independence and Brenham.

We pause in the neat little city of Navasota to stand and admire the statue of the ornate Frenchman, La Salle, on his pedestal. We read that it is erected at the spot in the forest where, in the arms of Father Douay, he breathed his last . . . a far distance from Rouen and the old cathedral on the hill above the wharves . . . The Eleventh Port . . . manned by G.I. stevedores and unloading L.S.T. boats that day when we looked down upon it from the cathedral of the Jesuits where La Salle was educated . . . there were pink-and-white candle-blossoms on the horse-chestnut tree in bloom . . . but here he died, ingloriously by an assassin's bullet . . . Frank Teich has done a magnificent image of him.

The trees are more uniform now, denser, and the moss begins to show. We are nearing the coast and this is where the Navasota and the Brazos Rivers meet . . . a cross-roads in the olden days. The La Bahia-San Antonio Road and the Nacogdoches Trail met the Indian path that came down from Waco. As one they head for the Lower Colony and the Gulf.

Before they started calling it Navasota, in 1858, it was called Nolanville, after James Nolan who built the first log cabin hereabouts for a stage-stop. It grew to be an important station. They still point out to you the wing of Freeman's Inn built in 1852 before fire and yellow-fever ravaged this part of the valley. Old colonial architecture and huge boles of the oaks indicate we are approaching the oldest part of the Brazos-land. Now we must cross the River and ride six miles to Texas' birthplace.

"Here a nation was born!" That is on the slab. And there is a tall pole with a Texas Lone Star banner flying . . . the

little old blacksmith shop where they declared Texans free
. . . some markers and monuments . . . an old fashioned house
once "The White House" of Texas . . . a modern stone
building . . . and a greensward that goes down to meet the
Brazos.

One wanders about, drinking in history along with the
sunshine. If old trees could talk! Once it was a busy place,
plenty of people flinging defiance, cheering and shouting,
planning to face a tyrant advancing with a modern army,
old Sam Houston, swinging up on his horse, headed for "the
sound of the guns."

A few little frame houses outside the State Park, some
Negro cabins and a bridge over the Brazos. Not much left
here today. The State Capital was here before Lamar wanted
to set it up at old Waterloo and call it Austin.

"Old Washington-on-the-Brazos," wrote Dr. John Lockhart.
"What a glorious place in which to die! It sat at the cradle of
the Texas Republic and likewise followed its hearse."

Randall Jones came to Washington in 1819 and built a
fort. Andrew Robinson came in 1821 and built a ferry across
the Brazos. For nineteen adventurous days it was the seat
of the Texas government. It was back here in 1842 after
being moved here and there. A move to Houston and then
it was back here to see the flag of the Republic come down
for the last time. Here the Stars and Stripes first flew over
Texas.

When the soldiers under General Gragg were marching
home from Mexico after Zachary Taylor had turned them
loose, they stopped and camped here at a spring to rest their
horses. There was abundant grass and the Kentuckians wrote
about the natural beauty of the springtime and its flowers.
Many came back to settle. It might have become a big city
— a capital city — but it refused to pay the railroad $11,000
as a subsidy. Navasota across the Brazos, six miles away, did;

and it spelled the difference between existence as a town and relegation to a shrine-status.

We visit Independence, hard by, eight miles from the flag pole at Washington. It dates from 1836 . . . crumbling, fading ruins. Baylor began here and the 1839 Baptist Church is still used. Old Sam Houston joined the Baptist Church here. Down south of town is Rocky Creek where Dr. Burleson "dipped him down under."

Across the road is the old Houston burying-ground where his wife, her mother, Nancy Lee, and two of the Negro servants of the family rest. There are intriguing old houses . . . the Lea House where Mrs. Houston died . . . J. M. Blue House of cedar wood and stone built by one of Austin's First Three Hundred . . . the Seward House, 1835 . . . the old Masonic Hall in the center of town . . . the Toalson House built by the Mexican government in 1835.

Near the River as we journey south is Chapel Hill where the Mississippi and Alabama planters came and built imposing replicas of their homes "back home." Colonel Browning, who came from Mississippi, built his of cedar in 1856, while the Sledge mansion was of brick and plaster and possessed ornamental woodwork, still preserved. The House of Routt was of pine and cedar. There were two colleges before the guns of the Civil War boomed — Hill Female College in 1852 and Soule College in 1856.

Along the country-roads one sees the real Brazos-land. Austin County with Waller by its side. Hempstead is a thriving town of modern enterprise. Bellville is the county-seat of Austin, where cotton, oil and busy commerce keep the wheels turning. The derricks rise in the Raccoon Oil Field against the trees. King Oil attends to his business in the lower as well as in the upper and middle Brazos. There are some old buildings reminiscent of lands across the waters. There is a church like that in Bayern and a stone barn of that sort in Prague.

[385]

We visit Liendo Plantation. Romance tarried here. Here are great oaks and dogwoods, wild grapevines and moss, magnolias and sweet shrubs. There is the great house that Leonard Groce built in 1851 . . . fifteen rooms!

Elizabeth Ney chose it to be the resting-place where she and her husband, Dr. Edmon Montgomery, might find peace from her busy life in Austin. They bought it in 1874. The gifted lady, a French artist, well-known in Europe, and a part of the early Texas tradition, sleeps in the old burial-ground of the plantation.

We travel down the old road with quickening thoughts as we near San Felipe for the first time. Here is the place. Austin said when he saw it shining in the sun: *"Here we build!"*

Greeting our eye is a seated statue of Stephen F. Austin on a white pedestal — courtly, stately, dignified — in bronze.

There is no bustling city about him. The tranquility of birds and grass, flowers and trees. There is the old well-site that furnished water for San Felipe. There is his old double-cabin with the "dog-run" in the middle and a chimney at each end. Yonder the ferry-line, and there the familiar River that leads us to this spot where so much of history was enacted . . . with which it is joined in history, legend, and story.

It was settled in hardship, built in discouragement, burned in retaliation, rebuilt in determination, and perpetuated in memory. The slab states:

The prosperity of Texas has been the object of my labors, the idol of my existence. It has assumed the character of a religion for the guidance of my thoughts and actions.

Those are *his* words. This is Austin's spot . . and we read:

If he who by conquest wins an empire and receives the world's applause, how much is due to him who, by unceasing toil, lays in the wilderness the foundation of an infant colony and builds thereon a vigorous state.

If the Texas nation was born at Washington-on-the-Brazos, here it was conceived.

We take up our trek on down the River. Here is the famed Bend where they built a Fort and after which a county is named — Fort Bend County. Here the colonist unlimbered his axe, the farmer opened the neck of his seed-bag and took out precious corn for the first planting. And logs were hauled to make a home. Here Virginians built their new Richmond in the Brazos' "green and pleasant land."

White colonial houses, green magnolia trees, huge oaks, moss and mocking-birds. Mirabeau B. Lamar, the artist of Texas, called this his home-town and lies buried there in the cemetery. It is also the resting-place of Jane Long — The Mother of Texas. In the heart of town, in the Episcopal church-yard, there is a monument to mark the grave of the man who cut Vince's Bridge that April day . . . Deaf Smith.

The first log house here was built in 1822. This was the place where both Houston and Santa Anna crossed to keep rendezvous at San Jacinto. It started when a Philadelphia man, Robert E. Handy, aide to Houston through "The Runaway Scrape" days, opened a store at the Bend and vowed he would stay. Both the Bordens helped him as did Tom Rusk and by August 1, 1837 he announced in *The Telegraph and Register* that lots in the townsite would be sold. Rusk had already named it for his home city on the James River.

Lamar loved this place and its River. When the Republic was ungrateful to him . . . refused him as commander of the Army after President Burnet had appointed him its Major-General . . . here in this spot he died December 19, 1859, just before the dawn of Secession's decade. He was the Brazos' first man of letters, a historian, a diplomat, a poet and a patriot.

This was the land of the Carancahuas and they tell an Indian story. It was in the summer of 1823 and the Cronks came to New Year's Creek — where the *empresarios* from the

Lively came first in 1821 — and stole some horses. The white settlers posse followed as far as Richmond, but hearing that the main body of the Cronks was at Big Creek, fifteen miles below Richmond, they sent back for reinforcements. Austin answered the call with eighteen men from San Felipe.

He parleyed with the Indian Chief at Carita. The Indians were talked out of the stolen horses and five of their braves were delivered up to be punished — fifteen lashes from Austin and fifteen from the Cronk Chief. But the gentle Austin could not go through with it and delegated Abner Kuyken-dall who laid them on with a vengeance. Abner was later killed by a man named Joseph Clayton who was convicted and hanged in 1834. That was the first execution in Austin's colony by law.

As we pass on down the River we come to the great State Prison farms. They are a macabre note in the pleasant places and historical points of interest.

We push on to East and West Columbia. The Republic's capital was here once and in October 1836 the Congress met, using log-sheds for committee rooms. There is a capital oak here and this is where Stephen F. Austin died.

We ask the way to old Peach Point Plantation where he is buried. There under the oaks and magnolias, in the bury-ing-ground of his people — the Perry's — in whose home he kept a room always, he is laid to rest not far from the River's banks. He rested here beneath this graying stone for seventy-and-five years. Then they tried to find his dust and carry it to Austin.

There is a little church nearby and the whole is bathed in a serene solitude this Sabbath morning, as the sunlight filters in through moss and leaves. He was the peer of his kind, gentle, courageous and the man who planned what should be in the valley of the River of the Arms of God.

Back to the highway and our journey coast-ward, where the palmettos and palms greet us. In place of great square Herefords, the cattle are of the Brahma strain. Deep gray with large ears and straight horns and a huge hump on their backs.

Here at Bell's Landing they loaded cotton in the days of 1836. Bolivar is the head of the Brazos tidewater . . . sixty miles to the Gulf by meanders . . . forty-five by land . . . fifteen from Galveston Bay as the sea-gull flies. Here was where the courageous Jane Long stood by until the word of her husband's death came to her.

Cabeza de Vaca called this section "Malhado" — Land of Misfortune — when he dwelt among the Carancahuas. Jean Lafitte called it "Campeachy" when he had his headquarters here for his pirate crew. On the old Spanish maps it is even marked as "Isla de las Culebras" or "The Abode of the Snakes."

"Say, Auntie," we pause to ask an old Negro woman, "what's become of all the old plantation houses — the places where the rich folks lived around here in the days before the War?" "Lawdy-me, suh," she grins until her blue gums are visible. "Dey's all gone. Dey died wid d' folks what lived in um, I spec."

That's as good an answer as any . . .

Walking in Old Brazoria we find there is much of the Brazos tradition and lore that still lives.

It is a land of peach-trees and magnolia blossoms, of sugar-cane and gray-bearded oak trees, of ruins of old chimneys and wild roses climbing over decayed columns. A tangled garden sends our memories and fancies about the task of reconstructing it as it once was. There is a new Brazoria on the highway, with filling-stations and stores and a neat little town, but here off the road among the stately trees we see what is left of a vanished past.

We pause and read the inscription on John Austin's granite monument . . . Alcalde of Brazoria in 1832 . . . fought at Velasco and marched in Long's Expedition . . . died in 1833 and missed San Jacinto. No kin of Moses and Stephen F. Here is the old Masonic Oak, but no tablet to mark the place. Here in March 1835, Anson Jones, John A. Wharton and four others met to petition the Grand Lodge of Louisiana for a lodge at Brazoria. It was called Holland No. 36. (There seems to be magic in the number "36" in Texas history . . . 36th meridian . . . 36th Texas Cavalry in the Civil War . . . the 36th Division in the two World Wars made up of Texas troops . . . Holland Lodge No. 36.) Jones was the first Worshipful Master and is said to have carried the charter in his saddle-bags at San Jacinto.

Down to the old River we go and stand upon its high banks to contemplate what once was here. Absently we gaze at that pyle out in the stream about which the driftwood gathers. There was a bridge here once. Many crossed it on their way to history's great events.

Jared Groce brought the first cotton-seed here and put up a gin in 1825. Austin built the second in 1826 and five years later, Edwin Waller, after whom the county of Waller was named, sent out of Velasco a shipload of cotton to Matamoras, Mexico, and got 62½c a pound for it. In 1834 the crop here in Brazoria ran over a half-million bales.

We have pointed out to us the place where the old courthouse stood . . . the wagon-bridge . . . the place where they loaded the boats in early days . . . and the sites where the great houses of the gentle-folk ranged. Slave-quarters, sugarhouse and the old plantation-bell.

They show you Anson Jones' grave in the small cemetery . . . the magnificence of the view where Albert Sydney Johnston, great Brazonian, built China Grove Plantation. We've run into his tracks all up and down the River — Fort Belknap, Palo Pinto County survey, Council House Fight, Civil War days, now here in the low country of the River — he must have loved the Brazos, too.

The first insurance company in Texas came into being

in this old county of Brazoria in 1837, capital stock $200,000.
We pause and see where Orozimbo Plantation stood. There
Dr. James A. E. Phelps took Santa Anna and the big Mexican "brass" after San Jacinto for safe-keeping until it could
be decided what would be done with them. We have a notion
it was to keep the other Mexicans from liberating their *El
Presidente.*

There are many of these old plantation sites . . . scattered
and apart. A. J. Strobel has collected much of their data
in his "The Old Plantations and their Owners of Old Brazoria County." It is an interesting pamphlet and a guide-
book to the Brazos in this section. Old Jim Hogg, when
Governor, bought one of these plantation sites for his children and told them to hold fast to it — there was oil under
it and it would make them rich. It did!

Eagle Island was William H. Wharton's place in 1826.
There is Durazno, Westall, Lowwood, Hawkins, and many
more. We see Ben Freeman's home where they held the
meeting in 1835 and drew up the memorials to the Mexican
government protesting the new customs-duties and harsh
laws. They armed the expedition that used the sloop *Ohio*
to storm Velasco out of Brazoria. That was how it all started.
We are here in the place where they planned Texas Freedom.

There were great plantations in through the Oyster Creek
community in the olden days. Much of the history was made
around the settlement they called "Bailey's Prairie." It seems,
according to the stories they tell, that another raft of the hapless folk who were with Cabeza de Vaca's expedition landed
here on November 5, 1528. Most of them perished at the
hands of the Carancahuas, who set them to digging roots and
gathering oysters in a region infested by mosquitoes and
other pests.

Back in the 1830's there was an old fellow here who died
of the cholera the year the flood of the Brazos was so bad.
His name was Bailey and they named the place after him.

[391]

He wanted to be buried with his rifle on his shoulder, standing up, facing west with a jug of whiskey at his feet. They did just that, piling the River loam in on top of him. The Negroes have sworn from that day to this that he walks by night —Brazoria's most distinguished ghost — in a land full of spectres.

Daniel Shipman gives us a chronicle of the old days:

We planted corn in holes that we made with sharp sticks. Here we grew thousands of bushels of corn and big crops of cotton. There were hundreds of wild cattle and hogs, the latter being only usable when female or young. The Mexican hogs would not cross with our own. In the Oyster Creek timber were spotted leopard, panther, bear and other game down to the cotton-field rabbit.

They did their part in the Civil War days . . . Frank Terry, John Rugely, of Matagorda, and John A. Wharton, of Brazoria, rode a stage-coach over to Austin. On the way they talked about organizing a Confederate regiment. Beneath these oaks, chinaberries and cypresses, the idea for "Terry's Texas Rangers" was born. Terry and Lubbock went off to Virginia to get commissions and got there in time to fight at First Manassas where Terry was cited for bravery. He shot down the halyard that flew the Yankee flag over the courthouse and came back a Colonel.

Oyster Creek and Fort Bend gave him their volunteers, among them his son, David. To the songs of farewell from the folk of the town, the slaves of the plantations and his own family, he rode away to fight in Kentucky until one December day they shot him out of his saddle. His body came home to rest on Oakland Plantation under the Brazos breezes.

When Lee surrendered they were not of that same mind in Brazoria . . . they drew up resolutions . . . "There is an ocean of blood between us which can never be crossed or dried up" . . . there were 80,000 Confederate troops west of the Mississippi and the resolutions went on to say . . . "With the aid of God, Kirby-Smith and General Magruder we can hold Texas against the world!"

We go on to old Velasco and Quintana and to Freeport, the new sulphur town. We do not look for the old fort or even for evidences of the former settlements at the mouth of the Brazos. They are gone . . . the sands of the dunes cover them . . . little frame houses now occupy the spot and Velasco is a name on the highway sign: Quintana, you have to inquire about.

We bring to this spot our memories and try to sketch in the history that we have gathered. It is not preserved here for you. The sights that Cabeza and Piñeda saw: the vast expanse of ocean, gulf, salt march, water-birds and sky, are there with a bright morning sun glistening over the scene.

We began our journey about eight hundred miles away in Bailey County from Muleshoe. Down the River we have cruised to arrive where the waters of the stream and the Gulf of Mexico are united. Velasco . . . a Mexican custom-house was here . . . a fort. Colonel Domingo Ugatechea double-crossed the colonists . . . they had a battle . . . a skirmish of sorts — before the commander of the redoubt hauled down his flag. They signed the treaty with Santa Anna somewhere in this neighborhood. It is not as easy to identify as San Felipe and Washington . . . no shrine. The State Capital tarried here overnight.

Stephen F. Austin paced the floor here once and prayed God to avert war between his people and the Mexicans who had trusted him. This was the town of the Wharton brothers. Rothschild decided to build a great sea-port here, but he never carried out his intentions.

Once this was a land of steamboats and banjos, cards and crinoline, great colonial homes with tall columns, gay society, fiddles scraping on the wide piazzas, and Negroes singing in the moonlight. Herndon's plantation had twelve rooms and could be seen out in the Gulf.

Here the *Lively* made port with The First Three Hundred and Mrs. Holley says in one of her letters:

Our sails are spread to a fair, light breeze upon the Brazos . . . the sun and air seem softer and brighter than elsewhere since we have left New Orleans . . . There is nothing in the whole course of the Ohio or the Mississippi for quiet beauty to be compared with the Brazos.

And so we go to land's end and feel the breeze from out at sea . . . out where sea-weed washes up on the beach and the wind is from the salt cedars . . . a fog out beyond the sunlight . . . the jetties to keep back the waves.

Cabeza de Vaca saw this . . . the builders of the Spanish fort who gave their General's name to it thought it a strategic place . . . they had a factory where they slaughtered and cured hides, meat and tallow, from the wild cattle on the coastal plain . . . there were clipper ships and barkentines at this mooring once . . . gamblers and pirates . . . ship-yards and Confederate batteries.

From Bailey to Brazoria . . . Caprock to Quintana . . . from butte to sand-dune . . . high mesa to level seashore . . . blackland to desert . . . rocky gulches to irrigation-ditches where hyacinths grow. Through it all, even as a thread through the warp and woof of the garment that is Texas, the Brazos flows. We feel as Julia Ward Howe:

> *I have made a voyage upon a golden river,*
> *'Neath clouds of opal and of amethyst;*
> *Along its banks bright shapes are moving ever*
> *And threatening shadows melted into mist.*

LLO

W

CK

ND

N

MEXICO